PRINCES OF WALES

PRINCES
OF
WALES

Alan Palmer

WEIDENFELD AND NICOLSON
LONDON

Weidenfeld and Nicolson
91 Clapham High Street
London SW4 7TA

ISBN 0 297 77691 6

Printed and bound in Great Britain at
The Camelot Press Ltd, Southampton

Contents

Illustrations

The Investiture of Edward VIII (*Press Association*)
Edward, Prince of Wales on the Western Front (*Royal Archives, Windsor Castle*)
George V with his two eldest sons (*Royal Archives, Windsor Castle*)
The Duke and Duchess of Windsor with Hitler (*Keystone Press Agency*)
The Investiture of Prince Charles (*Keystone Press Agency*)
Prince Charles (*Camera Press*)

Preface

In April 1284 Queen Eleanor of Castile, consort of King Edward I of England, gave birth to a second son at Caernarfon, the ancient centre of the Welsh princes of Gwynedd. The boy, named after his father, was born in a castle on which building work had only begun a few months previously and which was intended by the king to serve as a means of effective government and a symbol of imperial conquest. Nearly seventeen years later young Edward, now heir to the throne, was formally created 'Prince of Wales' by his father at the Lincoln Parliament. Thus began an association of the royal heritage of Gwynedd with the English Crown which has survived for nearly seven centuries. In 304 of the past 678 years there has been a Prince of Wales among the peers of the realm, but the title is not inherited at birth and is borne only after conferment by the sovereign.

This book traces the fortunes of the twenty-one Princes of Wales, thirteen of whom became King of England. Some, like the Black Prince and Henry of Monmouth, won fame on the battlefield; five remain shadowy figures, who died too young for their promise to be fulfilled; others were recognized abroad as emissaries of goodwill. At first sight such disparate personalities have little in common with each other. Yet, over the centuries, familiar problems emerge in differing forms. The Plantagenets and the Hanoverians were troubled by conflicts between sovereign and heir-apparent which had deeper significance than any normal clash of generations; and there was similar conflict in the reign of George V. Education in kingship has been a recurrent preoccupation of the princes' parents: it perplexed Queen Margaret in 1463; it prompted Princess Augusta to turn to Lord Bute in the 1750s; it propelled Prince Albert's pen through nineteen years of laboured memoranda; and it induced Queen Elizabeth II to set up an informal committee of wise counsellors as recently as 1965. Bride-hunting for a Prince of Wales, which was in earlier centuries an instrument of statecraft, excited tavern gossip in London long before the rise of the popular Press made it a speculative sport for the uninitiated masses at home and overseas. Uncertainty over the best 'employment' for a Prince of Wales, a favourite theme of nineteenth-century political writers, also worried the later medieval kings. Despite changes in the relationship of prince and people and despite long gaps in time when the title was in abeyance, there has remained a continuity of tradition linking the Princes of Wales through seven centuries and it provides a thread for this present book.

Apart from the first, second, fourth and fifth of the 'English' princes, all were descended from the best-known ruler of medieval Wales, Llywelyn the Great. Few, however, before the present century, took much interest in the Principality, its people, language or culture. Eight bearers of the title never even visited Wales, as prince or king. It is only in recent years that Welsh national sentiment has succeeded in changing placenames into the native language. Although I write as an Englishman who speaks and reads no Welsh, I have tried to observe current usage, preferring 'Caernarfon' and 'Conwy' to the anglicized 'Caernarvon' and 'Conway'. At times, however, I may have used alternative spellings of proper names more readily familiar to the general reader. For such linguistic solecisms I ask the indulgence of Welsh purists, to whom I apologize.

I would like to thank the staffs of the Bodleian Library and the London Library for their ready assistance, Mr Benjamin Buchan for his editorial guidance, and Mrs Mary Cumming for typing the manuscript so meticulously. My wife, Veronica, has helped me greatly, not least with the proofs. She also compiled the Index. I much appreciate her advice and encouragement.

A. W. P.
Woodstock, July 1979

CHAPTER ONE

Edward of Caernarfon

D URING the early days of March 1284 a straggling procession of carriages and carts, horses and oxen rumbled slowly along the rough roads of the northern Midlands from Nottingham to Chester. The peripatetic household of King Edward I, which had spent part of January in York and much of February in Lincoln, was returning to Wales.* On 15 March the great caravan crossed from Chester into Flintshire, travelling on to Rhuddlan where the walls of a new castle were beginning to rise starkly on the hill above the river Clywyd.[1] By now it was a countryside which the king had come to know well.

The 'Lord Edward', as he was called when heir to the throne, first fought in Snowdonia as a young man defending lands between the Conwy River and Chester entrusted to him by his father, Henry III. It had been a humiliating experience. For two hundred years the Anglo-Norman sovereigns of England had sought to conquer the Welsh people: they destroyed the old kingdoms of Wales, building up a military frontier against the wild Celts, policed by Norman earls and barons who enjoyed virtually royal powers in the lands they overran. In some parts of Wales – especially Pembrokeshire, Glamorgan and around Brecon – these 'Marcher Lords' held sway with all the ruthlessness of brigand chieftains. Only in the mountain lands of the north-west, in what had earlier been the heart of the kingdom of Gwynedd, did Welsh national princes continue to defy the invaders. The ablest of them, Llywelyn the Great, recognized the English king as a feudal overlord and modelled the administration of his lands on a Norman pattern but carefully preserved the identity of his Welsh inheritance. His grandson, Llywelyn ap Gruffydd, offered the Welsh the proud reality of independence; in 1258 he challenged the English crown by creating for himself the new title 'Prince of Wales', and the Lord Edward's

---

* For a map of medieval England and Wales, see p. 223.

mercenaries were unable to save north Wales from being overrun by Llywelyn's skilfully led army. After his accession King Edward I mounted two full-scale invasions of the principality and forced Llywelyn to render him homage at Conwy in 1277. Five years later a sudden revolt by Llywelyn's brother, David, took Edward by surprise. After initial reverses, the king met this new challenge by a carefully planned campaign which was intended to complete, once and for all, the Anglo-Norman conquest of Wales. Llywelyn was killed in a skirmish, while David was captured and executed. As neither brother had an heir, the king of England could claim that by feudal law the possessions of a Prince of Wales had passed into his hands as rightful and acknowledged liege lord of Llywelyn; and it was to impose a new settlement on the fallen principality that the king returned to Wales in the spring of 1284.

At Rhuddlan on mid-Lent Sunday (19 March) Edward issued a statute for Wales. It defined the character of the Anglo-Norman administrative system and consolidated the king's military conquests, substituting English criminal law for the ancient customs of the Welsh people. But Rhuddlan was not Edward's final destination. He was determined to make Caernarfon the setting for his English Court within Wales, partly because of Caernarfon's strategic position but even more because of its past associations. The town had been a seat of government for the princely dynasty of Gwynedd. Legend conjured up a more distant past: what was believed to be the body of Magnus Maximus, 'father of the noble emperor Constantine', was found at Segontium, only half a mile from Caernarfon Castle, in 1283; and one of the best-known myths of Welsh folk-lore associated Maximus and Constantine himself with a great fortified city, 'the fairest man ever saw', built at the mouth of a river in a land of high mountains and facing an island. The architecture of Caernarfon Castle, so different from Beaumaris or Conwy or Harlech, suggests that Edward wished a symbolic imperial city to be built at the mouth of the river Seiont, a city whose outer fortifications would resemble the massive land-walls of Byzantium. Caernarfon was to have its tower crowned by imperial eagles and, like Constantinople, a Golden Gate. As yet, in 1284, the castle by the seashore was little more than a collection of makeshift quarters hurriedly run up by royal carpenters at news of their sovereign's approach. There was, however, some prospect of comfort for the king and queen, a chamber with nine newly made glass windows in it. Here Edward and Eleanor of Castile arrived on 1 April, at the end of their long winter journey southwards from York.[2]

Queen Eleanor was a remarkable woman. Edward had married her at Burgos when he was fifteen and she a few weeks short of her ninth birthday. Her devotion to her husband's interests turned a contract of policy into a marriage bond of affection. Already she had accompanied her husband to Gascony and on to Tunis, Cyprus and the Holy Land; she travelled with him to the northern castles of his kingdom; and so, for the fifth time, she had come with him to Wales. It must, however, have been a hard journey for the queen. She was now thirty-eight and this spring she expected to give birth to her fourteenth child in twenty years. The high infant-mortality rate of the thirteenth century had taken a heavy toll of her family: four girls died as babies and two sons, John and Henry, failed to reach manhood; but there were six daughters still alive and an eleven-year-old heir to the throne, the Lord Alfonso. No doubt Edward wished for another son; he may have seen eventual advantages in having a boy born in Wales. When Eleanor was last pregnant, in the autumn of 1282, the king kept her with him at campaign headquarters in Rhuddlan rather than send her to safer and more comfortable accommodation with his mother in England: the child born at Rhuddlan was a daughter, baptized Elizabeth. Living conditions were better for Eleanor at Caernarfon than at Rhuddlan eighteen months before. Moreover she knew Caernarfon already: indeed since the royal household spent most of July and August in 1283 at Caernarfon, the child she was about to bear must almost certainly have been conceived there. King and queen celebrated Easter together, Edward ordering alms to be distributed to the poor in the queen's name (*pro regina pregnante*) on the Tuesday of Easter week (11 April).[3] Problems of government appear to have summoned him to Rhuddlan in the following week, and it was to Rhuddlan that a courier brought news of the birth of a son on the Feast of St Mark the Evangelist, 25 April.

A week later king and queen were together again, with at least three of their daughters, for the baby's baptism. He received his father's name; and, as there was no precedent for giving even a king's son a title of rank at birth, he was known as the Lord Edward of Caernarfon. Legend maintains that, shortly before the baptism, Edward presented his son to the Welsh people as a prince 'born in Wales who speaks no word of English'. Historians, understandably, will have nothing to do with this fable, especially as, in its most circumstantial form, it includes the emergence of the king with babe in arms on to a tower not yet constructed. The tale first appears in a *Historie of Cambria* by the Elizabethan antiquarian, David Powel, a work printed exactly three hundred years after the incident it describes. There is no evidence that in 1284 Edward was thinking of making Wales a titular appendage of his son; the dignity of prince was unknown in England at that time, and it would have been impolitic to advance the prospects of a newly born child while Alfonso, the heir-apparent, remained without a territorial title himself. Yet there may be a grain of truth behind the legend. David Powel, an expatriate Welshman writing in Oxford, could well have based his tale on an oral tradition still current in his homeland after the passage of more than ten generations. In statecraft and in war Edward I was invariably an opportunist: it would be in character for him to seek political capital from the birth of a son in a town so recently the seat of a native dynasty. Even if there was no dramatic presentation of their coming prince to the people of Caernarfon, the place and timing of his birth inevitably associated the boy with the fallen principality, and with Roman imperial traditions, at a decisive moment in Welsh history.[4]

The child remained in his birthplace through the summer months of 1284, cared for by a Welsh wet-nurse named Mary Maunsel, who was granted an annual pension of a hundred shillings by her former charge five years after his accession. Yet the employment of a Welsh girl was not in itself a sign of reconciliation between conquerors and conquered. Many young Welshmen were tempted into the king's service, especially when the household travelled back into England later in the year. Their sovereign, however, was not a man to spare their national feelings. He had returned to Wales that spring to impose a settlement: he lingered in the old principality to savour success. Relics, allegedly including the crown of King Arthur, were received and retained. Young Alfonso was sent to Westminster to present the Abbot with a golden necklace which had belonged to Prince Llywelyn and which the king now wished to adorn the shrine of Edward the Confessor. 'A cross captured by the king in Wales' (as a monastic chronicler noted) found its way to the Archbishop of Canterbury. Edward was intoxicated by his newly found

4

mastery of the Welsh. Late in July he staged a tournament and 'spectacle' at Nefyn, on the peninsula south of Caernarfon, which became so festive that the floor of the castle gave way under the accumulated weight of romping knights.

Less than a month later this euphoric mood of triumph was shattered. On 19 August Alfonso died suddenly, apparently from a fever caused by drinking infected water. The four-month-old Edward was now heir to the throne. Arrangements were made for him to be brought, with two of his sisters, to Chester and along a 'safe' route through Shropshire and Hereford, eventually joining his father and mother at Bristol, where they had travelled more directly through the difficult country of central and southern Wales. Young Edward never returned to Caernarfon. He did not visit the land of his birth again until after he was created Prince, when he was almost seventeen.[5]

Even though he was now the king's only son, Edward received no special favours, nor was any great attention given to his early upbringing. Indeed between his second and fifth birthdays he had no contact with his parents whatsoever. Early in May 1286 they crossed the Channel: Edward rendered homage to the French king, Philip the Fair, for his territorial possessions in France, and, with Eleanor, subsequently set up his court at Bordeaux in order to settle disturbances within Gascony. Not until the second week of August 1289 was the boy reunited with his mother and father at Dover. Much of this time he had spent at Windsor with his sisters in a household presided over by a veteran clerk in holy orders, Giles of Oudenarde: the royal children were protected by a band of knights and sergeants-at-arms. Occasionally Edward visited his grandmother, Eleanor of Provence, the widow of King Henry III, in the priory at Amesbury where she had taken the veil in the summer of 1286 and where Edward's sister Mary was received as a nun at the age of six. But for the most part the boy was left in the care of his nurse, Alice Leygrave, who succeeded Mary Maunsel in the autumn of 1284 and was to remain in his household for at least twenty-nine years. Alice Leygrave gained some of the influence enjoyed in the nineteenth century by the nannies of great families. Edward treated her with affection and lasting consideration. An official letter, written by a royal clerk in 1313, refers to her as 'the king's mother . . . one who suckled him in his infancy'.[6]

The responsibilities of Alice Leygrave increased in the closing weeks of 1290. That autumn Edward I and Queen Eleanor had travelled in Cheshire and Derbyshire. The queen contracted a fever in October, to which she succumbed on 28 November. Young Edward was now left motherless: his grandmother died eight months later, while the habit of early marriages deprived him of the company of his remaining sisters before his thirteenth birthday. He spent a lonely childhood, and frequently it was a stormy one. King Edward showed little understanding of an infant heir forty-five years his junior. Fortunately he entrusted the boy to a veteran knight and crusader, Guy Ferre, who had brought up a good soldierly son of his own. As the 'Lord Edward's governor' (*magister*), probably from the age of seven until he was eighteen, Sir Guy was responsible for training the heir to the throne in horsemanship, for safeguarding his moral welfare, and for seeing he received a grounding of book learning from ecclesiastical tutors in his household. Sir Guy showed a greater latitude than many later governors to heirs presumptive. Edward of Caernarfon became a good rider, who enjoyed hunting and breeding horses, and he is known to have appreciated music. To the surprise, and ill-disguised contempt, of many contemporary knights he did not joust, preferring to swim, row and even to amuse himself in the fields, hedging and ditching or thatching as though he were a serf. He was neither the first, nor the last, heir to the throne who gained pleasure from cultivating a strip of land and dabbling with horticulture. Sophisticates of the eighteenth century ridiculed such practices in caricatures; conventionally minded scribes of the fourteenth century censured them in chronicles: 'Had he devoted as much toil to the use of arms as he gave to the rustic arts, England would have prospered and his name would have resounded to the ends of the earth', wrote the anonymous author of the *Vita Edwardi Secundi* in the last years of his reign.[7]

Every effort seems to have been made to interest young Edward in jousting. Most of his schooling took place in the winter months when his household would stay for twenty weeks or more in Hertfordshire, a few miles from St Albans. Virtually nothing remains of the royal manor of King's Langley, although we know from contemporary records that it was a pleasant building on slopes above a brook; stables housed, not only horses, but a camel (a trophy from the crusades?) and Edward could enjoy the luxury of a private bedroom with a chimney for its own fire. Lest these comforts should make him soft, a heraldic artist was summoned to Langley in the summer of 1292 while Edward was absent and received the considerable sum of fifty shillings for painting fifty-two shields on the walls of the great hall, together with a mural depicting four knights riding to a tournament. This picture does not, however, seem to have inspired Edward. The following June his cousins Thomas and Henry of Lancaster, and a large following, breakfasted with Edward and his household at Kingston on their way to joust at Fulham and 'caused great expense' for their food and fodder; but there is no record of the heir to the throne joining them.[8]

In the summer of 1297 the king, who was preparing a new campaign against the French in Flanders, summoned the magnates of the realm to Westminster Hall where, on 14 July, he presented his thirteen-year-old son to them and required them to do fealty to him 'as heir, future lord and successor to the kingdom'. This dramatic episode was followed by seven months of regency during the king's absence: it was a period of discontent at home and of threatened invasion from Scotland, and it was fortunate for the young man that all decisions were taken by the experienced councillors whom his father had selected as the real governors of the realm. The king came home in March 1298, prepared to lead an army against Scotland, and the Lord Edward returned to his amusements, his studies, and his diligent observance of holy days and festivals. By now, however, his household had been strengthened by the introduction of a group of royal companions, *pueri in custodia*, young men chosen by the king as fit company for England's next ruler. They were joined that summer by a Gascon who had especially pleased the king during the Flanders campaign, Piers Gaveston, son of a much-respected crusader and a resolute enemy of the rulers of France.

Gaveston was a squire, a veteran of camp and court, and – it would seem – a gifted raconteur. 'When the king's son saw him, he fell so much in love that he entered upon an enduring compact with him, and chose to knit an indissoluble bond of affection with him, before all other mortals', declared a chronicler, with the benefit of thirty years' hindsight.[9] No contemporary observer has much to say for Gaveston: there are suggestions that he was handsome, good at the martial arts, which Edward still treated with disdain, but he was inclined to scoff irreverently at all pomposity of rank. No doubt to the *pueri in custodia* he was good fun, even though he was later blamed – not altogether convincingly – for having led the Lord Edward's household into degeneracy. Yet many of their pursuits at Windsor and King's Langley were harmless enough; and there is, in the wardrobe accounts for March 1300, an intriguing entry: 'To master John of Leek, chaplain to the Lord Edward, the king's son, for ready cash paid out for the said Lord's playing at *Creag'* and other games at Westminster . . . the sum of one hundred shillings'. The use of an apostrophe at the end of the word was a frequent abbreviation for '-et' and it is therefore possible that Edward and his friends may have been amusing themselves in some primitive form of cricket.[10]

But there were more serious occupations for Edward and his young companions a few months later. The Scots, under William Wallace, seemed to pose a threat to the king as grave as had the Welsh to his father's lands forty years before. Already Edward I had defeated Wallace in one campaign (1298): now he planned to bring the Scots to battle again; and this time he proposed to test his son's response to camp life and warfare on the borders. For fifteen of the last eighteen months the two Edwards had been in each other's company, living for the most part in amity. In May 1300, before the new war in the north, they spent some days of religious retreat and devotion at Bury St Edmunds, the boy staying a week longer than his father: 'He became our chapter brother,' recorded one of the monks. 'Each day he asked to be served with a monk's portion, such as the brothers receive in refectory.'[11] Yet the religious life was not for him. By midsummer he had joined Gaveston and his friends at Carlisle to await battle.

The campaign was unrewarding. The Scots very sensibly declined to take the field in force, relying on diplomatic pressure from the Pope to curb King Edward's latest imperial venture. Edward was told his son had distinguished himself during the brief siege of Caerlaverock Castle, but it was the only good news that he received. Discontent among the feudal magnates and the bishops at the exercise of royal rights in the forests and at financial levies induced the king, in September, to announce he would summon a parliament at Lincoln early in the new year. Meanwhile the king accepted a truce with the Scots – from All Saints' Day 1300 until Whitsun 1301 – and moved southwards for Christmas.

While still on the Scottish border the king appears to have decided to make some public show of confidence in his son at the Lincoln parliament. No doubt he was, in a sense, rewarding the sixteen-year-old lad for his fortitude during a tedious campaign. But there were more political considerations, too. Bishops, barons and knights were united in seeking to limit the king's arbitrary authority. They wished for confirmation of concessions won in the charters of the past ninety years. Some sought to subject appointments to the chief offices of state – Chancellor, Treasurer, Chief Justice – to parliamentary approval. Such novel theories were rejected outright by the king, but he had to accept petitions reaffirming the validity of the charters before he could be certain of a war subsidy and other taxes. During a constitutional crisis of this character it was natural for him to seek ways of emphasizing his sovereignty and the unique character of dynastic kingship within the ordered ranks of a feudal realm. Accordingly, by a charter dated 7 February 1301 at Nettleham (the royal residence north of Lincoln) Edward I bestowed on his eldest son all the king's lands within Wales, together with the earldom of Chester and the county of Flint.

The charter was a legal endowment of land, only unusual in its geographical concentration on a particular region. The term 'Prince of Wales' does not appear in the charter, but a second grant concerning the 'castle and town of Montgomery', and dated 10 May, refers to the king's son specifically as *principe Wallie et comite Cestrense* (Prince of Wales and Earl of Chester). At some moment in the fourteen weeks separating the Nettleham charter from the new endowment, young Edward was therefore created Prince and Earl. There is, however, no record of any investiture. Probably the ceremony took place in the chapter house at Lincoln before the assembled magnates of the realm on 7 February, immediately following the formal sealing of the Nettleham charter. Young Edward had been in residence at Navenby, seven miles south of Lincoln, for more than a fortnight before the charter was issued; he left the king's company when the parliament dispersed at the end of February, spent Easter quietly with the itinerant royal court in Worcestershire, and was thereafter engaged in his new duties as principal territorial magnate in Wales. Almost certainly the new Prince was presented by his father with a golden coronet, a ring on the finger and a silver rod, since subsequent investitures refer to such insignia as *juxta morem* ('according to custom'). But a monastic scribe at Canterbury, chronicling recent history a few years later, merely says that the king endowed his son with the Welsh and Cheshire lands at Lincoln, 'ordering him forthwith to be called Prince of Wales'.[12]

During the seventeen years since his birth at Caernarfon, little notice had been taken of Edward's Welsh origin. A gift of four herons was presented to him by someone living in Caernarfon about the time of his sixth birthday, and ten years later he received two greyhounds from the constable of Conwy Castle. In the Scottish campaign he encountered some Welsh infantry, employed by the king to harry the Scots among the jagged hills of the southern Glenkens. Three Welsh servants are mentioned by name in his household accounts at this time, but it is unlikely they would have made any impression on him. An unknown monk of St Albans, continuing the chronicle ascribed to William Rishanger down to 1306, maintained that the revival of the title Prince of Wales pleased the Welsh people who 'esteemed' the king's son 'their rightful lord, because his origin was derived from those parts'.[13] But St Albans – an abbey especially patronized by the new prince – was a long way from Wales. It is hard to see why the people of northern Wales, who had ravaged Caernarfon town and castle in a violent rising seven years before, should look with particular favour on the formal usurpation of Llywelyn's principality by its enemies, whatever they may have felt in later years. The prince travelled to Chester in the spring to exact homage and fealty for his new possessions. He crossed into Wales on 21 April. During an exhausting three-week journey he received vassals at Flint, Ruthin, Rhuddlan and Conwy. The extent of the principality was limited to what were, until recent times, the shires of Flint, Anglesey, Caernarfon, Merioneth, and Cardigan, with a segment of Carmarthen and additional isolated lands in Montgomery, Pembroke, Brecknock and the English county of Shropshire. Edward personally never went further south than Snowdonia: some tenants from west and south Wales travelled up to Conwy, but many took oaths intermittently over the next five years before special commissioners.[14] Most of the remaining areas of Wales were in the hands of Anglo-Norman 'Marcher Lords'. Government within the principality was carried out by justices in their prince's name: it was good and efficient; and soon Welshmen held minor posts within the administration. The principality was never simply a milch-cow for Edward; and there were several families in the north and south who readily acknowledged the soundness of princely rule in contrast to the misgovernance of Marcher Lords. Many of the Welsh developed a personal loyalty to their prince which survived his accession and was to influence his final fate in the autumn of 1327.

He did not visit Wales again during his six-year principate, but he retained an interest in Welsh affairs and in the distinctive culture of the people. Thus in the spring of 1305, while a parliament was in session north of the Thames at Westminster, the Welsh (who did not then enjoy parliamentary representation) were permitted to present thirty-two petitions to their prince at Kennington, south of the river; and, in records for the years 1305–7, there are several allusions to Welsh minstrels commanded to entertain the prince with music on the crwth, a primitive six-stringed violin which served as a lyre for the bards of Gwynedd. At times, however, Edward affected an indulgent contempt for his Welsh subjects: thus on 26 May 1305, shortly after receiving the petitioners at Kennington, he sent a palfrey and some dogs for hunting hares to Louis of Evreux, half-brother to the king of France, accompanying his present with a letter in which he said, light-heartedly, 'And, dear cousin, should you want anything else from our land of Wales, we can if you like send you plenty of wild lads (*gentz sauvages*) who know full well how to teach breeding to the young heirs or heiresses of the great lords.'[15]

The last two years of Edward's principate were marked by recurrent rows and reconciliations between father and son. Edward I had always been a man of violent temper, like his grandfather, King John. So long as she was alive his fury had, for the most part, been contained by his queen, Eleanor of Castile. Soon after her death his rages became worse: once he even threw his daughter Elizabeth's coronet into the fire, losing two precious jewels. In September 1299, however, the king – now sixty – married for a second time, and for five years his temper seemed to mellow. His bride was Margaret, the seventeen-year-old sister of the King of France. As usual, their marriage was a political device, intended to put an end to Anglo-French feuds in anticipation of a new crusade in the Holy Land. The marriage was a happy one. Two sons and a daughter were born, and there are many instances on record of good family fellowship, with entertainments shared by the king, his young queen, the

Prince of Wales and his sisters – at least until the summer of 1305. Then, with all the suddenness of a summer storm, the king turned angrily on his son at Midhurst on 14 June and banished him from the court. The prince himself, writing later that same day to a friend, said the king had been infuriated 'because of certain words which he was told we had had with the Bishop of Chester'; and the ostensible reason for the dramatic scene was a complaint from Bishop Walter Langton, the king's treasurer, that the prince, Gaveston and others had amused themselves by poaching deer on his land. It is, however, probable that the king was already irritated by reports of the prince's persistent frivolity at King's Langley, where he had travelled with Gaveston and his circle of bright young lads. The weather, moreover, at Midhurst that June was hot, dry and oppressive – a poor time for a son to pick a quarrel with his father's favourite minister.[16]

The prince did not expect the rift to last long. He kept close to the court, as it progressed through the southern counties, rather than return to King's Langley. The king ordered him to Windsor where he was to remain until the next parliament was summoned, but the prince had his allies and used them well: Bishop Bek of Durham was a good advocate; and an even more effective one was Queen Margaret. 'Our lord the king has now allowed most of the gentlemen of our chamber to resume their accustomed dwelling with us', the prince wrote to his stepmother at the beginning of August, 'and well we know that this was done by your request.' In the autumn the king recognized he needed his son's support too much to prolong the breach. They were reconciled on the Feast of the Translation of St Edward the Confessor (13 October) at Westminster, a fitting time and place.[17]

By the following spring there was a fresh crisis on the Scottish borders. Despite the capture and execution of William Wallace, the Scots were resolved to maintain their independence and found a new national leader in Robert Bruce, crowned as King Robert I at Scone on 25 March 1306. King Edward, so frail by now that he was borne from palace to abbey on a litter, prepared for yet another campaign, one in which the Prince of Wales was to hold independent command. At Whitsun a splendid ceremony was held at Westminster: the prince was endowed with the duchy of Aquitaine, 'adorned with the belt of knighthood' by his father, and then himself permitted to knight nearly three hundred young men –

many of them his close companions – before the high altar of the abbey. The king swore never to draw his sword again once the Scots were subdued, except on holy crusade. It was a safe oath for an old warhorse just four weeks short of his sixty-seventh birthday. His son's slightly curious oath not to sleep two nights in the same place until he reached Scotland stressed the urgency of the crisis.

Within a month the prince was leading the advance-guard across the border, accompanied by the new knights. Gaveston, too, was there, resplendent on a black charger with three white feet, presented to him by the prince. The army ravaged the Lowlands and, by early August, had moved as far north as Perth in vain pursuit of King Robert. With the coming of the autumn rains, the campaign was halted. The king spent the winter months at Lanercost Priory, ten miles east of Carlisle: the prince returned to England for much of November and December, but was otherwise close to his father at Wetheral. It was a strange winter, with a parliament summoned to Carlisle amid the deep snow of late January; and Scotland, as King Edward commented, lying 'wasted, destroyed and stripped bare in many ways'.[18]

At the end of February 1307 a fresh – and, as it proved, decisive – dispute flared up at Lanercost between the king and the prince. Four months previously the king had discovered that twenty-two of the new knights were no longer in Scotland, having preferred to return home rather than linger in winter quarters like Romans on the old imperial frontier. The king was angry: he ordered seizure of the estates and persons of the deserters, who included the prince's close friends, Piers Gaveston and Gilbert of Clare. Once again Queen Margaret intervened and in January secured a royal pardon for most of the offenders. But within a matter of weeks the Prince of Wales sought a new honour for Gaveston: he asked his old enemy, Bishop Walter Langton, to beg the king to transfer from the prince to Gaveston the countship of Ponthieu, a small region around Abbeville on the Somme, which the prince had inherited from his mother. Possibly Langton did not forward the request tactfully. Certainly the king reacted violently. He sent for the prince, and berated him; 'You base-born whoreson, do you want to give away lands now, you who never gained any?', he said, seizing as much as he could of the prince's hair, and pulling it out with his hands. The king decreed that Gaveston should 'leave England for Gascony' at the end of

April, remaining 'beyond the sea during the king's pleasure and awaiting his recall'. The Prince of Wales was made to swear that, during this term of exile, he would not receive or retain Gaveston 'near him or with him'. A northern Franciscan chronicle, edited and interpolated in Lanercost itself, declared firmly that Gaveston's exile was 'on account of the undue intimacy which the younger lord Edward had adopted towards him, publicly calling him his brother'. Another chronicler, writing a few years later, commented reflectively, 'I do not remember to have heard that one man so loved another'. Across the Channel the scribes were less indulgent: the prince was 'too much given to sodomy', says a chronicle of Meaux Abbey.[19]

There is no doubt the prince enjoyed flouting the conventions of the age and, on this occasion, he treated his father's outburst with near contempt. He accompanied Gaveston southwards to Canterbury and Dover, bestowing generous gifts on him. Meanwhile the king ordered concentration of a new army at Carlisle for yet another punitive expedition into Scotland. Slowly the Prince of Wales set out again for the border wilderness: on 8–9 June he was at Lambeth, a week later in Northampton, whence he sent a gift of sturgeon preserved in brine to his father, no doubt as a gesture of reconciliation. By now, however, Edward was a sick man, scarcely able to move from his bed; and on 7 July he died in the arms of servants who were helping him take food. It was another fortnight before the prince, riding up from the south, reached his father's bier.

Edward II's accession was hailed 'with the greatest rejoicing' (*cum ingenti laetitia*) recorded one of the monks of Westminster Abbey.[20] Other chroniclers noted the widespread pleasure at having a youthful king 'fair in body and of great strength' and known for his religious observance, his affability with ordinary folk, and his declared intention of curbing the Scots. His first political act surprised no one. Walter Langton, his father's treasurer for the past twelve years, was arrested even before the dead king's burial: he was a bitter personal enemy of the Prince of Wales, but he had antagonized others, too; and with exchequer debts of more than £60,000 and customs' levies already mortgaged to an Italian banking-house, Langton's imprisonment for alleged misappropriation of funds was accepted without protest from his fellow bishops or from the barons. Soon, however, Edward was in disfavour. He summoned home Gaveston and created him Earl of Cornwall. This dignity, rich in landed endowments, was customarily held only by members of the royal family. Its bestowal was followed by further honours heaped on Gaveston: the regency of the kingdom when Edward crossed the Channel to marry the twelve-year-old daughter of the King of France; and pride of place in the coronation ceremonies. It was even said Edward had presented to Gaveston wedding-presents rich in jewels. The costly and ambitious policy of Edward I's later years was bringing the English feudal kingdom to the verge of collapse. Only a skilful successor could have prevented conflicts between the crown and the landed magnates and between rival barons. Edward II's folly in elevating Gaveston brought feudal anarchy rapidly nearer.

Briefly in the winter of 1308–9 it seemed as if Edward had broken with Gaveston. Under pressure from the earls and the Archbishop of Canterbury, the king suspended his favourite from his territorial titles and sent him to administer Ireland (a task he did well). But by the summer of 1309 Edward was concentrating his mind on dividing the baronial opposition, building up a party which allowed him to recall and reinstate Gaveston as Earl of Cornwall. He returned as arrogant as ever, mimicking his enemies, scarcely bothering to conceal nicknames coined to amuse the king. To be dubbed 'Black Dog' or 'Burst-belly' or 'Joseph the Jew' by a Gascon upstart was intolerable for the landed magnates. Ordinances drawn up in the winter of 1310–11 sought to impose on the king English-born baronial advisers; and once again Edward agreed that Gaveston should leave the country. But within weeks king and favourite were openly celebrating Christmas together at Windsor. Their opponents – the Ordainers – took up arms and, in a brief civil war, captured Gaveston after a siege at Scarborough. While travelling under safe-conduct to London, he was seized in north Oxfordshire by an armed force and beheaded on Blacklow Hill, near Kenilworth. King and Ordainers reached a compromise settlement; and in mid-December 1312 a 'final peace' was proclaimed throughout England and Wales. It was hoped Edward would no longer allow himself to be beguiled into 'evil pursuits'.

Meanwhile the Scots under King Robert kept up their pressure on northern England, taking advantage of the disorders to burn Corbridge, Hexham and even Durham. At last the king agreed to mount the full-scale invasion of Scotland which his subjects had long desired. It was an unmitigated disaster. At Bannockburn on 24 June 1314 the English were trapped between a wooded hillside and a deep marsh; and Edward's army, 20,000 strong when it reached Falkirk two days before, suffered 16,000 casualties. The king himself fled eastwards to the coast at Dunbar, eventually escaping by sea to Northumberland, a fugitive afraid to risk ambush in the hills of Lammermuir.

Moralists, sheltered within the scriptoria of priories and abbeys, blamed the catastrophe on Edward's evil and slothful habits – although, in fact, defeat at Bannockburn sprang less from laziness than from over-eagerness to launch a premature attack.[21] There was little prospect of Edward recovering prestige or winning a national following. King Robert established a hold on Ireland, as well as sending raiding parties into Cumbria and as far south as the Yorkshire dales. It was feared he would incite the Welsh to rebellion. But, significantly, Edward was able throughout his reign to count on the loyalty of his subjects in the old principality. There was in 1316 a brief rising in Glamorgan – which was not part of the principality – but its causes were local, and it evoked no response further north. Edward's accession had put an end to his titular relationship with Wales, all revenue from the lands of the principality automatically reverting to the crown; but administration through his 'vice-regent' or Justice continued to be sound, and spokesmen for the Welsh gentry always received a fair hearing. At Lincoln in 1316 the king made important concessions to freemen in Wales over their rights to sell land, meeting requests they had laid before him, as Prince of Wales, at Kennington eleven years before. And in May 1322 the king summoned a parliament to York which included, for the first time, twenty-four spokesmen for the principality of Wales.

This recognition of Wales as a political community was, in part, a reward by the king for the support he received from Welsh knights during the renewed baronial disorders of 1321–2. For eight years after Bannockburn the king was forced to accept the dominance of his first cousin and old rival, Thomas Earl of Lancaster, the man whom he regarded as chiefly responsible for Gaveston's execution. Earl Thomas was a prototype of the late medieval over-mighty subject, reaching ambitiously for the crown. To his original title he added the earldoms of Leicester, Derby, Lincoln and Salisbury. Such landgrabbers inevitably provoked hostility and, in March 1322, the king was able to raise a sufficiently powerful army to defeat Thomas at Boroughbridge; he was brought to trial before the king and his magnates in council, and duly beheaded. Thus, when the parliament met at York two months later, Edward II for the third time had an opportunity to turn his difficult inheritance into firm and just kingly government. The task was beyond him. He repeated the folly of earlier years, raising up a new favourite – Hugh Despenser the Younger – whose avarice and tastes reminded his fellow barons of Gaveston at his worst. He possessed, moreover, a territorially greedy father, whom the king was also pleased to reward. The combination of the two Despensers completed Edward's alienation from his English subjects and led to his deposition within five years of his victory at Boroughbridge.[22]

In this final phase of the reign the role of Edward's queen, Isabella, was crucial. As a child bride she had resented Gaveston's presence and greed but was too young to oppose him. Now, as a woman of twenty-seven with two sons and two daughters, she had no intention of tolerating insults from new favourites, especially when – in September 1324 – the Despensers deprived her of revenue from certain estates. That winter a war crisis between England and France led the king and the Despensers to a rash decision: on 9 March 1325 they allowed Queen Isabella to sail for France on a diplomatic mission to her brother, King Charles IV; and six months later they agreed that the twelve-year-old heir to the English throne should join his mother at the French court. By the end of the year the queen and her son had attracted to Paris several leading members of the English baronage with grievances against the Despensers. Foremost among them was Roger Mortimer, a Marcher Lord who had fallen foul not only of the younger Despenser in south Wales but also of the king's principal supporters among the native Welsh gentry, Sir Gruffydd Llwyd and his kinsman, Sir Rhys ap Gruffydd. The queen's open liaison with Mortimer caused scandal and embarrassment at her brother's court, and the couple were forced to withdraw to the Netherlands, where they received support from the Count of Hainault. In September 1326 the queen and Mortimer landed on the Suffolk coast with a mere 700 mercenaries. So widespread was hatred of the Despensers that, within a month, most of southern and eastern England had deserted to Isabella's side, and the king was in flight from an insurgent London to Wales, where he knew he still had some following.[23]

On 26 October Edward reached Cardiff, by boat, setting foot in

Wales for the first time in twenty-five years. The Welsh had no liking for Mortimer, but it was too late for the king to rally the mountain people around him. He fled to Caerphilly and Neath Abbey, going into hiding. On 16 November Henry of Lancaster (heir and brother of Earl Thomas) found him at Llantrisant Castle, and at Monmouth, on 20 November, Edward II duly surrendered the great seal. Early in the new year a parliament at Westminster declared him deposed. A thirty-man deputation from parliament cajoled him into formal abdication at Kenilworth on 16 January 1327: nine days later his first-born son was proclaimed his successor, reigning as King Edward III.

The fallen ruler, now officially 'the Lord Edward, sometime King of England', remained at Kenilworth until the spring. By then the Despensers and most of their supporters had suffered the barbarous death of traitors, but Edward was not himself harshly treated. On 3 April he was escorted from Kenilworth to Berkeley Castle in Gloucestershire, where Mortimer, the effective authority in the kingdom, could keep him under closer surveillance. It is possible that, even so, a group of outlaws succeeded in raiding Berkeley and briefly taking Edward into their custody during July. Early in September Mortimer's deputy as Justiciar of Wales, William de Shelford, informed him of a conspiracy in which a band of Welshmen, headed by Sir Rhys ap Gruffydd, planned to free Edward from Berkeley and set him up as champion of Welsh liberties against the Justiciar and the Marcher Lords. Thirteen Welshmen, including five members of the York parliament of 1322, were imprisoned at Caernarfon: others, including Rhys ap Gruffydd, fled to Scotland. The plot sealed Edward's fate. Mortimer could not afford for him to remain alive, a once-crowned talisman of rebel Welsh hopes. On 21 September it was announced the 'sometime King' was dead: almost certainly he was murdered by Mortimer's henchmen who thrust a red-hot spit into his bowels. Outwardly the corpse, viewed by many dignitaries from Gloucester and the surrounding countryside, showed no signs of violent death.[24]

Shortly before Christmas the embalmed body was interred in the abbey church of St Peter at Gloucester. It was an impressive funeral, worthy of a great king. Soon, however, rumour began to claim Edward was not dead: he was said to have escaped from Berkeley in July, crossed to Ireland, travelled back through England in disguise after the body was buried at Gloucester, taken ship to Sluys and then made his way to northern Italy where he allegedly lived for more than fifteen years, passing his days in prayer and repentance within a cloistered hermitage. An inscription over a tomb in the abbey church of Sant Alberto di Burtio in Lombardy claims to mark the final resting place of King Edward II of England.[25] It is probable an English refugee who believed himself to be the deposed king did, indeed, find sanctuary in Lombardy; but there is no corroborative evidence that the real Edward of Caernarfon eluded Mortimer's murderers. For thousands of ordinary folk, prepared to accept the fact that his life had ended in Berkeley Castle, Edward's burial place at Gloucester became a shrine. There was a widespread demand for the dead king's canonization, especially in 1330 when Edward III overthrew Mortimer and sent him to his execution. The young king was clearly troubled in conscience and came himself to Gloucester Abbey, a pilgrim to his father's grave. Nor did he limit himself to prayer: a two-canopied limestone and marble tomb, with a delicately carved alabaster effigy, survives today in what is now the cathedral church at Gloucester, a memorial erected by Edward III to his father.

A hundred and forty miles to the north-west another effigy still stands over the castle gateway of Caernarfon. It is weather-bitten, with none of the serenity of the memorial at Gloucester; and yet it is in many ways a more fitting monument. For prologue and epilogue to Edward's reign were both set in Caernarfon. Four years after the king's death Hywel ap Gruffydd, one of the Welshmen detained at the castle on Mortimer's orders in September 1327, brought an action against William de Shelford, accusing him of complicity in Edward's murder. The authorities were embarrassed: all the alleged conspirators, including those who fled to Scotland, had received royal pardons from Edward III; he did not wish the matter raised again, and the case was allowed to lapse. But Hywel ap Gruffydd had voiced in his king's court a sense of betrayal felt by the Welsh nation. His action was noticed far away, and remembered. Half a century later Thomas of Walsingham, a monk loyal to his abbey of St Albans and its benefactors, wrote an account of England's recent turbulent history. On Edward of Caernarfon he delivered a measured judgment:

When Scotland openly rebelled against him and all England wished to rid herself of him, then did the Welsh in wonderful manner cherish and esteem him and, so far as they were able, stood by him, grieving over his adversities both in life and in death and composing mournful songs about him in the language of their country, the memory of which lingers to the present day, destroyed neither by fear of punishment nor by the passage of time.[26]

CHAPTER TWO

Woodstock and Bordeaux

O N 15 June 1330 Queen Philippa of Hainault, the sixteen-year-old consort of Edward III, gave birth to a son at the royal manor of Woodstock, eight miles north of Oxford. Like his father, grandfather and great-grandfather the boy was named after the Confessor king whom Henry III revered as patron saint of the dynasty, and it was thus as 'Edward of Woodstock' that the prince was first known to his contemporaries. Soon, however, he was accorded formal rank in the peerage: he became Earl of Chester in May 1333 and Duke of Cornwall in March 1337, the first creation of a territorial duchy within England. On 12 May 1343 King Edward III, 'with the consent of the bishops, earls, barons and knights of the shire in our general parliament at Westminster assembled', invested his eldest son with the insignia of a Prince of Wales: coronet on his head, ring of gold for his finger, silver rod in his hand. Finally, at the age of thirty-two, Edward of Woodstock was created Prince of Aquitaine and Gascony, rendering homage to his father for this new lordship at Westminster on 19 July 1362. Yet he is remembered by none of these high-sounding titles. Antiquarians were referring to him as the Black Prince as early as the reign of Henry VIII, perhaps because of the colour of his armour or possibly because of harsh deeds associated with his name in oral traditions across the Channel.* Whatever the reason, he was 'the Black Prince' to Shakespeare's York in *Richard II* and to his Archbishop Chichele in *Henry V* and this appellation has survived through four centuries, becoming as familiar in usage as the cognomina affected by the great families of Rome.

Much of the Black Prince's boyhood was spent in his birthplace. Woodstock, a straggling manor where the queen had her own rural pavilion with cloistered gardens and enclosed orchard beside the river Glyme, was Philippa's favourite summer residence. The young prince

---

* For the Hundred Years War, see map on p. 222.

could learn riding, fishing and hunting in the meadowland and forests of north-west Oxfordshire, for the most part under the discerning eye of his mother; and there was no hint that he dabbled to excess in the rustic arts (as his unfortunate grandfather was said to have done). Philippa, too, appears to have supervised the general character of his more formal education: her almoner, Walter Burley, was a scholar of repute, with an interest in philosophy; and Burley was appointed tutor to the prince as soon as he was 'of age to go to school'. Burley died before the boy was fourteen years old and there can have been little affinity of mind between master and pupil. The prince could write and he is known to have possessed some richly decorative books, but no contemporary ever claimed he was bookish. His character and tastes probably owed more to Burley's two successors, the prince's master of the household Sir Bartholomew de Burghersh and an anglicized Hainaulter in the queen's service, Sir Walter de Mauncy. These two knights trained the heir to the throne according to his father's wishes, emphasizing the allurement of soldiery: the Black Prince was taken to his first tournament at the age of six, given a complete set of armour (including two helmets) before his eighth birthday, and formally knighted in active service on French soil three weeks after his sixteenth birthday. Unlike the first Prince of Wales, Edward of Woodstock became a hearty extrovert who delighted in the skill of arms and loved the ceremonial aspects of chivalry. He consistently fulfilled his father's expectations, and throughout the thirty-three years of his life there is no record of quarrels, or even of petty friction, between father and son. From an early age the king treated him as a companion in the brotherhood of arms: an entry in the household accounts shows Edward III and his fifteen-year-old son gambling at dice together as they journeyed by boat down the Thames to the Kentish coast on pilgrimage to Canterbury. Three years later – at Christmas 1348 – the young prince gambled away £105 in a single day while entertaining his father at Sandwich as they travelled, yet again, to offer prayers at Becket's shrine.[1]

For most of the Black Prince's life, England was at war with France. He was still a child when his father threw the Scots back over the Cheviots, gaining a decisive victory at Halidon Hill, north of Berwick, in July 1333. This feat of arms ensured the prince would fulfil his military service in more rewarding parts of Europe than the bleak Scottish borderland. The Anglo-French conflict, which continued intermittently from 1337 until 1453 and flared up again on three occasions in Henry VIII's reign, had its origins in the 'Gascon Question', the obligations incurred by a king of England as duke of Guienne (Gascony) towards his overlord, the king of France. A compromise settlement of this long grumbling dispute was reached in 1327 but broke down within three or four years. English resentment at French encouragement of the Scots, and French resentment at English economic pressure which sought to manipulate wool prices in Flanders and the Rhineland intensified the cold-war atmosphere of the exchanges between London and Paris. There was no direct cause of war but merely 'a known disposition thereto'. Edward III's attempt to claim, through his mother, the throne of France itself was followed in May 1337 by Philip VI of France's formal confiscation of Edward's possessions in Normandy: these acts provided moral justification for a war from which the English king, his lords and their retainers hoped to gain material rewards in land, ransom money and plunder. The misnamed 'Hundred Years War' was not a trial of strength between two nations: for the landed class it was a speculative mercenary enterprise, in which the military sports of the tourney and the tilting yard were given professional status. The archers, lancers and footmen summoned for service across the Channel showed a xenophobic patriotism, though at a regional rather than a national level, but for them, too, war in France held out the prospect of rich booty. Contemporary chronicles describe how the soldiery robbed and pillaged the small towns and villages on the Cherbourg peninsula at the start of the invasion of France; they emptied the town of Barfleur of 'so much gold, silver and jewelry . . . that boys and servants in the baggage-train set no store by good fur-lined gowns'.[2] This march along the coast on 13–14 June 1346 constituted Edward of Woodstock's introduction to active campaigning. Twelve days later his men pillaged Caen. Small wonder if the Black Prince came to refer to France as a land 'rich in splendid spoils' for Englishmen.

A month after the sack of Caen the prince distinguished himself by his courage at the battle of Crécy, fought some twelve miles north of Abbeville in a terrain not dissimilar from the countryside he had known in those Oxfordshire summers of his boyhood. He was in the thick of the fighting throughout that afternoon. At one point he was thrown to the ground, defending himself in hand-to-hand combat. The French sent in fifteen waves of attack, their cavalry suffering heavily from the crossfire of longbowmen and the tenacity of dismounted men-at-arms grouped around their lords' standards. The laurels of victory belonged rightly to Edward III: he had chosen a sound defensive position with tactical skill; and he knew how to exploit the long-range effectiveness of archers against charging cavalry. But it suited the king to give credit to his eldest son: provided he exalted his family, he need not fear the advancement of other nobles, distinguished by their heroism and enriched by the spoils of war. In the preamble to the charter of 1343 creating his son Prince of Wales the king declared that, just as the rays sent forth from the sun do not reduce its brightness, so the eminence of a throne is heightened by the honours conferred upon his kinsmen by a sovereign. It was this principle which the king followed in lavishing praise on the prince for his role at Crécy. There is no doubt the young man fought bravely, displaying to advantage the physical strength that made the Plantagenets the most muscular of English dynasties. But the legends of Crécy – the winning of the boy's spurs, the appropriation of ostrich feathers badge and '*Ich Dien*' motto from the fallen King of Bohemia – are embellishments by chroniclers and poets, eager to find edifying stories in kingly propaganda. Certainly, after Crécy, it was known in Europe that the ruler of England was a first-rate commander and that his heir was as skilled in arms as any knight on the jousting field.

There followed, for the prince and his father, eleven months of siege warfare as the king sought to starve out Calais and thus acquire a foothold in Europe only twenty-one miles from his castle at Dover. Occasionally the prince raided the surrounding countryside, but for most of the year he was with the king, the queen and the court at the improvised hutted town of Villeneuve-le-hardi, outside the ramparts of Calais. He was present on 4 August 1347 when the king, apparently at Queen Philippa's intercession, showed clemency towards the burghers who, at last, surrendered to him the keys of their town. By mid-October the prince and his parents were back in London: all major operations on land were suspended for seven years by a series of truces.[3]

The Black Prince saw action of a different kind on 29 August 1350 when the king's warships intercepted a Castilian fleet, which had been raiding English and Gascon merchant craft, off Winchelsea and fought a sharp engagement called by the chroniclers the battle of Espagnols-sur-mer. Tactically the prince and his father used their ships as though they were sea cavalry charging down an enemy: the English vessels ran alongside the Spanish, while knights and men-at-arms sought to board them sword in hand. Probably the Black Prince – who was accompanied by his ten-year-old brother, John of Gaunt – was in greater danger that August evening in mid-Channel than at Crécy three years before: his ship was sunk soon after he had leapt aboard a Spanish vessel, leaving him the choice of taking the enemy ship as a prize or perishing in the savage fighting on its decks. The vessel was captured, as indeed was almost half the Castilian fleet, the remaining ships slipping away westward under cover of darkness. It was a notable victory, confirming Edward III's claim to mastery of the straits. Yet, although parliament tactfully congratulated him on becoming 'King of the Sea', neither father nor son rated the battle of great significance, and no attempt was made to build up a permanent fleet. It is curious that Edward of Woodstock, who courted fame as a commander on land, should be the only Prince of Wales to have fought at sea.[4]

Edward III's respect for the ceremonies and ritual of chivalry led him to establish the most famous of all secular orders of knighthood, probably on St George's Day 1348. An oral tradition, first put on paper by Polydore Vergil two hundred years later, describes how a lady's garter, accidentally falling to the ground during festivities to mark the capture of Calais, was picked up by the king, who fastened the blue ribbon around his knee, rebuked amused onlookers with the comment '*Honi soit qui mal y pense*', and declared that he would soon make the garter ribbon the most highly honoured decoration worn by a knight. This tale may well be apocryphal, but there can be no doubt of the esteem in which the Order was held within a few years of its foundation. Edward of Woodstock was the youngest of the twenty-six original knights of the Order of the Garter: he seems, moreover, to have been in effect organizing King of Arms for the Order. Surviving accounts show that, shortly before Christmas in 1348, the keeper of the prince's wardrobe purchased twenty-four garters of blue ribbon which were presented to the knights companion. The prince also provided them with clasped brooches of gold, belts, buckles and batons. His influence on the early years of the Order was considerable: thirteen of the knights had served with him, either at Crécy or before Calais; and, since the average age of the founder knights was under thirty, it is probable that Edward III intended the Order to bind the young nobility in a comradeship of arms which was dependent upon his eldest son. Significantly, few founder knights among the prince's friends were elevated to the peerage : the cult of chivalry enabled the king to find in the symbolism of the blue garter a bond of loyalty more exclusive – and politically less threatening – than the landed endowments with which the early Plantagenets had been forced to reward the services of soldiers of fortune.[5] The Order of the Garter was no mere jousting club, nor was it a prototype for later oath-swearing sword-and-cape fraternities of fact or of fiction: it was a secular brotherhood of distinguished companions and rooted in religious observance. The hearing of mass within the chapel of St Edward and St George at Windsor is a central injunction of the Order's earliest statutes : to the prince and his friends it was a solemn obligation, however contrary to Christian ethic their conduct may appear to later eyes.

War with France was renewed in earnest during the autumn of 1355. The prince, appointed as the king's lieutenant in Gascony, set sail from Plymouth on 9 September at the head of a fleet of more than seventy vessels which anchored in the Garonne off Bordeaux eleven days later. On 5 October the prince and his expeditionary force set off on the first of their great raids (*chevauchées*) into the heart of France. It took them across Armagnac and through Languedoc; passing south of Toulouse the raiders harried farms, villages and small towns up to the walled cities of Narbonne and Carcassonne, firing houses outside the citadels in both instances. This systematic devastation of four hundred miles of countryside took eight weeks. In one sense it was the medieval equivalent of the indiscriminate terror-bombing of the Second World War, causing havoc deep in enemy territory and seeking to disrupt the economy. On the other hand, unlike aerial bombers, the raiders returned with fat booty : 'You should know that in this journey, the prince and his men had very great profit', writes Froissart. The army not only lived off the land as it marched but continued to thrive on its gains for many months after it came back to winter quarters. All that was missing from the first raid was a decisive engagement, with the opportunity of taking prisoners who could be held to ransom.

This deficiency was rectified in the second raid. King John II of France tried to cut off the Black Prince as he was returning to Bordeaux from a profitable *chevauchée* northwards from Bergerac to the Loire, and the two armies met in battle a few miles south-east of Poitiers on 19 September 1356. By closely following his father's tactics at Crécy, the Black Prince tempted the French to concentrate their cavalry on a narrow front, where the horsemen were caught in the crossfire of well-placed archers. Lack of co-ordination between the various wings of the French force allowed the English defenders to destroy a succession of attacks by dismounted knights in isolated combats. Finally King John, showing the personal courage of a knight rather than the sagacity of a sovereign commander, went into the attack, was surrounded by the prince's men and taken prisoner, as also was his second son, Philip, a boy of fourteen. In all, the English and Gascons took nearly two thousand captives at the battle of Poitiers, including fifty noblemen. The final attack on the king's bodyguard killed off some of the finest names in France: among the dead were two dukes, a Marshal of France, a viscount and Geoffrey de Charny, bearer of the sacred banner, the *oriflamme*. Most were buried in Poitiers, either at the Dominican or Franciscan churches, but the captive king was permitted to pay for the exhumation of Charny's body and its re-interment in Paris with all the honour due to a champion of the standard of Saint-Denis. The Black Prince insisted on observance of every nicety in the chivalric code.

Froissart, picking up stories of the campaign from veterans in London a dozen years later, writes prettily of the Prince of Wales entertaining 'the King of France and most of the captured counts and barons' at supper that evening, serving his guests 'in all humility' and kneeling before King John 'in honour and friendship'. This episode, if it ever took place, went unrecorded at the time. The army is known to have spent that night close to the battlefield, enjoying provisions from the ransacked French camp and sharing out booty. The Black Prince personally did well from the battle: he acquired some of the French King's jewels and his crown, together with a silver vessel shaped like a warship which had been the central decoration on the king's table; and in later years the prince offered these jewels as security for borrowing money. He bought custody of some distinguished prisoners from the knights who had taken them, and then made a profit on the business by selling three important captives to his father for £20,000. The rest he held until good ransom money came from France. He was also entitled to a share – frequently as much as half – in ransoms collected by any knight in his service. Yet he was expected to reward his knights and squires generously, and always did so with lavish prodigality. Since he had already contracted loans on the prospects of future revenue, he did not emerge from the campaign with so comfortable a fortune as did many of his captains in the field.[6]

To return to England with a captive king of France in his baggage train was a unique triumph, one in which the Prince of Wales gloried to the full. He wintered, with King John, in the archbishop's palace at Bordeaux, only crossing to Plymouth in the spring of 1357. A leisurely journey through Sherborne, Salisbury and Winchester brought prince and king on 24 May to Southwark where they were greeted by a procession of city aldermen and guildsmen. There followed a state entry into the city unmatched in splendour until the prince's great-nephew came back victorious from Agincourt nearly sixty years later. Edward III greeted his son and King John at Westminster: the captive king was housed in the Duke of Lancaster's palace of the Savoy, and in due course Edward III fixed his ransom at half a million pounds, payable by instalments in gold crowns. A truce brought two years of uneasy peace, while Edward III sought restoration of the old Plantagenet possessions. Renewal of the fighting took the prince on a fresh campaign around Rheims and the upper Seine in the winter of 1359–60. Eventually the treaty of Brétigny of May 1360 conceded some, but not all, of Edward's demands: he was recognized as full sovereign of Gascony; his territories were extended as far east as Poitiers, Perigueux, Cahors and Limoges; he was confirmed in possession of Calais and the Somme estuary; and a complicated arrangement was reached for the handing over of King John II's ransom. Brétigny was not a good settlement: it left enough questions unanswered to provide the pretext for further war when the two main combatants were ready to offer each other a new challenge. Each continued to intrigue against the other on the periphery of the main battle zone, notably in the Low Countries and south of the Pyrenees; although technically the Anglo-French war was not renewed until the summer of 1369.

By 1360 Edward of Woodstock had, as the chroniclers assure us, won renown for the title of Prince of Wales 'throughout Christendom'. Ironically, Edward knew little about the principality whose name he was thus honouring. He showed none of his grandfather's interest in Welsh music and cultural traditions, nor did he ever visit Wales. In

August 1353 he may well have caught a distant view of Snowdonia as he journeyed hot-temperedly to Chester, where he believed casual lapses in the administration of justice were denying him the full customary dues of the earldom. He always looked upon Chester – and, indeed, upon the Duchy of Cornwall – as a source of steady revenue. Wales was in a different category: the net income from the principality could never be high because of the heavy cost of maintaining peace within its borders. In 1343 Edward III had proposed that tenants of the principality might mark the investiture of his son by a voluntary contribution towards repair of the Welsh castles, but this suggestion was received with deaf ears and tight fists – such a levy would form an unfortunate precedent, if the eldest son of every sovereign was to be invested Prince of Wales. The Black Prince regarded Wales primarily as a recruiting ground: it was the home of good bowmen and tough spearmen, or foot lancers: more than three thousand Welshmen served under their prince in the Crécy and Calais campaigns, and the archers of North Wales could rightly claim credit for unseating French knights in the decisive battle of August 1346. The Welsh troops, archers and spearmen, wore a uniform short coat and hat, of green and white, with the green on the right side of the body. Presumably this innovation was intended to identify the Welshmen to their English comrades in arms, and later to Gascons, Spanish and Flemings; for the barrier of language must, at times, have made it difficult to recognize the Welsh as allies. A smaller group of Welshmen accompanied their prince to Gascony, took part in the two *chevauchées* and fought at Poitiers.

The Black Prince's Welsh soldiery were mere numbers on a pipe roll. They are known to have marched to Chester and down the long route through Shrewsbury, Worcester, Bristol to Plymouth or across to the east coast where they took ship from the Orwell estuary. Some deserted, others were too ill for foreign service by the time they reached the port; and for the most part their names remain unrecorded. Among the prince's retinue, however, were a few members of the Welsh knightly class. Sir Rhys ap Gruffydd fought at Crécy and his kinsman, Hywel ap Gruffydd at Poitiers: both had served Edward of Caernarfon and remained loyal to his memory. Hywel, knighted in 1355, lived on until the early years of Richard II's reign, passing into Welsh legend under the graphic appellation 'Sir Hywel of the Axe'. At least three other Gruffydds distinguished themselves sufficiently on the Gascony expedition for their names to appear in a journal of special payments kept by the prince's chief cashier: so, too, did a Llewelyn, a Ken ap Eignyon and David ap Blethin Vaughan, leader of thirty Welsh archers from Flintshire (who took with them to France their own chaplain). But most of the Welshmen had to be content with low rates of pay and with blame for the more violent instances of pillage and vandalism. The Black Prince looked upon them as loosely disciplined arrow fodder. He suspected that the principality was avoiding its first full financial obligations and in 1348 he instituted *Quo Warranto* proceedings, sending judges from his council to make certain that the full revenue in fines and taxes was coming to the princely coffers. To the Welsh, the first of their English-born Princes was not the supreme instance of knightliness, 'the flower of chivalry', but a tough and grasping absentee landlord.[7]

In October 1361 the prince at last put his bachelor days behind him and married, not for political advantage, but for love – and money. His bride, Countess Joan of Kent, was his father's first cousin, a daughter of Edward II's half-brother, Edmund. Through her mother she was descended from Llywelyn the Great (by a similar relationship to that linking Princess Anne to Queen Victoria), but although this Welsh princely ancestry assumed importance later in the century, there is no evidence the titular Prince of Wales was even aware of it at the time of his marriage. Joan was 'a great prize, beautiful, pleasant and wise', said the Black Prince's earliest biographer, the herald of his friend, Sir John Chandos. Froissart found her 'the loveliest woman in all the kingdom of England, and the most attractive'. Later romantic writers dubbed her 'the Fair Maid of Kent': this was a generous misrepresentation of her character. She had gone through a form of marriage with a dashing young knight, Sir Thomas Holland, at the age of twelve. In his absence, fighting for knightly causes as far away as Prussia and Granada, she had also married – somewhat reluctantly – the Earl of Salisbury, who was a godson of Edward III, and probably his offspring, too. The king and Joan had a romantic attachment: legend says it was her garter that fell during the famous festivities at Calais; and if it did not, one feels that the fault can hardly be hers. A papal bull invalidated Joan's Salisbury marriage in 1352 and she lived as Holland's consort until his death in 1360, bearing him two sons, for whom the Black Prince was godfather, and a daughter. The prince had known Joan, who was two years older than himself, since childhood: she had spent many summers at Woodstock with Queen Philippa. By 1361 she enjoyed a good income from her lands as Countess of Kent and, in her widowhood, this wealth was augmented by the considerable war profits of her late husband. The Prince of Wales became her third husband in a splendid ceremony at Windsor on the eve of the Feast of St Edward the Confessor. Archbishop Simon Islip of Canterbury is said to have warned the Black Prince that doubts might later be cast on the legitimacy of any offspring of the marriage since the Earl of Salisbury was still living (and, indeed, survived until 1397). Significantly, among the official papers sent by Pope Innocent VI to Archbishop Simon a month before the ceremony was an assurance of absolution from any pains or penalties inadvertently incurred by the marriage. Dynastically it was not a wise union.[8]

The 'Prince and Princess of Wales, Aquitaine and Gascony' – for such, from July 1362, was the highest form of their titles – sailed from Plymouth for the Garonne on 9 June 1363 and were received in Bordeaux three weeks later with the splendour due to a Viceroy and Vicereine. For the next eight years they lived in great style, when the prince was not away at the wars: sometimes the court was at Bordeaux but by preference at Angoulême. It was at Angoulême that their first son was born in March 1365: he was baptized Edward; and in the following month the prince presided over a tournament to mark the birth of a grandson to the founder of the Order of the Garter. So magnificent was the scale of festivities that the prince had to pay for the stabling of 18,000 horses, while forty-eight peers or knights were honoured by attachment to the retinue of the princess for the ten days of celebration. The birth of a second son, Richard, at Bordeaux on the Feast of the Epiphany two years later caused less excitement: he was not in the direct line of succession; his father was about to leave for a campaign in the south; and, no doubt, the extravagances of a long Christmas had already imposed a strain on the prince's domestic finances. The luxurious life at the prince's court aroused adverse comment, especially in Paris, but his biographer, the Chandos Herald, looking back nostalgically a few years later, could wistfully write, 'There abode all nobleness, all joy and jollity, largesse, gentleness and honour; and all his subjects, and all his men loved him dearly.'[9]

Yet did they? Sir John Chandos was the prince's Constable in Aquitaine, his chief administrative officer, and the herald-biographer was therefore not a disinterested commentator on events. No doubt the prince's administration was beneficial: it was certainly efficient. Although war had harmed the wines of the region and the Black Death so ravaged the towns and villages that commerce failed to flourish, opportunities for trade were improved by practical measures, such as the construction of the first lighthouse in these waters, the Phare de Corduan, set on a rock in the Gironde estuary, off Royan. The prince did more for Aquitaine than he did for Wales or Chester. All classes, however, resented the unusually high level of taxation, and the Gascon nobility grumbled at their exclusion from office, for every major post seemed to go to a veteran campaigning friend of the prince. Moreover, he was soon out of his depth in continental politics. He conceived the grand design of supporting the exiled ruler of Castile, Pedro the Cruel, in alliance with King Charles of Navarre, against the French puppet king of Castile, Enrique II. It was hoped a combined English, Gascon, insurgent Castilian and Navarrese army could defeat Enrique and prevent the French from using the formidable Castilian fleet. The strategic purpose of the expedition was admirable, provided it could pay its way and not impose yet another tax upon the prince's Gascon subjects.

The Black Prince's Spanish campaign of 1367 is one of the epic adventures of medieval warfare: across the Pyrenees by way of the Pass of Roncesvalles in February snow and frost; through the mountains of Avala, uncertain of Navarrese loyalty, to the natural amphitheatre of Vitoria (where an English army, fighting its way northwards, was to win fame in 1813); and so in driving rain down slippery mountain trails to the valley of the Ebro, where Enrique's army awaited the invaders around the small town of Nájera. Spanish morale was low – some troops deserted Enrique and joined Pedro before battle began – but Enrique's army was strengthened by a French force under the inspired leadership of Bertrand du Guesclin. The battle of Nájera was a sharp engagement lasting no more than a few hours in the morning of Saturday, 3 April 1367: once again it was a striking triumph for the prince, although on this occasion some credit is also due to his brother, John of Gaunt, whose men-at-arms launched the first assault on du Guesclin's troops. Enrique fled, du Guesclin was taken prisoner, Pedro was back in Burgos, the capital of Castile, by Monday; and it only remained for the prince to secure from the restored king fit payment for the services of his English and Gascon troops and an assurance that the Castilian fleet would never again sail in support of the French. With over two thousand French and Spanish noblemen taken at Nájera, there seemed good prospects for ransom money. Emissaries sent from the battlefield to Bordeaux and on to Edward III represented Nájera as a second Poitiers.

The euphoria of victory lingered for several months in the English and Gascon courts. There was a week of celebration in Bayonne when the prince and his men crossed back into their own possessions early in September and further festivities when they reached Bordeaux. Thirty years later the monastic chronicler, Henry Knighton of Leicester, could still describe Nájera as the greatest victory of the fourteenth century, although this judgment may owe something to the Leicester canon's wish to please John of Gaunt (who seems to have dined out on tales of Nájera well into old age). Yet in reality Nájera created more problems than it solved: Pedro, restored to his Castilian throne, showed scant respect for agreements he had made with the prince before the start of the campaign: the army remained unpaid and it proved impossible to obtain the full value of ransoms, as money was wanted quickly. The prince distributed to some of his commanders jewels given to him by Pedro, retaining for himself one large ruby, which eventually was mounted in the English state crown, still worn by British sovereigns. There remained some six thousand unpaid mercenaries who were organizing themselves into companies of brigands along the Dordogne and other valleys. In order to pay these mercenaries and clear them from his domains the prince imposed a new hearth-tax: it enraged the Gascon nobility, some of whom refused to allow the tax to be levied on their estates. After making a formal protest to Edward III they went to Paris and appealed for support to the King of France, Charles V (who had succeeded the captive John II in April 1364). This process of appeal encouraged a full-scale rebellion in Gascony which reopened the Anglo-French war in earnest during the closing weeks of the year 1369, threatening every English gain conceded in the Brétigny treaty.[10]

By now the Black Prince was a sick man. He had contracted amoebic dysentery in Spain and never fully recovered his health. His last years are racked with the elements of classical tragedy. 'All kinds of mischance . . . befell the noble Prince, who lay ill abed', wrote the Chandos Herald: the English were pushed back from the centre of France; several of the prince's closest companions were killed in ill-coordinated defensive actions; the city of Limoges was surrendered to the French by its bishop, and then razed to the ground on the prince's orders, as a warning to all defectors; and finally the prince's eldest son, Edward of Angoulême, died, a few months short of his sixth birthday. Saddened and chastened by adversity the prince handed over what remained of his Gascon lands to his brother, John of Gaunt, and in January 1371 returned to Plymouth with his princess and the four-year-old Richard of Bordeaux. The prince was so weakened by the voyage from the Garonne to the Tamar that he had to rest for over five weeks at Plympton Priory before resuming his slow journey to London. It seemed as if he had come home to die.[11]

In fact the prince lived another five years after his return to England. On several occasions he received spokesmen from the convocation of Canterbury and from parliament and bullied them into granting subsidies for the war in France. Each St George's Day from 1372 until 1376 he travelled to Windsor for the Garter ceremonies and in the summer of 1372 sailed, with his father, on a last attempt to halt the erosion of their possessions in Aquitaine, but south-westerly gales prevented them from reaching the French coast and, with the coming of autumn, the expedition was called off. In November he formally handed back the principality of Aquitaine to his father. Now he reverted to his title of Prince of Wales.

There were moments when even that dignity seemed in danger. In 1336 a great-nephew of Prince Llywelyn 'the Last' known as Owen Lawgoch entered the service of the French, and began to organize groups of Welsh soldiery to fight against the English. King Charles v gave him full backing, recognized his claim to be the righful Prince of Wales, and fitted out an invasion force of 3,000 men which was to sail with Lawgoch – 'Yvain de Galles' as the French called him – and land in Anglesey, calling on the people of Gwynedd to rally to his cause. The expedition was a medieval counterpart to Roger Casement's attempts to raise an Irish Brigade in Germany in 1915–16; but Lawgoch allowed himself to be distracted. Instead of sailing for Anglesey, the force landed on Guernsey where Owen Lawgoch gave an impressive display of his fighting qualities. He remained in the French service, distinguishing himself at La Rochelle, and later at the siege of Mortain. The author of the *Anonimalle Chronicle*, a monk of St Mary's at York, reckoned Lawgoch 'a great enemy of England'; and his threat was taken so seriously in London that warnings were sent to North Wales for the castles to be kept victualled and fully garrisoned, while any Welshmen suspected of giving Lawgoch support were to be held in custody so long as there was a risk of invasion. It is difficult to assess how much backing Lawgoch might have expected in North Wales. Away from the fringe of castles in Gwynedd, the bards were said to be calling on 'Owain, the son of prophecy' to return to the land of his fathers.[12] The Welsh people were suffering from taxation and from increasing dues levied on a diminishing population which had been hard hit by the Black Death and other pestilences. It was natural they should find solace in a bardic patriotism which looked to the future as well as to the past.

In London, too, people were tired of the war. As Bishop Thomas Brinton of Rochester recalled, there had been a time when 'God was wont to be English' and 'our princes . . . won manly triumphs over their enemies'. Now victory was a distant memory. When in 1373 John of Gaunt, Duke of Lancaster, cut his way in a spectacular march from Calais to Troyes and on to the upper Loire and down the Dordogne to Bordeaux, he brought small recompense and succeeded in losing half his men. The duke was far from popular in London: he was known to have costly ambitions to secure the throne of Castile for himself or his second wife, the eldest surviving child of the murdered Pedro; and there were also persistent rumours that, if the Black Prince and Edward III died, the duke would declare his nephew Richard of Bordeaux illegitimate and thus seize the English crown. This canard may have been planted by French agents during peace talks at Bruges, and there is no evidence for the rumours. Nevertheless, there were many intrigues at court and everyone around the king was suspect, except the ailing Prince of Wales and his consort. The chief grievance was the presence in the king's retinue of courtiers and merchants suspected of fraud on a large scale. Edward III, by now in his dotage and partially paralysed, seemed dependent on his former mistress, Alice Perrers. 'It is not fitting or safe that all the keys should hang from the belt of one woman', declared Bishop Brinton in another hard-hitting sermon.[13]

Demands for purging the court party came to a head after the failure of a half-hearted expedition to Brittany in 1375. The 'Good Parliament', which assembled at Westminster during the last days of April 1376, had every intention of making monetary grants dependent on cleaning up the financial scandals at court. The Black Prince, who was well enough to attend the opening of parliament, is said to have sympathized with the Commons in their wish to free the king from evil counsellors. But at the end of May the prince's health finally gave way, just as the Commons were completing their charges against six men and Alice Perrers. His illness hampered the activities of the court and blunted the attacks of parliament, although the Commons succeeded in ousting all seven scoundrels, at least temporarily. On 8 June, Trinity Sunday, the Prince of Wales died: Westminster, London and all the country were thrown into mourning; and the political crisis was overshadowed by public sorrowing, which the dead prince's brothers and the court had good reason not to assuage, even had they so desired. His embalmed body lay in state in Westminster Hall until Michaelmas, 102 days in all. Not until the first Sunday in October were his remains interred, as he had wished, in Canterbury Cathedral.

Parliament, meeting only a few hundred yards away from the prince's catafalque, was acutely conscious of the dynastic uncertainty caused by his death and the physical and mental infirmity of his father. On 25 June the Lords and Commons requested that Richard of Bordeaux should be brought before parliament. When he was presented on the following day, a speech of welcome was delivered by the chancellor who, as it happened, was the senior prelate from Wales, though himself an Englishman: Bishop Adam Houghton of St David's spoke of the honour and reverence due to Richard as heir apparent 'in the same way that his noble father the Prince was'. The Commons, however, went further than this: the parliament rolls record that 'they prayed with one voice' for the king forthwith to grant Richard the principality of Wales. This prayer brought a testy reply from Eltham, where the court had retired from the heat and tension of Westminster: such matters, the king said, were not for parliamentary discussion. But there were two sound reasons for this initiative by the Commons. If the king created his grandson Prince of Wales it would be difficult for the Duke of Lancaster to claim the throne; and it would also check the pretensions of Charles v's Welsh protégé, Owen Lawgoch. For Richard – unlike his English predecessors as Prince of Wales – was descended from the great Llywelyn, and therefore had as good a claim on Welsh patriotic loyalty as Lawgoch or any other Messiah invoked by bardic sentiment. The bishops and lords temporal assured the Commons they would mediate with the king over this question. And seven weeks after the Black Prince was finally entombed in Canterbury Cathedral, Edward III duly issued letters patent from his Essex manor of Havering-atte-Bower: the king 'out of his favour' bestowed on his grandson Richard of Bordeaux the dignity and possessions of the Prince of Wales, together with those enjoyed by a Duke of Cornwall and Earl of Chester.[14]

Richard was prince for only seven months. During this brief period of time there are few instances of his public activity, and he was never invested with the insignia of princely rank. On Tuesday, 27 January 1377, three weeks after his tenth birthday, he deputized for Edward III at the opening of parliament; and the records conjure up a picture of a frail, fair-haired lad sitting in the king's throne of the Painted Chamber at the palace of Westminster while around him prelates, lords, knights and burgesses marshalled grievances against the burdens of royal and papal taxation. The prince returned to his father's old manor at Kennington: there, on the following Sunday evening, over a hundred prominent London citizens, mounted and masked, serenaded Richard and his mother in a torchlight procession which ended with dancing and other festivities, thus bringing gaiety to a winter grim with portent. Less than three weeks later, on 20 February, Richard was still at Kennington when his uncle, Gaunt, was forced to flee there as angry rioters were attacking his palace at the Savoy. That night, when Gaunt's enemies followed him south of the river, Richard's mother, the redoubtable Joan of Kent, needed only to appear before the trouble-makers as 'the prince's widow' for them to disperse in respectful silence.[15] The legend and legacy of Edward of Woodstock remained powerful spellbinders.

On 23 April 1377 the Prince of Wales was created a knight of the Garter. Honoured with Richard in that last colourful ceremony of their grandfather's reign was another prince of royal blood, his cousin and almost exact contemporary, Henry of Bolingbroke, the eldest son of John of Gaunt, Duke of Lancaster. Within nine weeks Edward III was dead and there was no longer a Prince of Wales: a lad of ten ruled as

King Richard II, and at his coronation his cousin Henry carried the sword of state. Twenty-two years later Bolingbroke usurped the crown and, as King Henry IV, founded the royal dynasty of Lancaster. It is tempting to over-simplify the tragic reign of Richard II, presenting Bolingbroke as an envious cousin, spurred on by an ambitious father. But the facts deny the Richard-and-Henry tussle any dramatic unity. The two boys appear to have been good friends until the Peasants' Revolt of 1381. While Richard behaved with great personal courage at that time, he left Henry in the Tower of London with the drawbridge down and he was nearly killed by the mob who executed the Archbishop of Canterbury. Relations between the royal cousins were sour for some years after the Revolt. Nevertheless John of Gaunt, 'time honoured Lancaster', remained consistently loyal to his nephew: the suspicions of the 'Good Parliament' came to nothing, for at heart Gaunt cared less for palaces in England than castles in Castile.[16] Richard II's authority was undermined, not so much by Lancastrian intrigue, as by his rare capacity for self-destruction.

This failure of Richard of Bordeaux is a matter of English history, remote from any story of the Princes of Wales. He tried to create a new, benevolently despotic monarchy which proved as capricious as the tyranny of John. He cultivated a civilized life, seeking to end the French wars and yet providing no outlet for the energy of the landed magnates nor any means for them to pursue power and purloin wealth. From the fate of Edward II he had learnt nothing and forgotten nothing: for, while the confidence which he gave to unpopular favourites recalled the days of Gaveston, he remained so devoted to the cult of his great-grandfather that he twice sent agents to Rome to press the Curia for canonization; and in the autumn of 1390 Richard travelled to Gloucester so as to seek in person evidence of miracles around the shrine. At times, especially in the later years of his reign, it is as if he were defiantly courting the disasters that had sent Edward to Berkeley Castle.

Like Edward II, Richard had a considerable following among the Welsh, especially in Gwynedd. In 1387 Richard crossed into the lands of the principality from Chester and recruited pikemen who, together with his Cheshire archers, formed the nucleus of his personal bodyguard, with its famous livery of the white hart. Further recruits were enlisted from Wales and Cheshire in 1397–8, the king's affection for the area leading him in September 1397 to raise Chester to the status of a principality, which was to include the basically Welsh areas of Flintshire. Among those who served Richard in 1398–9 were two brothers from a family which was soon to start its rapid climb in social status, Gwilym and Rhys ap Tudor. With other prominent Welshmen they accompanied Richard when he sailed for Waterford in May 1399, intent on punishing the perennially rebellious Irish.

Richard's Irish expedition was the second major blunder committed in the course of a few months. It took him away from an England alarmed by his mounting contempt for property rights and the safeguards of common law. In the previous autumn he had sent Bolingbroke (Duke of Hereford) and Thomas Mowbray (Duke of Norfolk) into exile; and in March 1399 he declared forfeit the title and estates of the Duchy of Lancaster which should have passed to Bolingbroke on the death of his father, Gaunt, at the beginning of February. This act of sequestration deprived Bolingbroke of an annual income from land of at least £12,000. As soon as news reached Bolingbroke in Paris that Richard had gone to Ireland, he began to mount an expedition pledged to save England from Richard's misrule and to recover the Lancaster inheritance, and the properties of other magnates dispossessed by the king's command. Bolingbroke landed at the mouth of the Humber early in July. News travelled slowly and Richard was not able to leave Ireland until 24 July. By then Henry of Bolingbroke was being welcomed throughout England as though he were the Messiah, as one of the bishops recalled a few years later. Significantly, Richard – again like Edward II – made for Wales, confident he would find support among the men of the principality. He landed first at Haverfordwest and then journeyed northwards along the coast to Conwy, hoping to raise the men of Gwynedd and enter his second principality of Chester in triumph. These .plans were mere romantic illusions. Hardly more than a hundred soldiers awaited him at Conwy Castle: he was tricked into accompanying emissaries from Bolingbroke to Flint, where Henry treated him as a captive. Within a month both cousins were back in London, Bolingbroke at Westminster as King Henry IV, Richard in the Tower as his prisoner.

Richard had yet to reach his personal Berkeley. It was sited farther north than the castle in which Edward II had met his death; for King Henry ordered his captive to be taken to one of the strongest Lancastrian possessions, Pontefract Castle, in southern Yorkshire. In the first days of January 1400 a muddled conspiracy by Richard's supporters in London was ruthlessly stamped out by the new king. Before the end of the month it was known that Richard lay dead at Pontefract. Nobody knows if he was choked, stabbed or poisoned. It is probable that he was allowed to starve himself to death. For most Englishmen the fate of Richard of Bordeaux mattered little at the time. The reaction of the Welsh was different: disgust at his deposition and apparent murder aroused resentment which intensified during the summer months when increased taxes and local disputes with 'English' landowners added fresh grievances against Lancastrian rule. In the autumn of 1400 the smouldering discontent flared up in open rebellion as Owain Glyn Dwr (Glendower) claimed the authority of a Welsh prince over Gwynedd and Powys, challenging the overlordship of the House of Lancaster.[17]

CHAPTER THREE

Harry of Monmouth

NO usurper ever picked up the English Crown with so rapid a twist from fortune as Henry of Bolingbroke. On 30 May 1399 he was an exiled duke in Paris, his estates sequestered by his royal cousin: on 30 September he stood before an empty throne in Westminster Hall, acclaimed by a parliament newly told that King Richard had signed away his titles. A fortnight later Henry was crowned with all the traditional rites at Westminster. As if to emphasize the continuity of sanctified kingship, Henry had chosen for his coronation one of the holiest days in the abbey's year: October 13 commemorated the translation of Edward the Confessor's body, when the bones of the abbey's founder had been moved to a new and finer shrine.

The coronation was an impressive ceremony, magnificently staged. A sharp-eyed Welshman, Adam of Usk, was serving that week as one of Archbishop Arundel's chaplains. He later maintained that there had been three disturbing omens on coronation day: the king had shed one of his ornate shoes during the procession; later, a golden spur had fallen from his leg; and, more surprisingly, 'at the banquet a sudden gust of wind carried away the crown from his head'. Such portents could be interpreted in differing ways by the prelates and magnates around the king. Adam also recalled in his chronicle the contrast between the two ceremonial swordbearers in the sanctuary: Henry Percy, first Earl of Northumberland, a 57-year-old veteran of Gaunt's march from Calais to Bordeaux, carried the king's personal sword; and opposite to him was Henry of Monmouth, the king's twelve-year-old son, with the unsheathed sword representing justice with mercy, which Bolingbroke had himself borne at the coronation of Richard II. Two days later Adam was again in attendance on the Archbishop at another ceremony: 'The king', Adam wrote, 'promoted his son Henry by five symbols, to wit, by the delivery of a golden rod, by a kiss, by a belt, by a ring, and by letters of creation to be Prince of Wales.' Other eye-witnesses describe how he placed a coronet of precious stones on the boy's head while Edmund Langley, Duke of York – last survivor of Edward III's seven sons – conducted the new Prince of Wales to his seat in parliament. Further titles and endowments swiftly followed, each backed by resolutions of the Lords and Commons and on 10 November it was decided that henceforth Henry of Monmouth's full style should be 'Prince of Wales, Duke of Aquitaine, Duke of Lancaster and Cornwall, and Earl of Chester'.[1]

Henry IV's insistence on gaining parliamentary recognition for these titles of his son reflected his uncertainty over public reaction to the Lancastrian claims. For, though Henry had occupied the throne speedily enough, there was no doubt that the rightful successors to Richard II were not the stock of John of Gaunt but the descendants of Gaunt's elder brother, Lionel, Duke of Clarence (1338–68). In 1385 Richard II acknowledged that his heir-presumptive was Lionel's daughter's son, Roger Mortimer, fourth Earl of March. When the fourth earl was killed in an ambush by Irish rebels in August 1398, his title and claims passed to his eight-year-old son, and it was this boy – the fifth Earl of March – who was natural successor to Richard in 1399. Henry IV, however, saw to it that young March was kept in custody, although not in strict confinement, and the king also anxiously watched the movements of the effective head of the family, the earl's uncle, Sir Edmund Mortimer. Yet, however uneasy he may have felt, from November 1399 onwards King Henry could at least claim parliamentary backing for the impressive dignities bestowed on the new Prince of Wales. The lordships of the Earls of March looked puny by comparison. Occasionally, March's presence was tolerated at court, as a hostage for the good behaviour of the Mortimer family as a whole. Before Christmas 1399 the boy earl and his mother were with the king in Windsor.

At the previous Christmas festivities the new Prince of Wales had held an equally inconspicuous place in the suite of his godfather, Richard II. Young Henry had never expected such rapid advancement, and for much of the winter of 1399–1400 he was lost in a conflict of loyalties and confused emotions. When he was born, in the gatehouse tower of Monmouth Castle on 16 September 1387, the prince was fifth in line of succession. Since there was no known reason why Richard should not have a family, it seemed probable the throne would slip further away as the years went by. Henry was trained and educated to take his place among the magnates of the kingdom, not to lead them. His mother – Mary Bohun, before her marriage to Bolingbroke in 1380 – was co-heiress to three earldoms and therefore brought additional wealth to the already prospering House of Lancaster. At the time of Henry's birth Mary was seventeen : she had borne her husband a son about the time of her thirteenth birthday, but the child was too weak to live for more than a few days. Five more sons and daughters followed the coming of Henry at Monmouth before Mary herself died in yet another childbirth at the age of twenty-four. For most of these years of infancy, Henry remained under the same roof as his mother, principally at Peterborough; but he hardly knew her, and the chief feminine influence on his upbringing was his maternal grandmother, Countess Joan of Hereford, the sister of Archbishop Arundel. Her father, Earl Richard of Arundel, was so wealthy that at his death in 1376 his executors had found more than £60,000 in cash on his various estates; and Countess Joan was able to offer her grandson a fine style of living. He showed a lasting respect and affection for his grandmother, who survived until 1419, while her nephew, Thomas Fitzalan, Earl of Arundel, became one of his closest friends and companion in arms.[2]

Henry saw little enough of his father, either. As a young man, Bolingbroke was one of the most admired jousters in Europe and he was frequently abroad. He fought for the Teutonic knights in eastern Prussia in 1390–91 and again in 1392; he made a pilgrimage to Jerusalem which enabled him to assess and enjoy court life in Prague, Venice, Vienna, Rhodes, Zadar, Milan and Paris; and, of course, he was also forced into exile by his king in the closing months of 1398. Young Henry accordingly spent much of his boyhood with his father's father, John of Gaunt, and he received some tuition from his father's step-brother, Henry Beaufort, the future Cardinal-Bishop of Winchester, a Cambridge man who became an active Chancellor of Oxford University at the age of twenty-two. Certainly Henry of Monmouth was learning Latin by the time he was eight: he read widely and was able to express himself in English, Latin and French; and in later years he wrote letters and marginal notes in his own hand. A Benedictine from Westminster, who saw much of Henry in his boyhood, recalls how diligently he observed church festivals, hearing mass and making his confession regularly. While this recollection may be a dutiful exercise in hagiography, it accords well with later facets of Henry's character. Moreover the same monk refers happily to less edifying pursuits – falconry, fishing, riding and hunting. The household accounts of the duchy of Lancaster record the purchase of new strings for a harp or zither when Henry was ten years old, and an early biographer says he 'delighted in songs and musical instruments': so, indeed, did his father.

This combination of bookishness, religiosity and zest for outdoor life made Henry a lad of character. It is not surprising he should have been especially welcome at Richard's cultured court, where art was generously patronized and learning respected. In the impressionable years between Henry of Monmouth's eighth and twelfth birthdays the legendary charm of 'Cousin Richard the King' may well have left a greater mark on him than any influence from his often absentee father. The proposal that he should accompany the king to Ireland in May 1399 was therefore an honour in which the boy delighted, with no thought that he was being kept in the king's suite as a hostage. Richard continued to show favour to him. While they were in Ireland the king knighted Henry, allegedly counselling him, 'My fair cousin, henceforth be gallant and bold, for unless you conquer you shall have little name for valour'. At that moment the 'Lord Henry of Monmouth' can only have felt for Richard the proud obligations of a boy thrust into the fellowship of knighthood through the grace of his sovereign liege lord. In these events and their aftermath lie the origins of the conflict between father and son which bedevilled the later politics of Henry IV's reign.

Richard left the newly knighted Henry at Trim, a castle twenty-five miles north-west of Dublin, when he returned to Wales in that vain attempt to save his kingdom. At once Bolingbroke sent a ship to fetch his son across the Irish Sea and bring him to Chester, where Richard was detained by his usurper during the last fortnight of August. But on arrival at Chester young Henry took up attendance on his lawful king, despite his father's orders 'to come from the king and wait upon him', as one of the chroniclers wrote. Only when reminded by Richard of his filial obligations did Henry obey his father, 'taking leave of the king his godfather with a heavy heart'. Throughout the following months – the coronation, the investiture as Prince of Wales, the settlement of his full princely and ducal style – the young man retained a certain loyalty towards 'cousin Richard', was saddened by news of his death and attended a requiem for his soul at St Paul's Cathedral.[3] Henry, however, possessed much shrewd common sense. Although he might respect the memory of his former liege lord, he recognized that he owed his advancement and every promise for the future to his father's initiative in exploiting Richard's mistakes. Even had he been older, he could not have opposed his father's policy at such a time. The seizure of the realm, accomplished with such apparent ease in 1399, began to provoke opposition early in 1400 which continued in various forms until at least the autumn of 1408. Within less than a year of his investiture, Henry of Monmouth became the first and last English Prince of Wales forced to fight in defence of his princely title.

The new king did not expect trouble from the Welsh. In the summer of 1400 father and son marched northwards on a brief punitive expedition against the Scots, who tended to infiltrate south of the border with each successive embarrassment to the English crown. While they were travelling back to London in September news reached them that one of the most respected figures in North Wales, Owen Glendower, had raised a force which was attacking the estates of his neighbour, Lord Grey of Ruthin, a member of the king's council. Owain Glyn Dwr, as his countrymen called him, was the richest Welsh landowner of his time.[4] He had married the daughter of a distinguished judge, Sir David Hanmer, himself a Welshman, and in 1385 took a prominent part in an earlier English raid into the Scottish border country. Owain, who in 1400 was about fifty years old, was descended from the ancient princely dynasties of Powys and Deheubarth. He was no hothead: his act of defiance was a sign of genuine discontent with the territorial penetration of his homeland by an English nobility which seemed intent on high taxation, and offered little in return. On 17 September Owain was proclaimed Prince of Wales in his lordship of Glyndyfrdwy, on the River Dee between Corwen and Llangollen. Within a few days his cousins, Rhys and Gwilym ap Tudor, had joined the revolt and armed bands of Welshmen were ravaging a crescent of English settlements between Rhuddlan and the approaches to Chester.

Glendower's attack on Grey's estates brought the king and the prince hurrying to the Welsh border with the army returning from Scotland. Yet it seemed at first as if the Welsh revolt hardly merited royal intervention. The rebels were severely mauled by an English force levied from the north Midlands and Shropshire before the king and the prince arrived. Henry IV contented himself with a show of strength, marching as far as the Menai Straits and declaring Glendower's lands confiscated, although he was not able to penetrate the mountain fastness and ensure that the act of confiscation was carried out. The king then returned to London. Parliament, meeting early in 1401, warned him that more trouble might be expected from Wales: the Commons said that Welsh students were returning home from Oxford and Cambridge, and Welsh labourers were leaving farms in the west Midlands and crossing the border, ready to take up arms against the English. Responsibility for Welsh affairs was entrusted to the Justiciar of Chester, Lord Henry Percy, the eldest son of the Earl of Northumberland: he was granted the lordships of Denbigh and Anglesey, and appointed Constable of the castles of Chester, Caernarfon, Conwy and Flint. At the same time he was made military governor of the Prince of Wales, responsible both for his safety and for his training in warfare. The prince's household was established at Chester and he took an active part in the administration of Wales, under Henry Percy's supervision.

When Henry Percy took up his post at Chester, he was thirty-six, three years older than Henry IV. His jousting skills had made him – like the king – an idol of the tournament circuit: he was respected as a good fighter, though an impetuous one, and his nickname, Hotspur, was well deserved. At first the employment of Hotspur by the king brought rewards. When the Tudor brothers seized Conwy Castle on Good Friday 1401, Hotspur and the prince were able to raise an army speedily and recapture the castle. Soon afterwards they routed Glendower's troops in a sharp engagement on the lower slopes of Cader Idris, and John Charlton, one of the Marcher Lords in Powys, narrowly missed taking Glendower in the mountains: he captured some of the Welshman's armour and a banner which he described as 'painted with maidens with red hands', and these trophies were sent to the king for display in London. But Glendower, like later resistance leaders, had the gift of withdrawing into the mountains and waiting for his enemies to fall out before emerging to continue the war. Less than a month after the skirmish at Cader Idris, Hotspur resigned all his appointments. Early in July he retired to Northumberland incensed at the king's failure to send money to pay either his troops or himself. The Prince of Wales's military tuition, and the recovery of his principality, was entrusted to Hugh le Despenser, a Marcher Lord from Glamorgan. To the prince's evident regret he died barely three months after taking up his post: Hotspur's uncle, Thomas Percy, Earl of Worcester was appointed his successor.

These Welsh campaigns rapidly brought the prince to manhood. Some letters survive, written when he was fifteen years old: they show his concern for the well-being of his household officials, his eagerness to put forward ideas on strategy and government, and his utter determination to punish the rebels ruthlessly. In March 1403 he was freed from dependence upon the Earl of Worcester and officially proclaimed lieutenant of the king within the Marches of Wales as well as the principality. This was a formidable responsibility for a young man still six months short of his sixteenth birthday: he at once marched against Glendower's own possessions, burning his homes at Glyndyfrdwy and Sycarth, ravaging the countryside, and killing captives rather than holding them to ransom. He then led his troops into Merionethshire: 'There we wasted a fair land and one well-inhabited', he reported to his father. As so frequently with guerrilla warfare, the rebel fighters personally suffered far less than their families for they could continue their rebellion from a mountainous countryside which no English troops penetrated; and by the beginning of 1403 Glendower was becoming a figure of European significance who established contact with the kings of France and Scotland and with the rebellious Irish. In the previous spring Glendower had captured Grey of Ruthin, only allowing him to go free after payment of a ransom of 10,000 marks. A few weeks later (22 June 1402) he gained an even more important prisoner, Sir Edmund Mortimer, uncle to the rightful claimant, the young Earl of March. King Henry was unable, or disinclined, to raise ransom money for the head of the Mortimers. This was a major political error on the king's part: Sir Edmund married Glendower's daughter and, in alliance with the Welsh, called on his tenantry along both sides of the border to help him fight the Lancastrian usurpers.

The Mortimer episode also worsened relations between the king and the Percies, for Mortimer was a brother of Hotspur's wife. Moreover the Percies had an additional grievance. They complained that they should have received £60,000 from the crown for their services in Wales and on the Scottish border. In fact, Henry paid them considerably more than £40,000 in less than four years. To raise this sum he kept the Prince of Wales so short of money that he had been forced to sell jewels and pawn plate so as to pay his men; for, as the prince warned the king in a letter, 'The rebels hear each day whether we shall be paid, and they know that without payment we cannot abide.' The Percies, however, had no sympathy for the House of Lancaster's financial embarrassment: they could indeed have argued that much of it sprang from the king's determination to treat his very considerable family revenue as personal and separate from his income and expenditure as ruler of England. The conflict between the king and his northern magnates came to a head over the old problem of ransom money. In 1402 the Earl of Northumberland and his son, Hotspur, had checked a major Scottish-French incursion south of the border, capturing several Scottish earls at the battle of Homildon Hill. The king expected that all such prisoners should be handed over to the crown for the raising of a ransom but, as Adam of Usk wrote, the Percies 'were all puffed up'. They declined to surrender the most valuable of their prisoners, the Earl of Douglas, claiming they were holding him in lieu of the funds owed to them for their earlier campaigns. In the early summer of 1403 the king began to raise an army, ostensibly to mount another preventive raid into Scotland and later to support the prince in Wales. It is not surprising if the Percies suspected that he was marching north in order to curb their independence of initiative along the border. When the king reached Leicester he was told that Hotspur was raising troops in Lancashire and Cheshire, proclaiming that King Richard was still alive, and denouncing 'Henry Duke of Lancaster' the 'presumed King of England without title of right but only of guile'.[5]

Soon more bad news reached the king. The Earl of Worcester had joined his nephew; and the two former military governors of the Prince of Wales were heading for Shrewsbury, where the prince had his headquarters, intending to take him prisoner. There was clearly a risk that the barons would unite with Glendower, and even without Welsh support their levies would outnumber the prince's troops. The king's speedy reaction saved the prince from disaster: he headed at once for Shrewsbury, his army covering fifty miles in three days, and thus reaching the prince a few hours ahead of Hotspur's men. By the evening of 20 July 1403 two formidable armies faced each other some three miles north of Shrewsbury. Attempts at reconciliation failed; next day, from noon to dusk, the king and his recalcitrant barons clashed in the fiercest battle on English soil since Evesham in 1265.

In numbers the armies were evenly matched. Hotspur, however, had three advantages: experience; a defensive position on a low hill protected by a string of ponds; and a strong body of expert archers from Cheshire and Flintshire. Had the battle been longer delayed he might, too, have had the assistance of Glendower whose irregulars were fighting in west Wales at the time. But, even without the presence of Glendower's men, the Prince of Wales was faced with a grim initiation into the uncertainties of a setpiece battle. He was four months younger than Edward of Woodstock at Crécy. Like the Black Prince, young Henry commanded one of the three divisions in his father's army but, unlike his great-uncle, he was forced at Shrewsbury to attack uphill and through a hail of arrows rather than wait for the enemy to exhaust himself in futile onslaughts against prepared defences. The prince was wounded in the face by an arrow almost as soon as the fighting began, but he minimized the wound and continued to press home his attack. The fighting was more intense and confused than at Crécy, Nájera, or (later) at Agincourt, and the proportion of casualties during a protracted mêlée was unusually high. More than a thousand rebels perished either in the battle or in the merciless killings which followed it. Hotspur was slain, his uncle captured and executed for treason. The king's men, too, suffered heavily and the Prince of Wales was fortunate to survive. His father – and in due course parliament – acknowledged his courage and persistence. It was accepted that he was a natural soldier, a worthy great-grandson of Edward III. Yet never again as prince was he called upon to fight a set battle, although there were plenty of sharp skirmishes 'attended by great slaughter' before the Welsh rebellion was stamped out. The only other occasion in his life when he fought an engagement on the scale of Shrewsbury was at Agincourt.[6]

The prince continued his campaigns in Wales for another five years after Shrewsbury. It was Henry IV's intention, as he himself remarked, to leave 'his first-born son in Wales for the chastisement of the rebels'. At times it was by no means clear who was chastising whom. Glendower was master of the great castle of Harlech and of the lesser castle of

Aberystwyth; and he was in touch with the Earl of Northumberland and other baronial dissidents in the north. The King of France treated him as legitimate ruler of Wales, someone with whom it was possible to sign a solemn alliance against 'Henry of Lancaster'; large contingents of French soldiery landed at Milford Haven in the summer of 1405 and assisted Glendower to raid deeply into the west Midlands, coming within eight miles of Worcester; and French vessels caused panic along the Channel coast of England, raiding Looe, Dartmouth, Plymouth, Poole and some villages on the Isle of Wight as part of the grand design against the Lancastrian usurper. But the Prince of Wales had his successes: a sharp rebuff to the rebels between Abergavenny and Usk in March 1405; and a gradual wearing down of Welsh resistance by the institution of new tactics. Instead of marching in force through the valleys and then dispersing again after a punitive stroke, the prince formed smaller policing units for particular areas, while encouraging the rank and file of the rebels by promises of free pardon. This shrewd combination of counter-guerrilla tactics and statesmanship began to pacify the south and Anglesey in 1406. But Glendower was secure in Harlech and Aberystwyth, as well as within the inner recesses of Snowdonia.

The prince set about the systematic reduction of Aberystwyth in October 1407, leaving Harlech to two close lieutenants, Gilbert and John Talbot, Marcher Lords from Monmouthshire. Aberystwyth schooled the prince in siege warfare: 'machines, bastiles and other engines' were constructed in Gloucestershire and shipped round the coast in order to provide a primitive form of artillery. The castle defied its besiegers throughout the winter of 1407–8 but fell before the end of September 1408. Harlech was a tougher nut to crack: it held out until the coming of spring in 1409. These two prizes virtually ended the Welsh revolt: Edmund Mortimer was killed at Harlech, and most of Glendower's remaining family captured. The legendary leader himself survived – the Owain Glyn Dwr of the bards. The mountains, and their people, appear to have sheltered him for some years. The Prince of Wales offered him a pardon upon his accession as Henry V in 1413, repeating the offer three years later; but there was no response. It seems probable he died during the winter of 1415–16.

From 1406 onwards the Prince of Wales was concerning himself more and more with the affairs of England; the siege of Aberystwyth was the last occasion upon which the problems of the principality had his undivided attention. The five years following Hotspur's death had placed a severe strain on Henry IV physically and mentally. Hotspur's father, the Earl of Northumberland, remained a formidable adversary despite the chastening of the Percies at Shrewsbury. In the early summer of 1405 the king had to act swiftly and drastically against further baronial treachery in the north, instigated by Northumberland. On this occasion the dissidents were supported by the Archbishop of York, Richard le Scrope, a priest and pastor known for his holiness who was genuinely troubled by the high incidence of taxation and the king's failure to protect his people from brigandage. Northumberland used his Scottish connections to flee the country and escape the king's wrath – although he was eventually killed near Tadcaster in February 1408 – but the unfortunate archbishop was condemned to death. Despite protests from Archbishop Arundel of Canterbury and from his chief justice, the king ordered Scrope to be summarily executed at Clementhorpe, less than a mile from his Minster. This act of vengeance, determined by the king in a fit of choleric rage, shocked Christians throughout Europe, including the Prince of Wales who reckoned the archbishop's nephew, Henry Lord Scrope, as one of his most intimate friends and trusted companion in arms. Veneration of the archbishop's tomb in the Minster had to be officially discouraged: he could easily have become to York what the 'holy blissful martyr' Becket was to Canterbury.

Archbishop Scrope was beheaded on 8 June 1405. That afternoon, as the king was riding his horse not far from York, 'it seemed to him he had felt an actual blow' and he almost fell from the saddle.[7] Throughout the following night he was feverish, screaming out that traitors were casting fire over him. It would seem that the king had either suffered some form of thrombosis or, under the stress of the moment, had given way to a protracted nervous breakdown. He never entirely recovered his health. In the summer of 1408 a similar seizure left him unconscious for several hours: partial paralysis prevented him from riding; and his features were marred by a skin disease which reminded his courtiers of leprosy. So bad was the king's physical condition that his eldest son began to anticipate a rapid accession; and a Prince of Wales's faction emerged among the younger prelates and nobility. At its head was Henry Beaufort, the

king's half-brother, Bishop of Winchester since 1404 and former tutor to
the prince who was only twelve years his junior. In 1406 Bishop
Beaufort, while on a diplomatic mission to the French court, indicated
that he believed the Prince of Wales would soon be on the throne of
England: his father would either die or abdicate.[8]

In this prediction the bishop was wrong. In fact, Henry IV's reign had
run only half its course. To the chagrin of the prince and his followers
the king turned in his illnesses, not to the rising generation, but to
Archbishop Arundel, whom he appointed Chancellor in January 1407.
There was a moment in the winter of 1408–9 when the king seemed so ill
that all his sons gathered around his deathbed, and at Greenwich on 21
January 1409 he dictated an abject will which began, 'I Henry, sinful
wretch, by the Grace of God king . . .'; but he survived and, on the days
upon which he could not take decisions or shape policy, he was happy to
leave all such matters to the archbishop. It seemed to the Prince of Wales
and his faction as if the kingdom was floundering: financial policy and
diplomacy were determined by expediency and improvisation. By the
summer of 1409 the prince and his supporters were ready to take over the
direction of affairs.

For the last four years of Henry IV's reign there was, in consequence,
a contest which anticipated in many respects the political conflicts
between the sovereigns and their heirs during the eighteenth century.
The principal stake in the disputes of 1409–13 was mastery of the king's
council, the body of some two dozen royal nominees responsible for the
routine business of government. The Prince of Wales regularly attended
meetings of the council in London after the fall of Aberystwyth and
Harlech castles had freed him from urgent responsibilities in Wales.
Early in December 1409 the prince vigorously opposed proposals for
fresh taxes put forward by Archbishop Arundel. Four days before
Christmas the archbishop resigned as chancellor and by the end of
January the king was prepared to recognize a new council virtually
nominated by the Prince of Wales. Bishop Beaufort was a prominent
member, while his younger brother, Thomas, was chancellor. The
prince looked for support to those who had served him in Wales: Lord
Scrope became treasurer; the prince's close friend, the Earl of Arundel,
entered the council and so, too, did one of the most efficient members of
the prince's household, Henry Chichele, Bishop of St David's, a top-

ranking civil servant. At the same time the prince assumed new and significant personal responsibilities. In the previous February he had become Constable of Dover Castle and Warden of the Cinque Ports: now, in March 1410, he was appointed Captain of Calais, thus controlling the two great fortresses on opposite sides of the Channel at its narrowest point. Already his ambitions lay in the 'vasty fields of France'.

Government by the 'Prince's Friends' continued for twenty-two months, from January 1410 until November 1411.[9] By now the prince looked upon his father as a sick man burdened with a triple guilt: he had deposed a king; directly or indirectly he had caused his death; and he had ordered the execution of a Primate of England within sight of his cathedral church. It seemed natural to the prince for the realm to be entrusted to others, men whose consciences were not racked by such memories. For England needed firm government: the merchants wanted revised trade treaties; the Commons sought redress of grievances before granting new taxes – the knights of the shires were particularly concerned over a breakdown of law and order in the countryside; and many members of the nobility argued that a forward policy in France would gain land and ransom money, for the authority of the French king was weakened by his own mental incapacities and by open warfare between the Burgundians and the Orleanists (Armagnacs). It was only a few years since the French had meddled in the Welsh rebellion and burnt English towns from Cornwall to the Isle of Wight. To the Prince's Friends – all, except the treasurer, landowners who had suffered from French incursions – the temptation to carry the perennial Anglo-French conflict back across the Channel was irresistible. Some attempt was made to balance the books of the royal finances, and a crude budget was drawn up in March 1411; better relations were established with England's old allies in Flanders; but France was the principal topic of discussion around the council table.

In the autumn of 1411 the Earl of Arundel with two thousand archers and a force of lancers supported Duke John the Fearless of Burgundy in operations against the Armagnacs on the hills north of Paris; and the earl promised that, in due course, the prince himself would come with a far larger army. But, suddenly and unexpectedly, Henry IV showed a resilience of spirit: he told the council he would cross to Calais and take command of an army in France, as his father and grandfather had done before him. Then he changed his mind, pleading ill-health. Bishop Beaufort, his half-brother, declared that if the king was unwell he should abdicate. Unfortunately the bishop did not keep his advice either within the family or within the council chamber: a new parliament was meeting at Westminster, and the Beauforts suggested that the Commons might wish to petition the king to hand over the crown to his eldest son. This was an ill-timed proposal: the prince was away from London, the new parliament was anti-clerical in temper and highly suspicious of the Bishop of Winchester in particular. Moreover the king had lost none of his guile: the Speaker of the Commons was informed that his sovereign had no intention of listening to constitutional novelties and that he would 'stand as free in his prerogative as any of his predecessors'. The hint was well taken by the king's faithful Commons: on 30 November 1411 they thanked the prince's friends in council for their past services; and each of them now found himself excluded by the king from all political power. Within three weeks Archbishop Arundel was back once more as chancellor. By the following summer a large English army was, indeed, fighting in France, and with much material profit. But it was fighting on the side of the Armagnacs rather than the Burgundians; and it was commanded not by the prince but by his oldest brother, Thomas, newly created Duke of Clarence. To add to the prince's mortification, the Duke of Clarence was assisted by the king's cousin, Edward Duke of York (son of Gaunt's brother, Edmund of Langley), and even by the dispossessed chancellor, Thomas Beaufort, who was made Earl of Dorset.

The dispersal of his council in November 1411 was the worst rebuff suffered by the Prince of Wales in the eleven years since he first took up residence at Chester.[10] It is difficult to trace his movements for the first half of the following year. Probably this was the period when madcap frolics created the 'Prince Hal' legend. The prince had acquired a former home of the Black Prince when he finally left Wales: it was situated, as the Elizabethan John Stow later wrote, 'up Fish Street Hill', between London Bridge and Eastcheap, and the council met there at least once during the government of the 'Prince's Friends'. Three separate and unrelated contemporary sources give the impression that the prince, much of whose adolescence passed in dreary campaigning against the Welsh, enjoyed himself recklessly in London. One sympathetic chronicler says he 'fervently followed the service of Venus as well as Mars', and that his extra-mural activities included roisterous rollicking and the occasional affray. The tale that, with some wild companions, he held up and robbed his own receivers is not improbable: it appears to have been a legend in Warwickshire and may be associated with Coventry, from where the prince on 17 June 1412 published an open letter denying slanderous reports which were being circulated by his enemies in London. The most serious accusation was that he intended to seize the crown and had come 'to our own city of Coventry' to recruit followers. He felt, so he explained in his statement, nothing but love, obedience and the humility due from a son towards his father.

There followed a crisis in the relations between king and prince marked by a little known and confusing episode.[11] On 30 June the prince arrived in London with a considerable following. He went, not to one of his own residences, but to the palace of the Bishop of Durham which was on the Strand and therefore strategically well-situated between the city and Westminster. The king was highly suspicious of his son's intentions: he was in Clerkenwell on 30 June and for twelve days he avoided going to Westminster, a move which would have required him either to make a humiliating detour to avoid the Strand or to cross the Fleet River close to Durham House, exposing himself to the risk of seizure by the 'abundant crowd' reported to be in attendance on his son. The obvious refuge for the king was the Tower of London: but he had sent Richard there at the time of his deposition. To go now to the Tower would leave the prince's followers with the opportunity of declaring that he had abdicated. Accordingly the king, closely guarded, spent five days in the small palace of the Bishop of London, adjoining St Paul's, and then moved eastwards to Rotherhithe, where he summoned his council. Emissaries from the prince pleaded his cause, asking in particular that his slanderers should be punished. As a compromise the king proposed that the prince should raise such matters with parliament, when next it assembled. The prince agreed, left Durham House, and was outwardly reconciled with his father over the second weekend in July.

Ten weeks later there was another dramatic incident: the prince came to town, again with a large following, prepared to answer charges that he had misappropriated funds as Captain of Calais; he is said to have disguised himself – in a singularly conspicuous blue satin gown with a golden collar – and, having reached the king's presence at Westminster, handed him a short sword, which he had concealed under the gown, and begged his father to slay him if he believed him guilty of treachery. There was, inevitably, an affecting reconciliation. This cloak and dagger story rests entirely on the hearsay of men at Westminster that autumn: it probably improved with telling, and was well written up over the years. But there is no doubt that the Prince of Wales did submit his accounts from Calais for scrutiny: on 21 October the king and Archbishop Arundel declared that he was fully exonerated.

By now Henry IV was very frail. He lost consciousness for long periods in December, rallied again when he went to Eltham for Christmas, but insisted on coming back to London for the opening of parliament in February. On Sunday, 19 March 1413, he appears to have suffered yet another seizure while in the sanctuary of Westminster Abbey, where he had been crowned. He was taken unconscious to the abbot's lodging and died there, in the Jerusalem Chamber, the next day. Shakespeare's famous scene, in which the dying king recovers sufficiently to see the Prince of Wales placing the crown upon his own head, is derived from a Burgundian chronicle: the details are suspect, although the incident may be allegorical, representing the prince's attempts to control the kingdom over the previous three years. Contemporaries indicate that the king did indeed receive his eldest son in the Jerusalem Chamber and urged him to work amicably with his brothers, especially Thomas Duke of Clarence, but there is no mention of the prince's eagerness to wear the crown.[12]

Several chroniclers remark that, immediately at his accession, the former prince became 'a new man, zealous for honesty, modest and grave'. He spent several hours on the night of his father's death in an anchorite's cell, within the abbey church. He certainly showed greater generosity of mind and statesmanship than during the disputes of the preceding year. The sixty-year-old Archbishop Arundel was replaced as chancellor by Bishop Beaufort; the archbishop died in the following February and was succeeded by the new king's confidant, Chichele. But there was no display of vengeance towards old enemies, even those who had slandered him as Prince of Wales. An easy and brotherly under-standing developed between Henry and Thomas of Clarence, who was to die in battle against the French dauphin at Baugé in 1421. The king sought to make amends for earlier misfortunes. He allowed the

Earl of March, now aged twenty-three, complete freedom of movement despite his better claim to the English throne. The earl was duly knighted at the coronation and allowed to inherit all the Mortimer lands, even though his uncle had fought with Glendower in the later stages of the Welsh rebellion. In December 1413 King Henry V paid a last homage to King Richard II, seeing to it that his remains were translated with due pomp and ceremony from an inconspicuous grave at King's Langley to the tomb in Westminster Abbey which Richard had himself commissioned. No doubt it suited Henry politically to let his subjects know that a truly dead and respected Richard was entombed at Westminster, not – as rumour said – living in Scotland and about to claim his throne from those who dishonoured him. Yet the reinterment of Richard was in keeping with the new king's character, a pious gesture towards the cousin who first raised him to knighthood.

Tudor historians, and Shakespeare with them, looked back on 'Harry of Monmouth' as the soldier king, 'too famous to live long'.[13] His triumphs against the French made him an archetypal royal hero for patriotic propagandists; and there is enough truth in these portrayals of a warrior prince to identify the man through the myth. But the first phase of Henry's nine-and-a-half-year reign was far from glorious. A Lollard rising in the winter of 1413–14 threatened both the established church and the monarchy, for its leader, Sir John Oldcastle, a former companion-in-arms of the new king in Wales, condemned Henry as 'the priest's prince' and planned to capture the royal family during the protracted Christmas festivities at Eltham. Oldcastle, an anti-clericalist fanatic, had so many sympathizers in southern England that he was able to live in hiding for four years after the frustration of his plot. Nor was his conspiracy the only threat to Henry's life. In the summer of 1415 the Earl of Cambridge, a younger brother of the Duke of York, planned to kill the king and his three brothers at Southampton as they embarked for France: Cambridge would then offer the crown to his wife's brother, the Earl of March. Among the ringleaders of this conspiracy was Henry's close friend, Lord Scrope, nephew of the executed archbishop. The plot was revealed to the king by the Earl of March on the eve of the assassination attempt. Henry accepted March's claim that he had become unwittingly a tool of the conspirators and took no action against him. But Cambridge was executed and Scrope dragged through the streets of

Southampton before dying a traitor's death. Only a few months previously the king had let it be known he would permit the faithful in Yorkshire to make offerings at Archbishop Scrope's tomb, as though he were a saint. But, after the Southampton Plot, Henry Scrope's head was impaled over the gate at Bootham Bar to remind the people of York there were limits to their sovereign's merciful indulgence.

Henry v sailed for France on 11 August 1415, a week after the executions at Southampton, with a fleet of some fifteen hundred vessels. He wished to recover, not just the lost possessions originally conceded in the Treaty of Brétigny, but the duchy of Normandy and the old Angevin Empire. Harfleur, at the mouth of the Seine, was besieged for a month before it surrendered. The king then sought to emulate the strategic plan of 1346: he set out northwards for Calais with reduced numbers, hoping to tempt the French to attack his columns at a good defensive position. The ruse worked: on 25 October the French threw their cavalry against Henry's longbowmen at Agincourt, where the king had found a commanding height facing a muddy defile. The battlefield was only eighteen miles north of Crécy. In under three hours' fighting the French lost more than five thousand men: English casualties were less than four hundred, although among the dead were the Duke of York, the Earl of Suffolk and several knights, including a Welshman, Sir David ap Llewelyn. Within a month the king was back in London, rapturously received by townsfolk who had shown strongly Lollard sympathies less than two years before.

Agincourt was a prestigious triumph, not a great strategic victory.[14] Many months of siege warfare were needed before Henry v could secure the mastery of Normandy which he had fixed as his first objective. Even before he had won Normandy, he gained two valuable diplomatic successes: an alliance with the Holy Roman Emperor, Sigismund, who could put pressure on France from his German territories; and, in 1419–20, alliance with Duke Philip of Burgundy against the natural heir to the French throne, the dauphin, whose Armagnac followers murdered the previous Duke of Burgundy, John the Fearless, in September 1419. The climax of Henry's diplomatic offensive was the Treaty of Troyes of May 1420 by which it was agreed that the mad King of France, Charles vi, would recognize Henry v as Regent of France and as his heir although retaining his titular sovereignty in his lifetime. On 2

June 1420 Henry V married the French king's daughter, Catherine of Valois, at Troyes Cathedral: and six months later the Regent of France and his bride were welcomed warmly by the people of Paris. Meanwhile the English soldiery were well pleased by the pickings of the Normandy campaign: lordships in the Duchy were being parcelled out as readily as Christmas gifts.

Henry brought Queen Catherine to England at the beginning of February 1421 and she was crowned by Archbishop Chichele in the abbey on her first Sunday at Westminster. The king returned across the Channel in June 1421, seeking to defeat the dauphin, who controlled two-thirds of France and was particularly powerful in the region south-east of Paris. Throughout the winter the king was besieging Meaux, a town on the Marne only twenty-five miles from all the comforts of the Louvre. It was a grim affair, even more cheerless than Aberystwyth, where Henry had learnt the science of siege warfare. Dysentery took a heavy toll, and many of the king's companions among the nobility shivered their way through fits of ague. Shortly before Christmas the king had good news from England: on 6 December Queen Catherine had given birth to a son at Windsor. A chronicler noted that 'King Henry's heart was filled with great gladness'. In time, no doubt the infant would be created Prince of Wales, and later still be crowned King of England and France: but not yet, prayed the king.

He never saw the boy. Even before the fall of Meaux in early May, Henry was struggling against illness. After Meaux surrendered he travelled to Vincennes and spent sixteen days with his queen, moving from Vincennes into the palace of the Louvre and out to St Denis and Senlis, seeking to escape from the intense summer's heat. Catherine had left the infant Prince Henry at Windsor, rather than risk his health in France. At the beginning of July, the queen returned to England, assuming that the king was recovering his strength. But as soon as he was back with his army, he collapsed again. He was borne back to Vincennes in a litter, and prayers were asked for his recovery on Sunday, 12 July, and through seven more weeks as he fought against an illness which baffled contemporaries and has puzzled later commentators too. Perhaps it was a protracted bout of dysentery, or smallpox, for there was an epidemic in Paris; or a 'marsh fever', contracted along the Marne. Whatever the illness, Henry lacked the strength to overcome it. In lucid moments he talked bitterly of unfulfilled tasks: the union of the English and French thrones; and a grand crusade to free Jerusalem from the Turk. Already an agent of his was reconnoitring the eastern Mediterranean, for his ambition vaulted easily over seas and mountains, and he had seen Harfleur and Troyes and Paris as mere springboards. But it was too late for such dreams. Death claimed him at Vincennes in the small hours of 31 August 1422, two weeks short of his thirty-fifth birthday. He was buried with great solemnity, as he had wished, in Westminster Abbey, close to the tomb of Richard II. Henry IV, the usurper, lay interred at Canterbury.[15]

CHAPTER FOUR

Three Prince Edwards

OR thirty-one years after the death of Henry V there was no heir-apparent eligible to be created Prince of Wales. The new king, Henry VI, was nine months old at his accession: he did not marry until 1445 nor become a father until October 1453, when his queen gave birth to a son who became Prince of Wales by a charter confirmed in parliament the following March. After this long vacancy in the principate the title was held for another period of thirty-one years by three successive boy princes, each named Edward and each destined to serve as a mere chessman in the contest of great territorial magnates. Only one of these Prince Edwards became king: none lived to full manhood.

The realm of England changed considerably in character between the premature death of Henry V and the hurried investiture of his infant grandson at Windsor on Whitsun Day, 1454. The Troyes dream of an Anglo-French dual monarchy was dispelled by the revival of French arms between 1429 and 1435, a change in the fortunes of war originally inspired by the leadership of Joan of Arc. There followed a gradual crumbling away of English possessions across the Channel: English troops were expelled from Paris in 1436; Rouen was lost in 1449, and all Normandy soon after; Bordeaux and the last possessions in Gascony fell in 1451. By 1453 nothing remained of Plantagenet designs on France except the citadel and port of Calais and a hollow claim to a crown now firmly on the head of Charles VII, the dauphin whom Henry V had roundly despised. These defeats in France exacerbated discontent in England: there was a general lack of governance; soldiers were unpaid and their commanders denied hope of enrichment in war overseas; merchants complained of heavy taxes and lost foreign trade; power and wealth were concentrated in the hands of a few mighty landowners who lived lavishly in their homes and at court. In the summer of 1450 popular discontent exploded in a series of violent crimes: the Duke of

61

Suffolk, a favourite minister of the king but long distrusted by parliament, died mysteriously while at sea in the Channel not long after his friend, Bishop Adam Moleyns of Chichester, had been murdered by seamen at Portsmouth; and Bishop William Ayscough of Salisbury, the king's confessor, was dragged five miles in full canonicals from Edington Church to a hill above Westbury, in Wiltshire, where he too was done to death. At the same time the men of Kent rose in rebellion under Jack Cade, marching on London and from their camp on Blackheath threatening the city with a reign of terror unless government was reformed and corrupt officials punished. These disturbances were not an immediate threat to the king's continuance on the throne, but they were a portent: public feeling was turning against Lancastrian rule.[1] No one doubted Henry VI was a man of faith and holy charity; around his head a saintly halo would have shone more naturally than the burnished lustre from a crown. Yet Henry was as feeble a king as any of his predecessors in English history, politically too naïve to lead his people and too trusting in character to choose good councillors. He showed none of the guile that John of Gaunt had brought to the House of Lancaster, nor did he possess the soldierly qualities shown by the father he had never known and by his uncle, Duke John of Bedford. As he passed into his thirtieth year it seemed as if Henry was becoming as remote from the realities of government as had been his maternal grandfather, King Charles VI of France. Inevitably the nobility and the Commons in parliament began to consider the merits of other claimants to the throne.

So long as Henry remained childless, the two principal contenders for the succession were Richard, Duke of York, and Edmund Beaufort, Duke of Somerset. York was descended from both the second and fourth sons of Edward III: his mother, Anne Mortimer, was the only child-bearing offspring of the Earl of March, Richard II's rightful heir; and York's father was the Earl of Cambridge who had been executed by his cousin, Henry V, after the Southampton conspiracy of 1415. These considerable dynastic claims were backed by much wealth, for York inherited the estates of his uncle, the Duke of York killed at Agincourt, and this legacy was equalled in value by the Mortimer lands which passed to him in name in 1425. By 1432, when he came of age, Richard of York was the wealthiest landowner in the kingdom: he could count on £7,000 a year from his estates in England and Wales alone, and to these might be added revenue from lands in Ireland.[2] The French wars showed York was also an efficient soldier, with money to raise an army of his own; and his political ambitions were supported by another great territorial magnate, his wife's nephew, Richard Neville, who had himself married Anne Beauchamp from whom in 1449 he inherited the lands and title of the earldom of Warwick. Although Henry VI ignored proposals in parliament that York should be declared the rightful heir of the kingdom, there was no doubt he had a better prospect of pressing a claim to the throne than had his rival, Edmund of Somerset. The king personally favoured Somerset, who had inherited much of the wealth and the political affiliations of his uncle, Cardinal Henry Beaufort of Winchester. But outside court circles Somerset was blamed for the loss of Normandy and ridiculed as an incompetent commander in the field. He possessed, however, one advantage over Richard of York: he enjoyed the full confidence of the queen, Margaret of Anjou, who hated and distrusted York and all his followers. By 1453 the will of Queen Margaret counted for more in the day-to-day conduct of government than the wavering indecision of her ineffectual husband.

Margaret of Anjou was a princess of character. She had been brought to England by Suffolk and the Beaufort faction in April 1445, and, at the age of sixteen, married to King Henry by the unfortunate Bishop Ayscough of Salisbury. It was hard for a girl of spirit, a natural leader and tenacious fighter, to accept the strange passivity of the king in a court where disgruntled magnates seemed ready to back a fresh usurpation of royal power. With remarkable speed Queen Margaret schooled herself in English politics, even though she was distrusted as a Frenchwoman born less than forty miles from Joan of Arc's village in Lorraine. In practice, Margaret was determined to bolster up the dynasty, bringing firm support to her husband, as Cardinal Beaufort and the Duke of Suffolk had hoped when they encouraged the Anglo-French marriage proposal during the truce of 1444–5. But it was easy for the queen's enemies to blacken the name of a young and fiercely combative Lorrainer, especially after war was renewed in 1449. Margaret was left in no doubt of her unpopularity at Westminster and in London.[3]

The violent summer of 1450 came as no surprise to her, although she was saddened by the killing of Suffolk and the two bishops on whom she had most strongly relied for support. The queen was convinced Richard of York had encouraged the rebels, especially in Kent where Cade freely used the name 'Mortimer' as a rallying call for opposition to the Lancastrians. York himself was out of the kingdom, serving as Lord Lieutenant in Ireland when Cade's rebellion began; but he returned to Anglesey in August 1450 and marched towards London with 4,000 retainers, showing his strength rather than threatening to unleash civil war. Early in 1452 he again advanced on the capital from his castle at Ludlow, seeking to have the Duke of Somerset removed to the Tower as a traitor who had sold out to the French. On this occasion the Bishop of Ely and the Earl of Warwick acted as mediators: Somerset went unmolested and York was himself fortunate to avoid detention. But it was clear to the queen that the only effective way of checking York was to weaken his claim to the succession. In the spring of 1453 Margaret discovered she was at last pregnant: the birth of a healthy son would trump Richard of York's pretensions.

Then suddenly, when Margaret was seven months pregnant, Henry suffered a nervous breakdown. While he was in residence at the royal hunting lodge of Clarendon in Wiltshire, early in August 1453, his mind was unhinged by a shock; he could neither speak nor move his limbs. Contemporary sources put the blame for the king's paralysis on necromancy, and in particular on the activities of sorcerers among a group of Bristol merchants; but the sources give no indication of the nature of that shock which finally tilted the precarious balance of his nervous system. Was it bad news from France, where the Earl of Shrewsbury's attempt to recover the English hold on Bordeaux had ended disastrously at Castillon a few weeks previously? Or did the king find reason to doubt the paternity of the child his queen was about to bear? Margaret's enemies certainly maintained that Somerset was the father rather than prudish, holy Henry: but there is no factual backing for the slanderous gossip of the time. Perhaps Henry's sensitive soul was injured by a visionary torment: did some sight suggest to him the suffering of his friend Bishop Ayscough on the hill at Westbury, for Clarendon was only a few miles from Westbury across Salisbury Plain and the king had not stayed in this part of the country since the bishop's murder? Whatever the cause of the king's breakdown, its effect was disastrous both personally and politically. For months at a time he could recognize no one and decide nothing. Margaret was able for two months to conceal the full gravity of the king's illness, but autumn brought the court back to Westminster where its true nature became apparent to all observers.[4]

In this crisis, the good of the realm demanded the setting up of a regency. The natural choice for regent was the heir presumptive, Richard of York. He was favoured by the Commons in parliament and by many members of the nobility. Yet if York once enjoyed the prerogatives and patronage of a protectorate, it seemed unlikely he would surrender these rights to a king restored to health. Bleak, indeed, were the prospects for the child whose birth the queen anticipated at any time after the court's return to Westminster. Both Margaret and her political ally, the Duke of Somerset, had every reason for postponing the establishment of a regency.

The queen duly gave birth to a son on Edward the Confessor's day (13 October 1453) and he was baptized by Bishop William Waynflete of Winchester some three weeks later, with the Duke of Somerset and Cardinal Archbishop Kempe of Canterbury as his godfathers. Before Christmas the queen hustled her husband and Prince Edward away to Windsor, where there was greater security of person and fewer prying eyes. A pathetic private letter written a few weeks later describes how the queen and the Duke of Buckingham carried the infant prince to the king at Windsor in the hope that he might bless his son, 'but all their labour was in vain, for they departed thence without any answer or countenance, saving only that once he looked on the prince and cast down his eyes again, without any more'.[5] Not until the following Christmas did the king show signs of recovery. Soon afterwards – on the Feast of the Epiphany, 1455 – he discovered he was father of a sixteen-month-old son; and gave thanks for a miracle.

For Margaret the king's recovery was miraculous in itself. Momentarily it improved her prospects and those of her son. Parliament had consistently denied the queen any powers of regency, and the lords spiritual and temporal had nominated Richard of York as 'Protector' in March 1454. York behaved with discretion: at Whitsun he allowed the investiture of young Edward, whose title as Prince of Wales had received parliamentary sanction twelve days before the protectorate was established. But York was filling the council with his nominees and had sent Somerset to the Tower. The king's recovery put an end to York's protectorate, led to Somerset's release, and marked the beginning of a period when the queen made no attempt to conceal her domination at court. The extraordinary conditions which had existed at the time of her son's birth intensified Margaret's determination to ensure that the Lancastrian heritage passed in full sovereignty to the young Prince Edward. Lest any doubt should be cast on his son's titles, Henry 'ratified, approved and confirmed' the creation of the fifth Prince of Wales at a parliament summoned to Westminster in July 1455. No previous prince had received a double parliamentary sanction of his title.

If Margaret believed her son's heirship was now guaranteed, she was mistaken. Already – at St Albans on 22 May 1455 – the armies of the king and of Richard of York had clashed in battle: for the duke, intent on discrediting Somerset, took to arms and, during confused fighting in the streets of the town, succeeded in killing his hated rival. Subsequently York and the king were formally reconciled, attending a service of thanksgiving together at St Alban's Abbey. Yet Somerset's death marked, not the end of a contest, but its intensification. For the next thirty years civil war simmered throughout England and Wales, occasionally boiling over in armed encounters between royal or baronial factions. The fighting was not continuous. In retrospect the civil war was over-simplified both by Tudor historians, who saw it as a conflict between Lancaster and York, and by Sir Walter Scott who, with a romantic novelist's licence, gave the campaigns the name of 'Wars of the Roses' when he came to write *Anne of Geierstein* in 1828–9. It is probable that bloodshed was less extensive in these disturbances than during the insurrections of Edward II's reign or the tedious quarrel between Henry IV and the Percies: little material damage was done to towns or castles. But the Wars of the Roses dominated, and eventually terminated, the seventeen-year life of the fifth Prince of Wales. The boy seems to have had no identity except as a puppet of his mother. Yet there is no reason for thinking he would have wished for any other form of existence. Even as a child, it was said, 'the Prince of Wales would talk of nothing else but cutting off heads or making war'. He was, thought the courtiers, his mother's son; but he was also grandson of Henry V.[6]

The prince saw little of his father. Henry suffered another breakdown about the time of the boy's second birthday, when the court was in residence at Hertford. Margaret took husband and child to Greenwich and the king recovered his senses within five months, but the illness strengthened the hold of Richard of York on the government and it was with difficulty that the queen reimposed the formal authority of the crown. She did not risk bringing the king or the prince to London until Easter in 1458 for she knew that the London merchants favoured York. Even then she remained only a few months in the capital. Much of the young prince's education was therefore conducted in an itinerant court, based on the Midlands and particularly in Coventry, which was held to be a reliable Lancastrian stronghold. The boy appears to have accompanied his parents westwards from Coventry in the autumn of 1459 when a royal army marched against Ludlow Castle, where Richard of York and his ally, the Earl of Warwick, were concentrating their forces. On this occasion the Yorkist cause collapsed without a major battle: York fled to Ireland and Warwick to Calais, where he held a key position as Captain of the citadel and effective keeper of the town. Yet the hollowness of the royal victory was emphasized by the uncertainty of the parliamentary proceedings which followed the Ludlow campaign: Lords and Commons were summoned to Coventry (rather than to Westminster) in the third week of November and the Lords were required, not merely to deprive York and his allies of their rights by passing an act of attainder for treason, but also to reinforce their oath of loyalty to Henry with an oath of loyalty to the Prince of Wales, and a pledge to support and protect the king's wife and son.

Seven months later (June 1460) the Earl of Warwick led a raiding party from Calais which landed at Sandwich and marched on London, virtually unopposed. On 10 July Warwick attacked the royal camp at Northampton and took the king captive. In the autumn Richard of York returned from Ireland and, entering London in triumph, claimed the throne. He found, however, that parliament was less acquiescent than in 1399: the Lords were reluctant to go against the oaths they had sworn so recently at Coventry. Eventually, on 28 October 1460, Henry agreed to a compromise: he would rescind the Coventry attainders, recognize Richard of York as his heir, and assign to him the revenue of the principality of Wales. In a gesture of family loyalty the king insisted that the title of Prince of Wales should remain with the seven-year-old Prince Edward.

By good fortune Margaret and the prince had left the king at

Coventry some days before Warwick's invasion force landed at Sandwich, and they were in Staffordshire when news came of the king's capture. At once the queen and her son fled to Wales, where the stout walls of Harlech Castle offered them several months of sanctuary. Margaret was infuriated by her husband's abandonment of the prince's rights; and in December she sailed from Harlech to Scotland, where she learnt that the Percies and other dissident families in northern England were prepared to rise against Richard of York's threatened usurpation of the crown. While the queen and her son were still in Dumfriesshire, a Lancastrian force surprised Richard of York outside Wakefield. In a brief battle York himself was killed and Warwick's father, the Earl of Salisbury, captured and executed. This victory improved the standing of the queen who was able to muster an army, part Welsh, part Scottish and part northern English, which marched southwards in late January 1461. The young Prince of Wales accompanied the army, which bore his insignia, 'a white ostrich feather on crimson and black'.

Warwick, who held the king captive in London, was able to rally some support by denouncing this motley army in the king's name as an invading rabble and by playing on southern English hatred of the Scots. Taking the king with him, Warwick awaited the invaders in a good defensive position around St Albans. The morale of his troops was, however, low and when the second battle of St Albans began on 17 February 1471, there were mass desertions in Warwick's army. In order to save his own skin the earl broke off the engagement and withdrew westwards with as many reliable men as he could extricate from the clash of arms. At Burford Warwick was able to join the Earl of March (Richard of York's heir) who had raised a large army from the Mortimer strongholds in Wales. Meanwhile, at St Albans, there had been a Lancastrian family reunion, for horsemen bearing white ostrich-feather badges found King Henry sitting under guard beneath a tree near the battlefield and brought him to his wife and son. The Prince of Wales was knighted on the evening after the battle by his father: it is said he was wearing a child's suit of armour covered with purple velvet and ornamented in gold. One contemporary source maintains that, after being knighted, the seven-year-old boy took delight in watching the execution of his father's former captors. Although this tale may well be a piece of Yorkist propaganda, it is not out of character. The queen wished her son feared as a ruthless warrior, not respected for his chivalry.

In London the merchants were certainly afraid that (as one of them wrote) 'the queen and prince would descend in fury with their troops', but the victory of St Albans brought the Lancastrians nothing except the liberty of their King's person.[7] Margaret distrusted the Londoners and consistently minimized the importance of the capital city. Possibly she saw the wars too much through a Frenchwoman's eyes, mistakenly rating London as low as the dauphin had rated Paris. For, as the Earls of March and Warwick approached from the west, so the queen and prince withdrew northwards, back to Yorkshire. It was thus the Earl of March who entered London, less than a fortnight after the Lancastrian victory, and he speedily showed that he knew his own mind, even if he was still two months short of his nineteenth birthday. On 4 March 1461 he was proclaimed King Edward IV. Parliament at once passed an act of attainder condemning 'the late King Henry the Usurper', together with 'Margaret lately called Queen of England and her son Edward, lately called Prince of Wales'.[8]

This Yorkist usurpation of the throne rallied some of the wavering nobility to support the queen and the prince. By the last week in March they had gathered an army of some 26,000 men. Edward IV brought this force to battle at Towton on Palm Sunday (19 March 1461) in a strange and bloody encounter fought in a snowstorm and against a background of church bells summoning faithful non-combatant villagers to their religious observance. Towton was a staggering defeat for the Lancastrians. The queen, her pathetic husband and her son fled once more to Scotland. Fighting continued in northern England for another three years; but there was now no doubt that Edward IV was master of the kingdom.

The Prince of Wales spent the first period of his exile at the court of the Queen Mother of Scotland, Mary of Gueldres, while Queen Margaret journeyed to France and back to Northumbria in the hope of kindling fire from the embers of Lancastrian resistance. By the summer of 1463 it became clear that she could not rely on Scottish support indefinitely and she believed she could do more for her cause on the continent than in the comparative isolation of the Scottish lowlands. In the third week of July 1463 the queen and her son parted from Henry in Edinburgh; they were never to see him again. From Scotland they crossed to Sluys; the prince was left in Bruges while his mother travelled to Béthune for a conference with the Duke of Burgundy. By the autumn of 1463 she had resigned herself to the frustrations of a long exile; and, with a small pension from her father, Margaret established herself at the castle of Koeur near Saint Mihiel, in the wooded hills of the Meuse valley, twenty-five miles south of Verdun. There, in the late summer of 1465, she heard that Edward IV had at last captured her husband, as he sought to escape for Wales after holding out for many months at the Percy stronghold of Bamburgh Castle. With Henry's disappearance behind the walls of the Tower of London even Margaret's hopes began to flag.

These years in exile enabled the Prince of Wales to receive a sound education.[9] He had a good tutor. Sir John Fortescue, a Devonshire man who had sat in seven parliaments during the king's minority, was appointed chief justice of the King's Bench in 1442 and remained consistently loyal to Henry VI, accompanying the queen to Flanders and acting as chancellor of her household at Koeur. It was natural she should entrust him with the education of her son. While he was at St Mihiel Fortescue wrote a series of legal treatises analysing the concept of monarchy and the nature of law in England: like Machiavelli fifty years later, he liked to write in the style of a tutor addressing a prince. Certainly no previous heir to the throne had been so well trained for the future 'governance of England' as the dispossessed Edward of Lancaster.

By 1469 there seemed a possibility all this learning might soon be put to good purpose. News reached the exiles of discord at Edward IV's court. In May 1464 Edward married Elizabeth Woodville, the young and beautiful widow of a Lancastrian knight killed at the second battle of St Albans. This marriage angered several members of the nobility, not least because the Woodville family showed themselves as expert and ruthless as the more experienced Nevilles, Greys and Mortimers at finding short cuts to riches and influence. Soon 'Kingmaker' Warwick found himself in conflict with Edward IV, not only over the advancement of the Woodvilles but also over foreign affairs, where royal preferences did not always coincide with Warwick's self-interest. Twice, in 1469 and early 1470, Warwick encouraged local risings against Edward IV who was, at one time, briefly in the hands of the Neville family. But Warwick's ultimate intentions were confused and it was not until midsummer in 1470 that he accepted the need to rescue Henry VI from the Tower and restore the Lancastrian dynasty.

On 25 June 1470 Warwick was brought by King Louis XI of France into the presence of his bitterest enemy and her son at the château of Amboise. Margaret and the prince never lost their distrust of Warwick, but they accepted the advice of Sir John Fortescue that there was no more valuable ally in England than the earl. Four weeks after the meeting at Amboise a ceremony of reconciliation took place in Angers Cathedral at which Warwick swore on a relic of the True Cross that he would be faithful to King Henry, Queen Margaret and the Prince of Wales. With marked reluctance the queen agreed that Warwick's daughter, Anne Neville, should marry her son. She insisted, however, that Anne should spend some months in her household. Moreover the marriage would not take place until the Prince of Wales was restored to his full inheritance.[10]

Warwick, with a group of Lancastrian supporters, landed in Devon in the second week of September. Edward IV was in Yorkshire, and Warwick received enough support from the discontented nobility to be master of London and of southern England within three weeks. On 3 October Henry was freed from the Tower and placed once more on the throne. Edward IV, with some three hundred followers, fled from King's Lynn to the Netherlands and eventually to Duke Charles of Burgundy, who had married Edward's sister Margaret two years before. Now was the time when Queen Margaret should have brought the Prince of Wales and his fiancée across the Channel, and Warwick prepared festive ceremonies to amuse the people of London. But the Queen hesitated. She feared capture of the prince by Burgundian vessels, placed by Duke Charles at his brother-in-law's disposal. As evidence of good faith, the queen waived her objections to Anne Neville's marriage. The prince's wedding was celebrated at Amboise in December 1470, although Anne was never accorded the title of Princess of Wales. Not until Saturday, 13 April 1471 did the queen, her ladies and the prince sail from Honfleur for England. By then it was too late: Edward IV had returned to London on the previous Thursday; and Henry was back in the Wakefield Tower.

Edward IV, with Burgundian troops and some English followers, had landed at the mouth of the Humber in mid-March. He found the towns of the North and East Anglia so apathetic that he had no difficulty in out-manoeuvring Warwick and making his way to London. On Easter Sunday, 14 April, his troops met Warwick's army at Barnet and, in a confused battle fought in thick grey mist, he gained a narrow victory, Warwick perishing on the field of battle. It was on this same Sunday morning that the queen and the prince landed at Weymouth; they heard the disastrous news late the following day. Good sense suggested a return to France, but there were still strong Lancastrian forces in South Wales and the queen was encouraged by contingents raised in the West Country by Edmund Beaufort, Duke of Somerset, son of the trusted friend killed at the first battle of St Albans. The army headed for Wales, hoping to cross the Severn before troops mustered by Edward IV could intercept it.

The Lancastrian force almost won the race. Skilful deception gave Edward IV the slip around Bath and Bristol on 1 May, enabling the queen and the prince to head for the bridge across the Severn at Gloucester. On Thursday, 2 May, the Prince of Wales slept at Berkeley Castle, a place of ill omen indeed. It was, in fact, the last occasion upon which he had any opportunity for sleep. Next day the gates of Gloucester remained shut and the army was forced to continue marching northwards towards the next bridge over the Severn. Late on Friday afternoon the exhausted Lancastrians reached Tewkesbury, while Edward was only nine miles away at Cheltenham. Somerset, as commander-in-chief of the queen and prince's army, chose a good defensive position with the abbey behind him and open ground pitted with dykes to hamper the Yorkist attack. He commanded one wing of the army himself: the centre of the line was entrusted to the seventeen-year-old Prince of Wales. Like his predecessors at Crécy and Shrewsbury, the prince was accompanied by experienced campaigners capable of giving prudent advice. Yet, in a sense, Tewkesbury was a young man's battle: Edward IV at twenty-nine was already a veteran of six bloody encounters, but the left of the Yorkist position was commanded by his youngest brother, Richard of Gloucester, who was only twelve months older than the Prince of Wales.

Fortune had favoured the Black Prince at Crécy and Henry of Monmouth at Shrewsbury: it turned against Edward of Lancaster at Tewkesbury that Saturday morning. Queen Margaret and his wife, Anne, watching the battle from a vantage point half a mile south of the massive tower of the Norman abbey, saw Somerset's men mount a courageous flank attack on Richard of Gloucester's division, only to be outflanked themselves by Yorkist horsemen, held in reserve. A resolute advance by the Yorkist centre pitched the prince's own men into hand-to-hand fighting. After initial resistance the sheer weight of the Yorkist onslaught triumphed; the Lancastrians fled to the abbey, seeking sanctuary within its walls. During the stampede 'the Prince of Wales, several other great lords, and a great number of common soldiers were killed upon the spot', as the French chronicler, Philip de Commines noted succinctly at the time. News of her son's death reached the queen before noon: she collapsed with grief, and was hurried by the widowed Anne and her other ladies into a carriage and away to Malvern, where a few days later she was captured by Yorkist patrols. She was too valuable a political hostage to be executed, as Somerset and so many leaders of the Lancastrian cause had been; and in January 1476 she was allowed to return, as a ransomed prisoner, to the land of her birth, where she lived in obscurity for another six and a half years. But nothing now could save the pathetic Henry. On 21 May 1471 Edward IV returned to London from his victory at Tewkesbury: that night 'between eleven and twelve of the clock', Henry was murdered in his cell at the Tower of London.

The remains of Edward of Lancaster were buried in Tewkesbury Abbey, as were the bones of many nobles who had fought for him. A brass plaque in the floor of the choir of the abbey church marks his burial place with a Latin epitaph: 'Here lies Edward, Prince of Wales, cruelly slain while still a youth, 4 May 1471. Alas the fury of men! You are the sole light of your mother, the last hope of your House (*gregis*).' He was the only one of the Princes of Wales to perish in battle.[11]

Within eight weeks of his death, there was a new Prince of Wales. While Edward IV was in exile in Burgundy in the previous winter, Queen Elizabeth (Woodville) had taken refuge in Westminster Abbey. There, on 2 November, she gave birth to her fourth child and first son, who was named after his father and known from the circumstances of his birth as 'Edward of the Sanctuary'. He was formally created Prince of Wales at the age of seven and a half months, and acknowledged by the Lords in parliament on 3 July 1471. His boyhood passed happily enough: no serious challenge was offered to Edward IV's authority for the rest of his reign, and his government was able to carry out a series of valuable reforms, which regulated prices, helped the cloth trade, and made the king as acceptable to the city merchants as their wives and daughters were to himself. The young prince benefited from this period of peace and prosperity. Yet it is probable he saw no more of his father than

Edward of Lancaster had done. For Edward IV believed court life harmful to a child's upbringing. When the boy was three years old he was put in the care of his mother's eldest brother, Anthony, Earl Rivers, and Ludlow Castle was assigned to the Prince of Wales as an official residence. At first the queen accompanied the boy to Ludlow, but she was to have five more children and she never showed the possessiveness of Margaret of Anjou.

Earl Anthony was a highly educated and strict, though kindly, guardian. Careful instructions regulated the prince's day, apparently from about his fifth birthday onwards. He was to get up 'at a convenient hour according to his age', spending the morning 'in such virtuous learning as his age shall suffer to receive'. During his midday meal he was to listen to a suitable reading from a book. In the afternoon he should take exercise, with play permitted after supper. There were to be moments of prayer during the day and careful observance of religious duties. No one should be permitted around the prince who was suspected of bad character, or given to bad language. His attendants should 'enforce themselves to make him merry and joyous towards his bed', and his curtains were to be drawn by eight o'clock until the age of eleven, when he was permitted to stay up for another hour. He became a precociously intelligent young man, like his great-nephew, Edward VI. Technically the prince was head of the Council of the Welsh Marches, which functioned from Ludlow. As he was a child the presidency of the council devolved upon his principal tutor, Bishop John Alcock of Worcester (who was later to found Jesus College, Cambridge), but it was Edward IV's intention that his son should come to know the Welsh borders and the problems of the principality. Occasionally the prince was brought to London. When the king planned a joint attack on France with the Duke of Burgundy in the summer of 1475, the Prince of Wales was knighted, declared to be 'Keeper of the Realm', and left with his mother at Westminster, while Bishop Alcock was appointed deputy Chancellor. And in May 1481 the king and the Prince of Wales went on a solemn, though hasty, pilgrimage to Canterbury. But for months on end the prince remained on the old Mortimer estates at Ludlow, with his uncle Anthony Rivers. Sometimes they spent some weeks at Tickenhill, a manor house near Bewdley in Worcestershire which the king had fitted out for his son as a home for rest and recuperation.[12]

They were in Ludlow on 14 April 1483 when news reached them that Edward IV had died at Westminster five days previously. He was three weeks short of his forty-first birthday and, although overweight, he appears to have been in good health until he developed a feverish cold after fishing at Windsor in the last days of March. His sudden and premature death threw the kingdom into confusion. The Prince of Wales was only twelve years old. England was therefore faced for the second time in the century with the prospect of a long royal minority. The prince's mother, Queen Elizabeth, was as unpopular as Margaret of Anjou: her Woodville relatives had continued to benefit from Edward IV's patronage throughout the years of political stability, grabbing high office, titles and rich heiresses. The older nobility also resented the rise of the Greys, the queen's two sons by her first marriage: Thomas Grey, Marquis of Dorset, was in 1483 constable of the Tower of London, controlling both the royal ordnance and the royal treasure; and Sir Richard Grey enjoyed considerable influence over his half-brother, the Prince of Wales. Since Edward IV knew the nobility hated the Woodvilles and Greys, he changed his will (apparently on his deathbed) and entrusted the care of his elder son, not to Queen Elizabeth as he had resolved in 1475, but to his brother, Duke Richard of Gloucester. But when Edward died, Duke Richard was in York, where he had shown himself an efficient, popular and just Lieutenant of the North: the Woodvilles and the Greys, controlling both London and the royal council, wished to set aside Edward IV's will and safeguard their own position. They proposed that the boy king should be crowned immediately, thus technically ending his minority and allowing him to choose his own advisers.

Anthony Rivers informed the Prince of Wales of his accession on 14 April but lingered in Ludlow for over a week, awaiting instructions from the Marquis of Dorset. Eventually Rivers and King Edward V set out for London on 24 April with an escort of two thousand men. Five days later Rivers was enticed away from the main body of the king's escort and, after an amiable meeting with Duke Richard of Gloucester at Northampton, placed under arrest by the duke's retainers. Next day Richard secured custody of his nephew at Stony Stratford, dismissed the royal escort, and took the young king to Northampton. By 1 May news of Duke Richard's coup had caused consternation in London: the Queen-Mother, with six of her children, found sanctuary in

Westminster Abbey, where they were joined by one of Elizabeth's brothers and by Dorset, who feared for his life if he remained in the Tower. On Sunday, 4 May, Edward v and Richard of Gloucester reached London: the king formally confirmed his uncle's title of Protector, to which was now added 'Defender of the Realm'. The king was lodged that night in the bishop's town residence, beside St Paul's. He seems to have remained in the bishop's palace for at least a week. But there was talk of coronation, and on the eve of being crowned, England's sovereigns traditionally went into residence in the royal apartments of the Tower of London. Edward v was conveyed to the Tower in the third week of May: his mother was induced by the Archbishop of Canterbury to allow Edward iv's other son, Richard of York, to leave Westminster Abbey on 16 June in order to join the king. Neither Edward v nor his ten-year-old brother ever emerged from the Tower.[13]

Protector Gloucester had good reason to suspect plots against his authority, not only from the Woodvilles but from other dissident families among the nobility and from Lancastrian claimants. He believed his hold on government and the continuance of peace within England depended upon recognition of his own tenuous claims to the throne. In the fourth week of June a whispering campaign, which was supported by a sermon at St Paul's Cross, maintained that Edward iv's marriage to Elizabeth Woodville was invalid and that Edward v and his brother and five sisters were illegitimate. On 26 June a petition from the Lords and Commons of England was handed to the Protector asking him to assume the royal dignity, since Edward iv's union with Elizabeth had never been a true marriage. On 6 July he was crowned Richard iii in Westminster Abbey in an elaborate ceremony which was followed by a banquet of five and a half hours. No doubt the formal acclamation of the new king could be heard by Elizabeth Woodville and her five daughters, still within the protection of the abbey buildings.

Crowned with Richard that Sunday was his consort, the kingmaker's daughter, Anne Neville. Twelve years before, when she was sixteen, Anne watched as the horsemen of her husband-to-be pursued the foot guards of her husband-of-five-months across the meadows beneath Tewkesbury Abbey. Soon afterwards she was captured, with Queen Margaret, by the Yorkists at Little Malvern. She was then sent north, to

Middleham Castle in Wensleydale, which had once been her father's favourite Yorkshire home but passed to Richard of Gloucester when the Earl of Warwick's estates were dispersed after his death at Barnet. Richard had, in fact, already spent most of the years between his ninth and fifteenth birthdays at Middleham, for Warwick was his first cousin, although considerably older, and there were several companionable youngsters in the earl's household at that time, including Anne herself. Before Richard of Gloucester took up his duties as his brother's Lieutenant in the North, he asked Edward IV's permission to marry Anne. The marriage seems to have been celebrated in Yorkshire before the end of the year 1472 and a son was born at Middleham, probably in the autumn of 1473. Edward of Middleham was not a robust child: perhaps for that reason his parents seem to have been especially fond of the boy, who remained their only child. He was created Earl of Salisbury in February 1478 and with his father's accession he became automatically Duke of Cornwall, but Richard had every intention of seeing him invested Prince of Wales, if only his health could stand the strain of a public ceremony.[14]

A fortnight after the coronation Richard left London and set out on progress through the west Midlands – Reading, Oxford, Woodstock, Gloucester, Tewkesbury. In August Anne met the king at Warwick and the progress continued through Leicester and Nottingham into Yorkshire. At Pontefract Castle they were joined on 24 August by their son, who had journeyed slowly south from Middleham with an impressive retinue of his own. On that same Sunday King Richard created the boy Prince of Wales by royal patent rather than in a charter made with the assent of parliament, the procedure followed for the creation of the previous five princes. The patent referred to 'the singular wit and endowments of nature wherewith, his young age considered, he is remarkably furnished' and held out a pious hope that through these gifts 'by the favour of God, he will make an honest man'.[15] Such language may be mere decorative verbiage but, if so, it has an unusually personal quality: Richard III was proud of his son's attainments.

Richard and Anne were popular in northern England. As Edward IV's Warden of the West March Richard had held the border effectively against Scottish raiders and carried the fighting as far north as Edinburgh without having to impose heavy taxes on the townsfolk he was defending; and his lieutenancy in the North was marked by good and impartial justice. He was, as the archives record, 'our full tender and especial good lord'. The city of York, in particular, responded to these years of sound administration by offering gifts and honours to the royal pair: in 1477 both Richard and Anne were admitted to the Corpus Christi Guild, the most powerful and select of the merchant fraternities of York. It was therefore natural that the king's entry into York on 29–30 August should be the high point of the sovereign's progress through his realm. The streets were decorated with hanging screens of arras tapestry, and three pageants were staged at different points along the route: the royal procession included, not only the new Prince of Wales, but six bishops, five earls, the chief officers of the Household, and the Spanish ambassador. The civic dignitaries of York were determined to impress 'the many southern Lords and men of worship' who had come for the first time to their city. So pleased was the king with this enthusiastic reception that he decided, not merely to invest his son in York, but to ensure that the investiture was enriched with the full majesty of a state occasion. Couriers hastened to London with orders for gowns, cloth of gold doublets, heraldic coats of arms, holy banners, satins, velvets, thirteen thousand badges of coarse fustian fabric depicting the king's emblem of white boar, and 'three coats of arms beaten with fine gold for our own person'. Incredibly, the king's Wardrobe was able to meet these demands within a week. On Monday, 8 September, Edward of Middleham was welcomed to York Minster by the archbishop and a fanfare from forty trumpeters. He was duly invested by his father with the gold coronet, ring and rod of a Prince of Wales; and when the ceremony was completed, a procession was formed of 'three princes wearing their crowns – the King, the Queen and the Prince of Wales'. They moved down the crowded, narrow streets with great dignity to the 'honour, joy and congratulations of the inhabitants, as in show of rejoicing they extolled King Richard above the skies'.[16]

The records conjure up splendid theatre, even after the lapse of five hundred years. Yet this week of festive performance was the only occasion in Edward of Middleham's life when he held the public stage. By the end of September he was back in Wensleydale and his mother and father moved south, carrying the king's progress to Lincoln. There, early in October, Richard learnt of a rebellion instigated by the Duke of

Buckingham, whom he had regarded as one of his staunchest supporters. The king overcame this threat without great difficulty, but throughout the winter of 1483–4 there remained a danger of fresh insurrection and Richard had to stay at the centre of government. In the first week of March 1484 he summoned 'nearly all the lords of the realm, both spiritual and temporal' to the palace and made each subscribe to 'a kind of new oath', pledging loyalty to the Prince of Wales 'in case anything should happen to his father'. Richard and Anne then left for Cambridge, where the university entertained them for a week, and began to travel slowly northwards. At Nottingham a courier brought tragic news: Edward, Prince of Wales, had been 'seized with an illness of but short duration'; and on 9 April – the first anniversary of his uncle Edward IV's death – the prince died in the apartments where he had spent almost all his life, at Middleham Castle.

'You might have seen his father and mother in a state almost bordering on madness by reason of their sudden grief', wrote one of the king's councillors in the Croyland Chronicle.[17] It seems as if Anne never entirely recovered from the blow: her health deteriorated, and she died less than twelve months later, still under thirty. No one can tell the full effect of his son's death upon Richard. The chronicler was chiefly concerned with the political impact, seeing the king mourning 'this only son of his, in whom all the hopes of the royal succession, fortified with so many oaths, were centred'. But there is no doubt Richard's private sorrow was intense and lasting, darkening the last year of his reign with an iron bitterness of soul.

Edward's body was interred, not at Middleham, but on his father's estate at Sheriff Hutton, much closer to the city where the trumpets had sounded on that 'great day of state' in September. It seems as if the king intended to found a chantry collegiate church for his son at Sheriff Hutton, as he had already done for the souls of other members of his family both at Barnard Castle and at Middleham. But in August of the following year Richard III was 'piteously slain' at Bosworth, 'to the great heaviness of this city', as the mayor of York wrote at the time: no chantry was founded, nor was there even an inscription placed upon the tomb. A worn, stone effigy of an eleven-year-old boy survives in Sheriff Hutton Church: Yorkshire's Prince of Wales lies buried, as he had lived, in almost total anonymity, remote and known only to a handful of people.[18]

CHAPTER FIVE

Sons of Prophecy

RICHARD III's crown was toppled in 1485 by an 'unknown Welshman' whose name had only recently slipped into the list of claimants to the throne. Henry Tudor, Earl of Richmond, was born on 28 January 1457 at Pembroke Castle in south-western Wales, but the origins of the Tudor family lay well to the north of Pembroke in Anglesey, that traditional offshore refuge of Celtic culture beyond the Menai Straits. Only four miles inland from the Straits, and six miles from the mainland cathedral city of Bangor, lies Plas Penmynydd, long the home of a family descended from Tudur ap Ednyfed, who died in 1278 while serving as seneschal to Prince Llywelyn the Last. By the end of the fourteenth century these lands, and others in Anglesey and on the mainland, were held by Maredudd ap Tudor, principal steward to the Bishop of Bangor, and shortly before 1400 a son, Owain, was born to Maredudd's wife, Margaret Vychan, probably at Penmynydd. During the child's infancy the whole of northern Wales was turned upside down by the rebellion of Maredudd's first cousin, Owen Glendower. Maredudd did not play so prominent a part in the revolt as his better-known brothers, Rhys and Gwillym, but it was enough to cost the family their Anglesey properties. Like many members of the Welsh squirearchy, Owain ap Maredudd ap Tudor thought it best to leave his homeland, anglicize his name, and enter the personal service of the Prince of Wales as a page. He accompanied his master, now King Henry V, to France and fought at Agincourt, remaining at court as a minor official when the campaign was over.

No other adventurer come to town made good so dramatically as Owen Tudor. When Henry died, Owen became Clerk to the Wardrobe of Queen Catherine, widowed in her twentieth year. She was cut off from her family in France and bored by the squabbling politics of Henry VI's minority: the Welshman was agreeable company, with good looks and a ready tongue; and at some time between 1425 and 1429 they were secretly married. Five children were born before Duke Humphrey of Gloucester discovered his sister-in-law's illicit union and induced her to retire to Bermondsey Abbey, where she died in January 1437.[1] After a brief spell in Newgate Gaol for having presumed to marry a queen dowager, Owen Tudor escaped from London and was able to live unmolested in Wales, where the family had recovered several of their confiscated estates. One son, named after his father, was accepted as a Benedictine monk and witnessed half a century's dynastic turmoil from the unique vantage point of Westminster Abbey. A daughter became a nun and the youngest child, the Lady Jacira Tudor, married a Yorkist baron, Lord Gray of Wilton. But it was the two eldest boys who received greatest attention from their half-brother, the king: the firstborn, Edmund, was created Earl of Richmond in 1452 and his legitimacy confirmed by act of parliament; and the younger brother, Jasper, was made Earl of Pembroke in 1453. These titles were accorded for sound political reasons, not fraternal sentiment. It was essential to have champions of the Lancastrian establishment in Wales, where the Yorkists could count on support from the Mortimer lands which stretched almost unbroken from the approaches to Chester through Ludlow and the border Marches down to the outskirts of Cardiff. The Mortimers and Tudors were natural enemies, bound in hostility by rival ambition.

Owen Tudor's advancement through marriage was equalled, and perhaps surpassed, by the achievement of his eldest son. For in 1455 Edmund of Richmond was encouraged by his royal half-brother to marry one of the most eligible child heiresses in the English nobility, Lady Margaret Beaufort, great-granddaughter of John of Gaunt, great niece of the rich Cardinal Beaufort, scholarly, devout, and twelve years old. But soon, after their marriage, the Tudor luck began to turn. Edmund of Richmond was taken prisoner by a Yorkist force in the summer of 1356 and died at Carmarthen in the following November. His thirteen-year-old widow, six months pregnant, took shelter from the civil wars in her brother-in-law's castle at Pembroke, where her son was born on St Agnes's Day and named after his step-uncle, the king. Four years later – on 3 February 1461 – the Lancastrian cause in Wales suffered a disastrous defeat at the battle of Mortimer's Cross. The sexagenarian Owen Tudor was captured and condemned to die in the market-place at Hereford: 'That head shall lie on the stock which was wont to lie on Queen Catherine's lap', he lamented as the final preparations were completed for his execution. His son, Earl Jasper of Pembroke, escaped by sea from south Wales and continued to resist the Yorkists at Harlech. It is probable he took young Henry with him: the chronicler, Commines, who met Henry at the French court in 1484–5, says that from the age of five he was compelled to hide in one Welsh castle after another. Certainly he saw little of his mother: she married the Lancastrian Lord Henry Stafford and, after his death in 1471, made her peace with the Yorkists and took Lord Thomas Stanley as her third husband. By 1468 young Henry was a ward of William Herbert and living at Raglan Castle in the care of Anne Devereux, Lady Herbert, who saw to it that he received a good education. But in 1470, during the kingmaker's brief restoration of Henry VI to the throne, Jasper recovered custody of his nephew. After the Yorkist victories at Barnet and Tewkesbury, Jasper and Henry were able to escape by sea from Tenby and find asylum in Brittany.[2]

Henry Tudor's importance increased considerably after the death of the Prince of Wales at Tewkesbury and the murder of the king in the Tower. For his mother was now heir to the Lancastrian titles, although the Beaufort rights were marred by a royal patent of Henry IV which expressly excluded descendants of his father's belated union with Catherine Swynford from the throne. The Lady Margaret, gifted with the grace of retreating into intense religious devotion at the onset of political emergency, never pressed her own claims, although she maintained a secret correspondence with her son in Brittany, sending him messages which to hostile eyes might appear treasonable. Yet the prospects for the Lancastrians seemed so poor that Richard III invited the Lady Margaret to carry Queen Anne's train as she moved in procession to the altar for the coronation of July 1483. No doubt it was a pointed demonstration of the rightful status of the Beauforts in Yorkist society; but had Richard regarded the Lady Margaret as a serious threat to his royal title she would more likely have been in the Tower than at the Abbey.

Nevertheless, Richard certainly distrusted the activities of Jasper and his nephew in Brittany; and with good reason. Duke Francis of Brittany made substantial loans to the Tudors and offered them protection of his ships when, during Buckingham's abortive insurrection of October 1483, Henry crossed the Channel, sought to land at Poole and sailed into Plymouth Sound. Attempts by Richard to bribe the duke's outstandingly venal treasurer into handing Henry over to an English emissary were narrowly thwarted; and Jasper and his nephew crossed out of the duchy and into the kingdom of France while they planned a more co-ordinated assault on Richard's realm. On Christmas Day 1483 Henry Tudor took a solemn oath in the cathedral of Rennes, swearing that, as soon as he obtained the crown of England, he would marry Elizabeth of York, the eldest child of Edward IV and Elizabeth Woodville. Present at Rennes that Christmas were the principal members of the Woodville family who were alive and at liberty; and with them were a number of Yorkists disillusioned by Richard III's failure to provide them with the high offices which they believed their past services merited. A Yorkist heir had better claims to the throne than any Beaufort or Tudor could present to the people of England, and the ceremony at Rennes improved Henry's prospects of uniting Richard's opponents behind his banner, at least momentarily. There was about all this bargaining in France an echo of old conspiracies, of Warwick's meeting with Margaret of Anjou at Amboise and the oath-taking ceremony in Angers Cathedral. A second Tewkesbury would ruin the Lancastrian cause and leave the Tudors buried in unmarked graves.

Yet Henry of Richmond possessed four advantages denied to the unfortunate Prince of Wales in 1470. He was gifted with an acute sense of political reality; he could count on wise counsel from the wiliest of uncles; and his mother, though a sympathetic supporter, was physically and spiritually distant rather than dangerously close at hand, as Margaret of Anjou had been. But above all Henry had the asset of being a Welshman. He was no titular Prince of Wales but the grandson of Owain ap Maredudd ap Tudur, someone who had spent half his life in Pembroke and most of the other half among his fellow Celts in Brittany. The Tudor cause was patriotically Welsh, not the latest expediency of a chronically rebellious baronage. Henry was conscious of his Welsh origin. At times it kindled the fire of romanticist lore in a mind habitually cold and calculating. As a boy the bardic poems were as familiar to him as tales from the bible and in exile he absorbed the *romans bretons*, the early-thirteenth-century cycle of legends linking Arthur and his knights with a Brittany which included Cornwall and Wales. Henry knew he was descended from Edward III through his mother and from St Louis of France through his grandmother, but what excited him was his descent, real or imaginary, from Cadwallader the Blessed who had ruled Gwynedd in the seventh century and was said by the bards to be coming again to claim primacy over all the lands of Britain. For Jasper made certain Henry was aware of the propaganda value of the Welsh bards. The fact that he remained in exile strengthened his messianic appeal: more than thirty bards are known to have kept Welsh national fervour on the boil during the last years of Edward IV. Long alliterative verses invoked the memory of Arthur, Cadwallader and Owen Glendower: the Welsh people were promised a deliverer who would free them from 'Saxon' oppression. By 1485 constant repetition of these vatic ballads was making the Welsh turn in hope to Brittany and see in Henry Tudor, Earl of Richmond, the promised 'son of prophecy', the *mab darogan* of whom the harpists sang.[3]

Henry's small invasion fleet set out from the Seine estuary on 1 August and arrived off Milford Haven in western Pembrokeshire seven days later. His force advanced unmolested up the coastal route from Cardigan to Aberystwyth, gathering enthusiastic recruits, including a contingent from Snowdonia and a large body of men from the south under Rhys ap Thomas. Letters were sent to all the gentry of Wales promising the restoration of former liberties and the abolition of the 'miserable servitudes', the laws which limited Welsh rights of citizenship; and Henry, somewhat blandly, spoke of 'the great confidence' which he felt in 'the nobles and commons of this our principality'. These assurances brought good results: by the time Henry entered Shrewsbury on 15 August all Wales seemed behind him and the nobility in England were deserting Richard III as speedily as instincts of personal safety permitted. Although Richard's army outnumbered Henry's at Bosworth, the king was betrayed by two members of the baronage in whom he had long felt little trust and killed on the field of battle. Henry VII was crowned in Westminster Abbey on 31 October. Eleven weeks later he was back at the abbey in order to marry Elizabeth of York and fulfil the vow made at Rennes the previous Christmas.

Among the standards flown by Henry at Bosworth was a white and green banner with the fiery red dragon of Cadwallader depicted on it.

The Welsh dragon remained his favourite heraldic beast, prancing still today in the sculptured furnishing of the chapel he completed at King's Cambridge, and over the king's tomb at Westminster. He knew more of Wales and the Welsh than he did of England, and Welshmen remained in favour throughout the first half of his reign. Most honoured among them was the king's uncle, Jasper Tudor. The earldom of Pembroke was restored to him, he received new lordships in Haverfordwest, Abergavenny, Newport and Glamorgan, and he was created Duke of Bedford and Chief Justiciar of Wales. Sir Rhys ap Thomas acquired so many offices and lands that he became virtual ruler of the south-western area of the principality. Other Welshmen were made bishops, sheriffs and given minor posts at court. Many Welsh veterans of the Bosworth campaign became founder members of the king's body of armed attendants, the Yeomen of the Guard. Among the earliest Yeomen Sergeants was David Seisyllt from Alltyrynys, who accompanied Henry and Jasper into exile and returned with them to Milford Haven. David Seisyllt anglicized his surname to Cecil and the family remained in royal service : a son was knighted and granted land in Lincolnshire ; a grandson became Lord Burghley and was principal minister to Elizabeth I; and a more distant descendant, Lord Salisbury, was the long-serving prime minister of Queen Victoria. There is no doubt the Welsh benefited from the rise of the Tudor family. St David's Day was celebrated in London by feasting subsidized from the king's privy purse. More seriously, in the principality itself men and women of Welsh blood found they were no longer humiliated by discriminatory practices encouraged by their overlords earlier in the century. The old Anglo-Norman ascendancy was re-asserted under later English rulers, but Henry of Richmond at least made some attempt to fulfil the promises with which he had rallied his compatriots to the Tudor cause.[4]

On 20 September 1486 Elizabeth of York gave birth to a son at Winchester. The prince was named Arthur so that he might bring life to a legend dear to the Celtic bards. Church bells were rung throughout the kingdom and the principality at the king's command, choristers assembled to sing the *Te Deum*, and bonfires lit 'in praise and rejoicing'. In November 1489 Arthur was created Prince of Wales, with the assent and advice of the peers 'in parliament assembled'. Three months later his investiture allowed free rein to the king's love of symbolic pageantry.

On the eve of the investiture – Friday, 26 February 1490 – the child prince embarked on the royal state barge near Kew. Slowly the oarsmen bore him down river to the 'Brigge', the king's landing-stage by Westminster Hall. Bishops, peers and knights waited in their barges between Mortlake and Chelsea. So, too, did the Lord Mayor of London, with vessels draped in the liveries of the craft guilds. Off Lambeth the Spanish ambassador's barge joined the procession, by now a gilded flotilla of high-pooped long-ships, rich in heraldic imagery. Trumpeters and minstrels accompanied the line of barges, and the prince was carried with great solemnity from the Brigge to his father's presence in the palace. A mass dubbing of knights followed on that same Friday while on the Saturday morning the prince was mounted on a horse which was escorted into Westminster Hall, where the king invested his son with the traditional regalia of a Prince of Wales. 'Then the King departing, the Prince that day kept his state under the Clothe of Estate'. He 'licensed' the knights to enjoy their meat, and a banquet was served in Westminster Hall while minstrels played and the festivities closed in a fine flourish of heraldic thanksgiving by the Garter King-of-Arms. King Arthur, it was said, had been borne slowly across the waters to Avalon, whence one day he would return and resume his kingdom. And now a new Arthur had come in slow procession down the waters of the Thames to a knightly ceremony at the king's court. The allegory was clear to those who, like Henry Tudor himself, were steeped in such neo-chivalric romanticism.[5]

No doubt to purists it was irritating that the new Arthur should be only three years and five months old at the time of the investiture. It is a remarkable tribute to a reputedly sickly child that he stood the strain of two February days of investiture ceremonies without any apparent ill effect on his health. His father, anxious to lift the status of the Tudor dynasty, pushed the boy beyond the normal responsibilities of his age. Even before his investiture Arthur had become a bargaining counter in his father's diplomacy, a means of securing a valuable alliance with Spain. In March 1488 Henry began negotiations for Arthur's marriage to Catherine of Aragon, youngest of the five children born to Isabella of Castile, who shared sovereignty over Spain with her husband Ferdinand. Formal betrothal did not take place until a treaty was signed at Woodstock in August 1497, but long before then Catherine was accustomed to being called 'Princess of Wales' at her mother's court in

Granada. Although diplomats continued to haggle over the size of her marriage portion, Catherine accepted as inevitable the long voyage to England and union with Arthur, who was nine months her junior in age. On 4 October 1499 he wrote to her, as a husband married by proxy. It was no more than a one-page letter and his stilted Latin compliments may have owed something to the inspiration of his tutor, but it was gratifying to receive from the Prince of Wales a letter addressed to the Princess of Wales and to learn he was longing for her company.[6]

The letter came from Ludlow. Already Arthur was learning at first hand the problems of Wales and its people. Henry VII, like Edward IV before him, had packed his son off to the Welsh Marches, with tutors and a trusted governor (Sir Reginald Bray) as an effective representative of royal authority. Probably Arthur went to the Marches as early as the spring of 1497, when he was ten and a half: he was certainly there in May 1499, when he went to Bewdley for a proxy marriage ceremony at which the Spanish ambassador made pledges in Catherine's name; and he was at Ludlow throughout the summer of 1501 while his father was waiting impatiently in London for the arrival of his daughter-in-law and the religious solemnization of the union formally made at Bewdley. It was important for Henry that he should see his son a husband and a father as soon as possible. The impostors Lambert Simnel and Perkin Warbeck had shaken the throne in 1487 and 1497, and there still remained at large Yorkists with good claims to the succession. A son's son would steady the dynasty, not least because the new Princess of Wales was herself a distant claimant: John of Gaunt was the great-great-grandfather of Catherine, as he was also of Henry VII, and in Catherine's case there was no Beaufort bar of illegitimacy to weaken her titles.

Catherine's ship and its escort reached Plymouth on 2 October 1501, long overdue. One vessel had been lost in a gale off the Basque coast which drove the surviving ships into the small harbour of Laredo where it took a month to make them fit to face equinoctial squalls in the Bay of Biscay. Couriers brought news of the princess's arrival to the king at Westminster in forty-eight hours but it took longer to reach Arthur in Ludlow and he did not set out for the south until the end of the month. He met his father at Easthampstead, a royal manor near Wokingham in Berkshire. There they learnt that Catherine was only ten miles away, at Dogmersfield, not far from Odiham. Her cavalcade of horses, mules and waggons filled with tapestries, jewels, clothes and plate could only make slow progress through the English countryside. Moreover the princess was protected, not merely by formidable Spanish chaperones, but by an archbishop and a bishop representing their sovereign. They were in no hurry to reach the English court: indeed they claimed that neither the king nor her affianced bridegroom had any right to see Princess Catherine until the day of the wedding ceremony.

To Henry these scruples of Spanish etiquette smacked of deception. Perhaps his son's bride suffered from some hideous deformity. He rode over to Dogmersfield: Catherine, he declared, was now his subject and he had every intention of seeing her that day, 'even were she in her bed'. This she was not: the princess duly received the king, and he admired her graceful beauty. Half an hour later Arthur was allowed to meet the girl whom he had first called 'my spouse' more than two years before. After supper the princess summoned her minstrels: Henry, Arthur, Catherine and their English and Spanish attendants 'solaced themselves with the disports of the dance' until the guttering candles began to flicker low.[7]

This almost merry November evening at Dogmersfield is one of the few occasions when the eighth Prince of Wales steps down from the anonymity of a formal portrait and assumes human likeness. So passive and so immature was Arthur that he seems constantly to have been upstaged by those around him – his father, his bride, even his ten-year-old brother Henry, Duke of York, who had inherited the lusty physique of his mother's father, Edward IV. Arthur did what was recommended to him by his tutor, by Sir Reginald Bray, or by the king: even at Dogmersfield the chronicler notes that the prince was encouraged to dance by his father, choosing an English lady-in-waiting as his partner rather than the princess he was soon to wed. So it was to be throughout November and December that year. The royal wedding at St Paul's cathedral and the days of pageantry in the city streets are better chronicled than the waterborne procession of February 1490 but in none of these events does the prince figure as a personality any more sharply defined than at his investiture, when he was a child of three. There was a tournament in a specially constructed tiltyard outside Westminster Hall, but Arthur took no part in the jousting. At the wedding banquet he sat with his brother and eldest sister while his bride and her ladies were seated at a higher table, beside the king and queen and the great officers of state. A contemporary noted how the Princess of Wales delighted the onlookers with Spanish dancing and how young Henry of York gave the king and queen 'right great and singular pleasure' by flinging off his gown and in doublet and hose partnering his sister Margaret in a boisterous romp. Prince Arthur danced unobtrusively with his mother's younger sister, the Lady Cecily.[8]

The Prince and Princess of Wales spent their first night together at the Bishop of London's palace, close to St Paul's. Many years later former courtiers recalled how they had assisted in the ritual of a nuptial bedding, in chambers freshly decorated with newly glazed windows, tapestries and specially commissioned ironwork, for Henry showed none of his traditional parsimony over Prince Arthur's wedding celebrations. Next morning the prince is said to have greeted his friend and kinsman, Maurice St John, with the hearty comment, 'I look well for one that hath been in the midst of Spain.' But by 1529, when these words were solemnly noted down by commissioners testing the validity of Henry VIII's marriage, interests of state were nudging courtiers' memories for salacious titbits: no such waggishly Tudor sayings were credited to Arthur at the time. More in character are the politely turned Latin phrases with which the prince wrote to Catherine's parents, 'their Catholic Majesties' in Spain, on 30 November, 'Never in my life have I felt such joy as when first I beheld the sweet face of my bride.'[9]

King and council were far from certain whether the two fifteen-year-olds were as yet sufficiently mature to live together. Common sense suggested that Catherine and her Spanish attendants might winter at the English court and allow Arthur to return to Ludlow and the administrative affairs of his principality. They lingered for a time at Westminster and at the new Thames-side palace in Surrey which the king had named Richmond, after the Yorkshire title he had borne as an earl in infancy and exile. At the end of November the court moved to Windsor with no decision taken over the young couple's future place of residence. No doubt Catherine would have remained at Windsor if there was reason to believe she was pregnant; but there was not, and before Christmas the prince's long column of palfreys, horse-drawn litters, and baggage waggons set out northwards through the Thames valley to Abingdon, and by way of Woodstock and Kenilworth to the comforts of Tickenhill Manor at Bewdley. By the new year they had reached Ludlow, the principal seat of the council in the Marches of Wales, where the old stronghold of the Yorkists stood watchful and menacing on its bluff above the river Teme. Rhys ap Thomas and other Welsh leaders travelled to Ludlow and offered homage to the first foreign-born Princess of Wales; and beside the castle's outer walls a walk was cut so that Catherine and her ladies might look out across the winding Teme and see the distant etched line of mountains which marked the true border of Wales.

It is a walk she cannot often have taken. Arthur's health gave way soon after Shrovetide (8 February) and Catherine, too, became ill. There was an outbreak of 'sweating sickness' in the West that winter and the epidemic may well have spread to Ludlow. But in its first recorded form 'sweating sickness' appears to have been akin to influenza; Arthur's illness showed different characteristics. Possibly he was asthmatic. He remained unwell throughout Lent and in Easter week he died, suffering it was said 'from a consumption'. His body lay in state at Ludlow for three weeks, until on St George's Day it was borne on a black draped hearse twenty miles to Bewdley. Two days later the cortege reached Worcester, where the prince was buried. It was an unforgettable journey: 'The day was the foulest cold windy and rainy day I have ever seen and the worst way, so that in some places they were fain to take oxen to draw the carriage', wrote one of the mourners.[10] Catherine was too ill to leave Ludlow.

News of the Prince of Wales's death reached the king at midnight on 2 April. He was personally distressed and politically embarrassed. There was now only Prince Henry to safeguard the male succession in the Tudor dynasty, although Elizabeth of York comforted her husband by reminding him, 'My Lady, your mother, had never more children but you only and God by his Grace ever preserved you.' The future of the Princess of Wales posed major problems: not all of Catherine's dowry had yet been handed over, and it was possible her parents might wish restitution of the hundred thousand crowns already paid to Henry for a match which promised for their daughter the eventual crown of England. Catherine herself came back from Ludlow to the Bishop of Durham's town house on the Strand in London. She was to remain at Durham House until December 1505, a mute player in the political drama centred on her future role in English affairs.

Within a few hours of hearing that their youngest daughter was a widow, Ferdinand and Isabella sent an ambassador to England with instructions to hold Henry to his alliance with Spain, seek a favourable settlement of the dowry problem, and – if possible – secure Catherine's marriage to her brother-in-law, Henry of York. Such a solution had also occurred to Henry VII. The marriage would be counter to canon law, unless it were established that the union of Arthur and Catherine had never been consummated. Catherine's chaplain and confessor at Ludlow and at Durham House, Don Alessandro Geraldini, had no doubt of the consummation of the marriage, and so informed the Spanish ambassador. But Catherine's duenna, Dona Elvira Manuel, whom Isabella had personally entrusted with the care of her daughter, vigorously disputed Don Alessandro's assertion and wrote to Queen Isabella insisting that the princess remained a spotless virgin. Don Alessandro was recalled to Spain. Catherine herself said nothing at the time; but many years later she told Cardinal Campeggio in the confessional that Arthur shared her bed on only seven nights in their five months of married life and that the marriage was not consummated. So convinced was the Cardinal that Catherine was telling him the truth that he broke the recognized seal of confession, repeating what he had learnt.

Cardinal Campeggio's studied indiscretion was not made until 1528. Henry VII, in 1502, had to weigh sentiment, religious conscience and diplomatic necessity before deciding on a policy. Characteristically, he hesitated a long time. In February 1503 Elizabeth of York died in childbirth. Henry was wretchedly miserable at this second death within a year but, despite his sorrow, he seriously considered taking the widowed Princess of Wales as his queen. Isabella was firmly opposed to such an 'unnatural' alliance, and hurriedly proposed a compromise arrangement over Catherine's unpaid dowry in the hope that the king would support her marriage to his twelve-year-old son, Henry. At the same time the Princess of Wales was advised by her parents 'to accept what the king offers'.[11] On 24 June 1503 a palace betrothal ceremony appeared to settle the matter. The prince and princess would marry as soon as Henry was fifteen, provided that by then the king had received a papal dispensation for the marriage, together with the second half of Catherine's original dowry. It therefore seemed probable there would be a second London wedding for the Princess of Wales, in July 1506.

Meanwhile there was a curious anomaly in the use of titles: a Princess of Wales was betrothed to the heir to England, who was titular Duke of York. On 18 February 1504 Henry formally created his son Prince of Wales, with the approval of parliament. If there was an investiture, it was held in private and without ceremony; and the king retained in his own hands the revenue from the principality which had, as usual, reverted to the sovereign as soon as there was a vacancy in the principate. Never before had the title passed from brother to brother; and never before had it been accepted so obviously as a rank of precedence, confirming the status of an heir apparent. Now that the Tudors were established as a respected European dynasty the king laid no stress on past links with the Heroic Age of Wales. The Tudors ceased to be essentially Welsh about the time of Jasper's death, in May 1495. Prince Henry was not a bardic 'son of prophecy', as his father and brother had been hailed before him; and he never visited the principality.[12]

The new Prince of Wales was better educated than his elder brother. From the age of seven until he was twelve, his tutor was the poet, John Skelton, a protégé of the boy's learned and redoubtable grandmother, the Lady Margaret (who was to outlive her son by a few weeks). Skelton's tuition was supplemented by the inspired gifts of William Blount, Lord Mountjoy, a courtier who was a friend of John Colet, Thomas More and the great Erasmus. It was Mountjoy who took Erasmus to Eltham Palace in 1499 to be received, in the absence of the king, by the eight-year-old Prince Henry, who showed himself to be a well-poised host with some understanding of Latin verse: 'In the midst stood Prince Henry, having already something of royalty in his demeanour, in which there was a certain dignity combined with singular courtesy', Erasmus wrote in his *Epistles*, adding a compliment to Skelton as a 'light and ornament of literature'.[13] Within a few years Prince Henry acquired other accomplishments: fluency in French, a flair for making music, good horsemanship, and a showy reputation at the butts, in the tiltyard, and at real tennis (*jeu de paume*). Although he did not contest tournaments until he was seventeen, Henry excelled in many of these skills even before his creation as Prince of Wales. No heir to the throne had shown such promise for a hundred years. His father looked on him with a combination of pride, possessiveness, jealousy and suspicion. There was no sharp conflict between father and son, as in

Henry IV's reign, but the prince was not so malleable as Arthur. It is possible that one of the reasons why young Henry was invested privately rather than with ceremonial pageantry was because the king saw no reason to spend money on enhancing the stature of a prince already standing high in his subjects' esteem. Over the next five years there were several occasions when the prince figured prominently in court festivals, but always as an aid to buttress the king's falling majesty. Henry VII never risked a spectacle of state in which the rays of the 'young Apollo' could outshine the lustre of the royal crown.

Young Henry seems to have hoped that once he was created Prince of Wales he would have an opportunity to leave the 'nursery palace' at Eltham and enjoy all the excitement of travelling to Ludlow. The king thought otherwise: the Council of the Marches could function efficiently and more economically without a princely presence; and there was much to be said for keeping the sole male heir close to the centre of government. In the summer of 1504 the prince was installed at Westminster. He was allowed a small establishment of his own, with servants, footmen and minstrels, but security demanded strict surveillance: nobody could visit him or ride with him for sport without the king's permission; and if the prince wished to leave his apartments, he could do so only by passing through his father's rooms where Yeomen of the Guard kept close watch on all going in and coming out. Skelton, an intellectual iconoclast, had already been supplanted as tutor by a colourless pedant, William Hone, but the king now had every resolve to train his son himself, perhaps even to tame him. The Spanish ambassador reported the prince's move to Westminster in a despatch to Queen Isabella: 'It is not only from love that the king takes the prince with him. He wishes to improve him. Certainly there could be no better school in the world than the society of such a father as Henry VII. He is so wise and so attentive to everything, nothing escapes his attention.'[14]

Probably Isabella read these words with wry amusement, for by now their Catholic Majesties were well aware that, over dynastic questions, Henry VII possessed the wisdom of a serpent and the eye of a hawk. Isabella was far from satisfied with his treatment of her youngest daughter. The papal dispensation for the marriage of the Prince and Princess of Wales had reached the Spanish court and was on its way to London. There was nothing more that Isabella could do: she was a sick woman, and died on 26 November 1504. It now remained for Ferdinand to send the residue of the dowry to Henry. But in Westminster the king was having second, third and even fourth thoughts. The betrothal ceremony had been premature: it deprived England of a useful card in the diplomatic game. For a struggling dynasty in the 1490s a Spanish marriage had carried a certain prestige, but by 1505 the Tudors looked established on the throne while there was no certainty Castile and Aragon would stay united now that Isabella was dead. A marriage alliance benefiting English trade had much to commend it, and the most valuable continental trade routes by now lay across the North Sea rather than across the Bay of Biscay. It would be as well for the Prince of Wales to recover the freedom to have a bride chosen for him. In June 1505 he was induced to sign a document which expressed doubts troubling his fourteen-year-old conscience: was a marriage contract with his brother's widow truly valid? For the moment he remained betrothed to Catherine, but by the autumn foreign envoys were reporting that there would soon be a new Princess of Wales. The favourite candidate was Eleanor of Burgundy, granddaughter of the Emperor Maximilian and, as it happened, daughter of Catherine's eldest sister, Joanna.

Meanwhile Catherine was still at Durham House, complaining she was rarely invited to state functions or allowed to see her 'husband', Prince Henry. In December 1505 the king decided it would be a prudent economy for her to leave Durham House and live at court, with an establishment comprising five ladies in waiting, a chamberlain, treasurer and a physician, all of whom were Spanish, for Catherine could still neither speak nor understand English. She lived in a wing of the palace at Westminster, well away from the prince, whom she would meet after her religious devotions in the chapel and on great occasions in the year. They both helped the king entertain Archduke Philip of Burgundy at Windsor early in February 1506, when Catherine had a chance to spend an evening and a day with her sister Joanna. Philip and Joanna had been shipwrecked when the vessels in which they were sailing from Walcheren to Corunna were caught in the famous 'great storm' of 15–26 January 1506. The Prince of Wales was much impressed with Philip the Fair, a handsome philanderer who overplayed the role of Renaissance magnifico. Catherine, on the other hand, found the revelry bitter sweet: she enjoyed the food and dancing after years of seclusion; she was pleased to see Joanna, although disturbed by the deep melancholia weighing on her sister's mind; but she was convinced that the king's expenditure on his guests' entertainment confirmed rumours of a new course in English marriage diplomacy.[15] During Philip's visit it was, in fact, agreed the king should marry Philip's widowed sister, Margaret of Savoy, and tentative proposals were made that Philip's son, Charles, should marry the king's daughter Mary, while the Prince of Wales would marry Philip's daughter, Eleanor of Burgundy. A political treaty and a commercial treaty, of great benefit to English trade in the Low Countries, were also concluded. All these proposals came to nothing: Philip died five months later, his schemes incomplete; Joanna's mind became so clouded that even Henry VII was eventually forced to strike her reluctantly from his list of eligible brides; Margaret of Savoy had sufficient independence to turn the proposals down; and the agreement over Eleanor of Burgundy, like the trade treaty, was never ratified. The Charles and Mary marriage remained a possibility long enough to benefit Henry VII's general foreign policy; but it is doubtful if there was ever any serious intent behind the negotiations. Rumours of a marriage treaty between Prince Henry and Margaret of Angoulême, a sister of the future King Francis I of France, provided a variant in the popular pastime of bride-hunting for the Prince of Wales.

Once the Prince had shed his adolescent hero-worship of Archduke Philip, he seems to have been content with his contracted obligation to wed Catherine of Aragon. The projected marriage date – July 1506 – went by unnoticed by the king, not least because the second half of Catherine's dowry had still not reached England. It is probable the prince found the proximity of his unattainable 'wife' tantalizing. She still possessed the russet golden hair, passive grey eyes and tiny hands and feet which had made her a figure of grace and beauty when first she landed in England. At the end of February 1508 a new Spanish ambassador, Don Gutierre Gomez de Fuensalida, arrived in London: he was prepared to pay the final instalment of the dowry, but demanded immediate fulfilment of the marriage treaty. The king procrastinated: the dowry was to be paid in cash, not through a combination of coin with the jewels and plate the princess had brought with her in 1501. Fuensalida was indignant but could do nothing to alter the king's decision. He was only permitted a few words with the Prince of Wales who gave no indication of his own feelings. The ambassador reported hearing of a violent scene between father and son, when the prince poured scorn on the king's marriage bargaining and was, in return, 'scolded' by his father 'as though he would kill him'. In confidence Catherine told Fuensalida that 'If the king were dead, I should have no difficulty with the prince'; but there was still no sign of a settlement of the dowry problem.[16] Envoys came to London to take up once more the Eleanor of Burgundy marriage project. There was talk, too, of a Bavarian bride for the Prince of Wales.

Yet by Christmas in 1508 everyone could see that Henry VII was a sick man, his body wasting away, his complexion unhealthily yellow. Somehow he survived until Easter when he staggered into his chapel for the last time. Death came to him in the palace he had built at Richmond on 21 April; and his councillors declared that his last command had been for his son to marry Catherine. This order Henry VIII obeyed within six weeks. On 11 June 1509 Catherine of Aragon, Princess of Wales, became queen consort of England in a private ceremony, conducted quietly at Greenwich.

The accession of Henry VIII marked the start of the longest vacancy in the principate of Wales, a gap of over one hundred and one years. Catherine bore Henry four sons: the first, born on New Year's Day 1511, lived long enough to be baptised Henry and proclaimed Duke of Cornwall before dying, 'short of breath', on 21 February; but none of the remaining three boys survived more than a few hours. A daughter, Mary, was born on 18 February, 1516. Her father's attitude to the child varied, if not from month to month, at least from year to year. There was no precedent for creating a female heir 'Princess of Wales' and the title was never formally bestowed on Mary, though used from time to time as an act of courtesy. Her mother feared that the king intended to advance the claims of his bastard son, the Duke of Richmond, rather than accept female succession to the English throne. Catherine was therefore pleased when, in August 1525, the king sent Mary to Ludlow as 'Governor' of the Council of the Marches of Wales, believing he was giving their daughter a status closely associated with the heir to the throne. But during the eighteen months Mary spent at Ludlow the king began to allow his conscience to be troubled by the thought that the Almighty was denying him a male heir for his sin in marrying his brother's widow contrary to the teachings of Leviticus. It was also during these eighteen months that the king found consolation for his worries by delighting in the company of Anne Boleyn. There was something to be said for keeping a daughter at distant Ludlow with so many distracting problems to hand at court in Greenwich.

From 1527 until 1533 the 'king's great matter' was the dominant political issue in London, simplifying the complexities of the English Reformation by concentrating on a personal and essentially domestic question, the validity of the marriage with which the reign had opened. When, on 23 May 1533, Archbishop Cranmer gave his decisive pronouncement at Dunstable Priory that the union of Catherine and Henry was null and void, the queen reverted in status to being once more 'Princess of Wales', accorded in life and in death the honours appropriate for a princess dowager.[17] She died at Kimbolton on 7 January 1536, and was buried at Peterborough where her tomb was destroyed by Cromwellian vandals in 1643.

Twenty-two months after Catherine of Aragon's death Henry at last became father of a son who, at least as an infant, enjoyed robust health. On 12 October 1537 Queen Jane Seymour, Henry's third wife, gave birth to Prince Edward at Hampton Court: the queen died within a matter of hours 'through the fault of them that were about her'; but great care was taken to protect and safeguard the child. He grew into a precocious lad who, as he once wrote, was accustomed to occupy himself 'learning of tongues, of the Scriptures, of philosophy and of the liberal sciences'.[18] The boy's physical, spiritual and intellectual well-being were matters of concern to the king. Yet, fond and indulgent father though he was to Edward, Henry made no preparations to create his son Prince of Wales. The title was accorded to him informally in speech from time to time, as if it were a courtesy rank of the male heir-apparent, but no approach was made by the king to parliament and no royal patent drafted which would have regularized the boy's standing among the nobility. It is possible that the king disliked the unreality of child investiture: the young creations – Edward of Lancaster, Edward of the Sanctuary, and Arthur – had all been unlucky; Henry himself had been eleven, the Black Prince and Henry of Monmouth twelve; and probably the king regarded what now would be called 'eleven plus' as a suitable age for advancing his son.

There may well have been sound political reasons why Edward was not created Prince of Wales.[19] In the late 1520s the old rivalry between powerful Welsh chieftains and English Marcher Lords broke out again, for the first time in over forty years. Sir Rhys ap Gruffydd, grandson of Henry VII's trusted supporter Rhys ap Thomas, resented royal favours shown to Walter Devereux, Lord Ferrers. A long feud ended with the execution of Rhys at Tower Hill in December 1531, the king having convinced himself that Rhys wished to become ruler of an independent Wales. This whiff of treason led to stricter control from the Council in the Marches. Yet, as the efficient Thomas Cromwell pointed out to the king, it was difficult to enforce sound government in a region subject to alternative jurisdictions, and gradually a system of shires was imposed on the whole country, ending the confusion of two and a half centuries of decaying feudalism. The two Acts of Union of 1536 and 1543 effectively integrated Wales in a 'Greater England' for administrative purposes: the Welsh were given a uniform system of law; they were allowed representation in parliament for the first time since Edward II's reign; and the local gentry were given opportunities for advancement as justices of the peace and as spokesmen for Wales at Westminster. This revolution from above virtually abolished the Marches. It therefore drastically changed the position of the Prince of Wales who was, in a sense, the greatest of all Marcher Lords. Small wonder if Henry hesitated over the advancement of his son at such a time of social and legal adjustment in Wales.

Yet soon after Prince Edward's ninth birthday there was talk of investing him with the traditional title. The king's customary progress in the autumn of 1546 had shown Henry to be ailing in health. There was a feeling that the boy's creation as Prince of Wales would strengthen his right of succession: a similar mood had prompted the Commons to demand recognition of Richard of Bordeaux as Prince in 1376. Parliament was summoned for January 1547 when it was expected that a royal patent would be laid before the Lords for creation of a Prince of Wales. There was, however, a tiresome obstacle. State ceremonies were the responsibility of the Earl Marshal; and on 12 December 1546 the Duke of Norfolk, Earl Marshal for the past thirteen years, was arrested and indicted for high treason in having spoken of the need to establish a regency for young Edward as the king's health was so clearly giving way. Instead of considering the creation of a Prince of Wales, parliament was expected to attaint the Earl Marshal who should have stage-managed the investiture. Before this confusion was resolved – and, indeed, before the axe could fall on the Earl Marshal – Henry VIII breathed his last. His son became Edward VI without being patented or invested as Prince of Wales.[20]

CHAPTER SIX

Four Stuart Princes

THE tenth and eleventh royal Princes of Wales were Scots by birth. Both were sons of King James VI and I, who in March 1603 was summoned south from Edinburgh to succeed his distant cousin, Elizabeth I, and unite the crowns of Scotland and England. The eldest of James's sons was born at Stirling on 19 February 1594. He was christened Henry Frederick: the first name honoured the memory of his great-great-great-grandfather, Henry VII, from whose daughter Margaret the Stuarts inherited their claim to the English throne; and the prince's second name commemorated his maternal grandfather, Frederick II, King of Denmark and Norway. Young Henry enjoyed good health as a child. The king's second son, Charles, who was born at Dunfermline Palace in November 1600, was far from strong as an infant, while a third son, Robert, born in January 1602, lived for only four months.

'A King's son and heir was ye before, and no more are ye yet', James reminded the nine-year-old Henry when he left Edinburgh for London in the first week of April 1603.[1] In fact, the 'King's son' already bore an impressive list of titles – Prince of Scotland, Duke of Rothesay, Earl of Carrick, Baron of Renfrew, and Lord of the Isles. But the prize, as he knew well, lay south of the border. Henry was trained for kingship on a grand scale. When he was still some months short of his fifth birthday his father completed a detailed primer on the nature of royal sovereignty, the *Basilikon Doron*, which was to serve as a standard of reference for the boy's tutors and was subsequently to be studied by Henry himself. The *Basilikon* laid down basic precepts for kingship: the sovereign's duty towards God, towards his subjects in general, and towards the Court in particular. A printed copy was presented to Henry for the first time as his father was about to leave for England: 'Study and profit in it as ye would deserve my blessing', James urged his son. But Henry, an alarmingly precocious boy in many ways, was bright enough to sense the hypocrisy behind much of this virtuous advice. The king would deplore effeminacy, and affectionately paw his favourites among the young men at court: he could tell his son to speak plain words honestly, avoiding crudities, and yet he would himself swear profanely when rain or any other misfortune hampered his hunting. As soon as the prince was granted a household of his own, he set up penance boxes in which anyone whom he heard swearing was required to leave a fine. It is hardly surprising if, now and again, the king spoke petulantly of his son's priggish code of behaviour. Henry did not necessarily endear himself to his father by diligently following the precepts of the *Basilikon Doron*.

From his earliest days in England the prince became a darling of the literary intelligentsia. There were three main reasons for his popularity: his sharp intelligence made him a good listener; his wealth – an annual income of £49,000 by the age of sixteen – promised generous patronage; and his independence of spirit marked him off as a possible champion of dissidents who had fallen foul of his father. Even as a boy of nine or ten the prince appears to have impressed Ben Jonson and his fellow poet, George Chapman. Both playwrights continued to be closely associated with Henry throughout his life, although from time to time they were out of favour with his father. Chapman was made Sewer-in-Ordinary to the prince, a household post with nominal responsibility for service at table. The appointment was, in reality, an example of literary patronage by which the prince was able to encourage Chapman to persist in his great Homeric translations, begun in the closing years of Elizabeth's reign. Henry delighted in Jonson's masks: the finest of them, the *Masque of Queens*, was presented in the new banqueting hall on 2 February 1609, under the sponsorship of the prince's mother, Queen Anne of Denmark; but the mask so interested the fifteen-year-old prince that he asked its author for a personal copy of the original manuscript, annotated so as to show the scholarly sources upon which Jonson had drawn. In January 1610 Jonson wrote speeches to be delivered by King Arthur, Merlin and the Lady of the Lake in a dramatic tourney arranged by the prince and known as *Prince Henry's Barriers*; and a year later Henry was Oberon in a 'very stately mask' which the prince commissioned Jonson to write for the protracted Christmas festivities. Originally the prince wished Jonson to prepare for a 'masque on horseback', but the king vetoed the suggestion. Henry liked the tiltyard and enjoyed wearing armour, tossing the pike, and playing at war. Life at court should have a martial ring. James preferred the arts of peace.[2]

Early in 1609 a Cornishman, Richard Connack, wrote to the prince as

Duke of Cornwall humbly petitioning him to give his mind to the affairs of the duchy. Henry at once examined his rights as Duke, discovered his rents were much in arrears, and ordered his agents to collect all outstanding dues. He also wrote to Connack suggesting that so diligent an antiquary might be interested in studying the other honours and monetary grants accorded by kings to their eldest sons. Connack replied with such a wealth of detail on the royal Princes of Wales that Henry was able to present his father with a carefully reasoned statement showing the merits of a title dormant for a hundred years. During the Christmas festivities the king announced his intention of creating his elder son Prince of Wales in the following summer.[3]

Six months' notice gave both London and the Court ample opportunity to prepare for the investiture. At first it seemed as if the ceremonies of February 1490 were serving as a precedent, for the king liked to emphasize the continuity linking Arthur Tudor with the Stuart princes. But the celebrations of 1610 were elaborate and far more protracted: they matched in pageantry the legendary coronation festivities of Elizabeth in January 1559. On Thursday, 31 May 1610, Prince Henry with a sprinkling of the young nobility embarked at Richmond and was rowed downstream to Chelsea where he was met by the Lord Mayor of London, aldermen and liverymen in their state barges 'with banners, streamers and ensigns and sundry sorts of loud-sounding instruments'. The barges towed two specially constructed rafts on which players from Shakespeare's company contributed to the water pageant. One raft, shaped like a whale, carried the boy actor John Rice representing 'Corinea, the Queen of Cornwall'; the other, shaped like a dolphin, was 'ridden' by 'Amphion, the Genius of Wales'. As Amphion, Burbage, making his last recorded appearance, delivered a 'grave and judicious' address when Henry stepped ashore at Whitehall stairs. The main ceremony was held on the following Monday (4 June): special stands had been erected in the building of the Court of Requests so that members of the Lords and Commons, the corporation of the City of London and other dignitaries could see James invest his son with symbolic and traditional ritual. The Prince then presided over an elaborate banquet in Westminster Hall, the king dining privately with the queen elsewhere in the palace. While the city worthies and the temporal peers honoured the prince, 'the hall resounded with all kinds of exquisite music'. Next day the Court was entertained by 'a most rich and royal mask of ladies', with the prince's nine-year-old brother Charles appearing as Zephyr and twelve daughters of noble families dancing attendance on him. One scene represented the landing of Henry VII at Milford Haven; and in another the queen appeared as Tethys, the 'Mother of the Waters', who was attended by four maidenly English rivers and by four maidenly Welsh rivers. Finally on Wednesday, 6 June, a whole week of festivity ended with jousting in the tiltyard, 'spectacles of naval triumph' on the Thames, and fireworks along the banks of the river.[4]

The prince, like every other Jacobean nobleman, enjoyed all this pageantry and trumpeting. Yet, apart from the tiltyard and the feasting, the entertainment reflected the tastes of his father and his mother rather than himself; and he was determined to create a miniature court which would give free play to his own interests. Although his household was not formally established until December 1610 the prince's officials were already being appointed at the time of the investiture. First on his list of officers is 'Mr Inico Joanes' who was named Surveyor of Works on 9 May. Inigo Jones had designed the settings for Jonson's *Prince Henry's Barriers* at the start of the year, and he was probably responsible for the plans of a new library built for the prince at St James's Palace. But Jones's liking 'for the Art of Design. . . in the Italian manner' may have served the prince in waterside work for his residence at Richmond and in modernizing the medieval 'bower' at Woodstock. Had he lived, the prince might well have shown himself an expansive patron of the arts, with a taste for Florentine grandeur. In June 1611 the Italian painter and architect, Gostantino de Servi, prepared extensive plans for a palace 'on a site in which His Highness is most interested' at Richmond. This scheme for fountains and grottoes beside the Thames received the king's approval at Michaelmas.[5]

Sir Charles Cornwallis, a former ambassador in Spain and one-time Member of Parliament for Norfolk, was appointed by the king as the first treasurer of the prince's household. It was a difficult post: James wished Cornwallis to check and control his son who was, as one of his intimate companions confessed, 'a little self-willed'; and, at sixteen, Henry was not inclined to pay too much attention to a retired envoy known by him to have favoured, and then rejected, a Spanish princess as his bride. Cornwallis, however, seems to have performed his tasks in the prince's household well. He liked Henry and won his respect. A few years later, in 1626, Cornwallis wrote a memoir of the Prince of Wales: he remembered a few faults – 'a kind of rough play and dalliance' with his brother Charles, a tendency to tease his sister Elizabeth by 'contradicting . . . what he discerned her to desire', a diet in which 'he showed too much inclination to excessive eating of fruits', and a delight 'at tennis-play . . . continuing oftentimes his play for the space of three or four hours, and the same in his shirt, rather becoming an artisan than a prince'. Before Cornwallis joined the prince's household, there had been a famous match between Henry and the third Earl of Essex (who was three years older than Henry) which ended when Essex disputed a point and, in a raging temper, hit the heir to the throne on his head with the racket. According to Cornwallis the prince's countenance 'whether he lost or won' was always the same. He seems, indeed, to have been a paragon: 'of a comely middle stature', writes Cornwallis, 'about five feet and eight inches high, of a strong, straight, well-made body (as if nature in him had showed all her cunning) with somewhat broad shoulders and a small waist, of an amiable majestic countenance, with hair of an auburn colour, long-faced and broad forehead, a piercing grave eye, a most gracious smile, with a terrible frown, courteous, loving and affable'.[6]

Others, besides Cornwallis, comment on his gravity. Francis Bacon noted the severity of his frown and the proud set of his mouth and, like Cornwallis, was surprised at his slowness of speech: he thought Henry had great powers of concentration, liking books but spending more time on outdoor skills. Both Bacon and the courtier churchman, Goodman, mention his growing opposition to his father's foreign policy. 'The Prince did sometimes pry in the King's actions and a little dislike them', wrote Bishop Goodman.[7] Like his mother and his uncle, Christian IV of Denmark, the Prince of Wales was convinced that his father had been wrongly prejudiced against Sir Walter Ralegh, whom James kept imprisoned in the Tower of London for allegedly being implicated in a plot 'to surprise the King's person' soon after his accession. Henry first visited Ralegh in the Tower as an escort for the queen who believed that Sir Walter had discovered during his voyages medicines capable of curing her ailments. Subsequently Ralegh became an unofficial tutor and adviser to the prince: they talked of ships and the insidious menace of Spanish power; they discussed the thought and action of past ages, for Ralegh was writing his *History of the World* during the long months of imprisonment; and they considered practical aspects of statesmanship. When in 1611 the pro-Spanish faction at court wished to marry Henry to a granddaughter of Philip II, Ralegh drew up a formidable memorandum against the project and a second memorandum against proposals for a similar marriage link binding Henry's sister, Elizabeth, to the Prince of Piedmont, Philip II's grandson: 'Whatsoever is pretended to the contrary, it is Spain that we ought to suspect', Ralegh wrote uncompromisingly, 'Spain to England is irreconcilable'. Prince Henry had no doubts of the policy he wished to pursue when he came to the throne: he would bring back the spacious times of Ralegh's primacy, championing the Protestant cause against Habsburg Catholicism on the European mainland and on the wider oceans of the world. Henry was at least able to induce his father to open negotiations to marry Princess Elizabeth to the leading German Protestant prince, Frederick, the Elector Palatine. But Henry did not succeed in persuading James to pardon and free Sir Walter Ralegh. 'Who but my father would keep such a bird in a cage?' Henry is reported to have exclaimed in disgust.[8]

By the beginning of the year 1612 James had come to resent his son's mounting popularity. He was irritated to see courtiers hurrying to St James's Palace to keep in favour with the heir to the throne: 'Will he bury me alive?' the king testily remarked, with typical Stuart resort to the rhetorical question. But Henry was wiser than his Hanoverian successors. He avoided a breach with his father. Indeed, he even tried to reconcile his parents, who from 1607 onwards had come together only on state occasions – 'They did love as well as man and wife could do, not conversing together', writes the judicious Bishop Goodman.[9] In September 1612 the Prince of Wales entertained his father and mother at Woodstock, apparently to mark the completion of work on renovating part of the royal manor for Henry's use. It was a merry occasion: the king enjoyed the hunting; the queen the feasting. Soon afterwards Henry returned to London by way of Windsor. The autumn was hot that year: the prince swam in the Thames, and he played tennis vigorously. His health gave way. When he was feverish his mother sent to the Tower and asked Ralegh to supply some of his mysterious 'Great

Elixir', which would cure any illness not induced by poisoning. The elixir was poured down the prince's throat: he recovered consciousness and spoke rationally, but not even Ralegh's balsam could fight off the fever of typhoid. On 6 November 1612 Henry died in St James's Palace, three months short of his nineteenth birthday. 'Numberless were the elegiac offerings to his memory, and sufficient might now be collected to fill a bulky volume', wrote Cornwallis's nephew, when he edited his uncle's memoir of the prince nearly thirty years later.[10]

Grief at Henry's death cast gloom over the marriage of Elizabeth and the Elector Palatine on the following St Valentine's Day; James shed tears as his daughter sailed from Rochester in a ship which the prince had helped to design. Three years later James decided to raise his only surviving son, Charles, to the dignity of Prince of Wales on the eve of his sixteenth birthday. This was a shrewd decision. Charles was shy, physically small, and inhibited. Throughout his life he spoke with a nervous stammer, as if carrying to excess the slowness of speech which, in his brother, had seemed a sign of measured deliberation. Henry, whom Charles greatly admired, had always outshone him. Until his investiture as Prince of Wales on 4 November 1616, Charles had never been at the centre of public attention. The king insisted that London should keep the accepted observances of the occasion, no doubt hoping a week of pageantry and celebration would boost Charles's self esteem.

The festivities fell slightly flat. They followed the traditional pattern well enough: a barge procession down river on Thursday, 31 October; the act of investiture at Whitehall on the following Monday; a banquet presided over by the new Prince of Wales; a mock tournament in the lists on Thursday; and celebrations in the City of London on Saturday. But 'the sharpness of the weather' hampered public participation and Charles's delicate health limited his activities, as well as requiring days of rest and recuperation. James played a more prominent role in the ceremonies than in 1610: not only did he view the prince's banquet from a gallery, but after a forty-part song had been rendered by the choir of the Chapel Royal it was the king who commanded an encore. Jousting in the lists reached a poor standard, and the introduction of live goats into a mask so as to recall Wales to the new prince proved an unhappy inspiration. Moreover the behaviour of the Lord Mayor's guests at a feast in Drapers Hall on 9 November was frequently 'rude and unmanly', writes a contemporary observer, some of the newly dubbed Knights of the Bath 'putting citizens' wives to the squeak'. It was hard not to make adverse comparisons with the summer celebrations of 1610 when the printing presses were turning out so many eulogies of the former prince. Queen Anne refused to attend Charles's investiture or any of the festivities: she was especially incensed that the king should choose a week which coincided with the fourth anniversary of Henry's death. Her son's ghostly shade seems to have been omnipresent. Even the Bishop of Ely, the scholarly Lancelot Andrewes, respected as a master of fifteen living or dead languages, became so confused that he offered a prayer for *'Henry*, Prince of Wales', and let the slip of the tongue pass uncorrected.[11]

It is impossible not to feel sorry for Charles, dull lad though he may well have been. 'The Prince is a youth of about sixteen, very grave and polite, of good constitution so far as can be judged from his appearance', wrote the Venetian ambassador a few months after the investiture, 'His chief endeavour is to have no other aim than to second his father, to follow him and to do his pleasure and not to move except as his father does .'[12] Charles would not match the legendary brilliance of the over-mourned Henry; he was confronted by a perversely garrulous father, whose temper became more and more choleric as age brought on arthritis and gout; and he had to watch James bestow greater affection on his latest favourite, George Villiers, than he ever gave to his own children. At first Charles detested 'Steenie', as Villiers was called: the king knighted him in April 1615 a few months after their first meeting, raised him to the peerage as a viscount in 1616, created him Earl of Buckingham a year later and a marquis in 1618. The Prince of Wales was publicly rebuked by the king for offending Viscount Villiers, boxed on the ears for adjusting a fountain so that it soaked the Earl of Buckingham's face, and roundly reprimanded for quarrelling with the Marquis of Buckingham while playing tennis. But in the summer of 1618 James encouraged a reconciliation: 'Steenie' and the Prince soon became close companions; and Buckingham had the insolence to write patronizingly to James of his regard for 'Baby Charles, whom you by your good offices made my friend'.[13]

Henry had deftly avoided the occupational hazard of all Princes of Wales, the marriage net: Charles, however, was enmeshed in its toils before his twenty-second birthday and never broke free. The king wished his son to take a Spanish bride, the Infanta Maria. He maintained that a Stuart-Habsburg marriage contract would be the prelude to a general pacification of Europe: the Spanish Habsburgs would put pressure on the Emperor in Vienna to call off his war against the German Protestants; and James's son-in-law, Frederick, would be restored to his possessions in the Rhenish Palatinate, which Spanish troops in the service of the Emperor had overrun. The subtleties of this intricate diplomatic design baffled parliament at Westminster, and no wonder. The Commons sympathized with Frederick and Elizabeth, the English princess who ruled briefly as a 'Winter Queen' in Prague when Frederick's cause appeared to prosper in 1619-20; but they argued that James could best help his daughter and son-in-law by joining in a grand Protestant crusade against the Habsburgs rather than by seeking a marriage bargain with Catholic Spain. This attitude angered the king. James told the Speaker in December 1621 that such questions were outside the competence of parliament: members had no right 'to meddle with . . . deep matters of State' such as 'our dearest son's match with the daughter of Spain'.[14] Rather than give up the idea of making the Infanta a Princess of Wales, James preferred to send the Commons packing. Parliament was dissolved so that the king could feel securely seated on his throne, as the Spanish ambassador explained to Madrid with studied irony.

It is hard to discover what Charles thought of all this. His father's affection for 'Steenie' was as warm as ever, and the Prince was content to seek comfort in its afterglow. If Buckingham favoured the dissolution of parliament then the Prince of Wales was prepared to say that the Commons should go; and if Buckingham told him he believed the Infanta was an angel of beauty, the prince was ready to fall in love with her from a safely uncompromising distance. Not until February 1623, when negotiations had dragged on for more than a year, did Charles show initiative in wooing the Infanta Maria; and even then his plans seem to have owed much to Buckingham's ingenious mind. The king, with some hesitation, agreed that Steenie and Charles should slip secretly through France to the Spanish Court and settle the marriage question, once and for all. On Wednesday, 19 February, 'Tom and Jack Smith' accordingly took a boat from Dover to Boulogne, suffering six hours of intermittent seasickness on the thirty-mile crossing. Late on Friday they reached Paris. There, disguising themselves 'artificially' in outsize periwigs, they joined the privileged Saturday crowd of spectators in the Grande Salle of the Louvre, where the ladies of the French royal family were rehearsing a balletic mask. 'Jack Smith' – as he wrote to 'Dad' in Whitehall – was pleased by the looks of the young Queen who 'wrought in me a greater desire to see her sister', Maria of Spain. He told James that there were in all 'nineteen fair dancing ladies'; among them was Princess Henrietta Maria, but he seems to have had no eyes for her on this occasion. After two days unrecognized in Paris the Smith brothers travelled south through Orleans and Bayonne to the Pyrenees, last crossed by a Prince of Wales at the head of an army in 1367. On 7 March, eighteen days after leaving London, they arrived unheralded in Madrid, making their presence known to King Philip IV and his chief minister, Count Olivares, next morning.[15]

The sudden appearance at her brother's court of a tongue-tied wooer from England did not sweep the Infanta off her feet. Charles reached Madrid at the end of the second week in Lent, a poor time to begin courting a Spanish princess who had said she would rather enter a nunnery than marry a heretic. Olivares treated Charles more as a hostage than a suitor: week by week the Spanish stiffened their marriage terms until Charles found he was being asked to approve in his father's name concessions to English Roman Catholics which no king could have forced on anti-papist London. By early June James wanted his 'two dear boys' to return to England brideless, and Buckingham would willingly have left Madrid. Charles, however, was easily convinced by Spanish assurances that 'all would end well': he was attracted by the porcelain transparency of the Infanta's complexion, and as late as 15 July could assure his father that 'she sits publicly with me at the plays and within these two or three days shall' be recognized as 'Princess of England' (*sic*). A month later, after Steenie had gone sick 'with a little fit of ague', even Charles admitted that 'we have wrought what we can' without success.[16] They left Madrid for Santander on 31 August, and sailed in an English man-of-war for Portsmouth where they landed on 5 October. The king created Steenie Duke of Buckingham in token of his wise counsel and there was public rejoicing that the Spanish marriage project was scotched for good. In 1631 the Infanta married her first cousin, the King of Hungary, who become Emperor Ferdinand III six years later. She proved herself to be an attractive woman of remarkable intelligence; and it is probable she found the pseudo-romantic charade of 1623 tedious and embarrassing. It certainly did not improve the standing of James or his son at the other European courts.

Buckingham, slighted by his rebuff in Madrid, became violently anti-Spanish. He took the lead in negotiating marriage terms between the Prince of Wales and the young French princess whom they had seen on their secret visit to the Louvre in the previous February. But the French, like the Spanish, wanted concessions for English Roman Catholics: James had promised parliament he would make no marriage treaty favouring his Catholic subjects; and in the last months of his life, he had no wish for a fresh tussle with the Commons. Once again the marriage negotiations of the Prince of Wales made no progress. Charles himself was in earnest: he sent a present of jewelry to Henrietta Maria; he told her by letter of the 'happiness. . . which I have already had of seeing your person, although unknown to you, which sight has completely satisfied me that the exterior of your person in no degree belies the lustre of your virtues'.[17] Cardinal Richelieu, beginning his career as chief minister in France, also favoured a marriage alliance, as a step towards uniting non-Habsburg Europe against Spain and the Empire. Only James procrastinated, a sick man, gloomily warning the Prince of Wales of trouble to come from the Commons and from the warring powers on the continent. On 27 March 1625 James died. Within two months Charles was married by proxy to the fifteen-year-old Henrietta Maria, having only seen her on that one occasion at the Louvre. By midsummer she was in England as Queen.

The first years of married life were marked by tension. The plague came to London soon after the Queen crossed the Channel: there were no royal entertainments, the theatres were closed, the court took refuge at Woodstock, and the Divinity School in Oxford became an impromptu House of Commons. Inevitably Henrietta Maria was forced back on the company of the priests and French ladies-in-waiting whom she had brought with her from Paris. But Buckingham's inept handling of foreign affairs threw England into war with both Spain and France; and rumour found traitors in the queen's retinue and hinted darkly at Jesuit intrigues behind King Charles's throne. The assassination of Buckingham at Portsmouth in August 1628 deprived Charles of 'the man whom the King delighteth to honour' at a time when he was facing a sustained attack in parliament; but it may well have saved his marriage. After three years of tear-stained neglect the queen found her singleminded husband offering her all the affection he had lavished on the dead Steenie. She became pregnant, but the boy lived only long enough to be baptised Charles. Almost exactly a year later – on 29 May 1630 – she gave birth to another boy, also named Charles, who lived to become the twelfth Prince of Wales. By the summer of 1637 Henrietta Maria was the mother of two sons and three daughters. That June her husband's nephew, Prince Rupert of the Rhineland, heard his uncle give thanks to God for allowing him to be the happiest king in Christendom.

'Yesterday at noon the Queen was made the happy mother of a Prince of Wales', wrote Viscount Dorchester, the king's minister responsible for foreign affairs, in a despatch to Paris on 30 May 1630.[18] But Dorchester was jumping the ceremonial gun. Although the heir to the throne was called Prince of Wales as a courtesy, his formal titles remained Duke of Cornwall and Rothesay until after the beginning of the civil war in the summer of 1642. There is, indeed, no patent creating him Prince of Wales and he was never invested with the sword, coronet and ring bestowed on his predecessors. Hitherto the creation of a Prince of Wales had been a joint act of king and parliament, most recently with the backing of the City of London. Charles I ruled without parliament for the first ten years of his eldest son's life and was thereafter in conflict with the Commons and many of the Lords. Moreover he was constantly on bad terms with the city worthies of London. Since there was no moment of calm when his son could be created Prince of Wales with all the traditional forms, the king was content to have him 'acknowledged' in the title soon after the raising of the royal standard at Nottingham Castle at the end of August 1642. Acknowledgement saved the festive expense of an investiture.

The prince enjoyed his boyhood; his mother was indulgent, although her habit of inventing games for which crucifixes were offered as prizes confirmed the worst suspicions of Protestants at court; and his father was kind, though grave in temperament. The king, who knew more about horses than children, was often awkward in their company, but he was never thrown into a temper, not even when he noticed his elder son ogling the ladies around him at church in Oxford. Young Charles's tutors, too, were easy-going. The governor of the prince's household, tactfully described as 'Groom of the Stole', was the Earl of Newcastle, who liked music, poetry and good talk but showed a sensible mistrust of narrowly bookish pedants. For three years Newcastle shared supervision of the prince's education with Brian Duppa, sometime Dean of Christ Church, and from 1638 onwards Bishop of Chichester. Duppa was a High Churchman of wit and courage, whose spiritual manual of devotions was reprinted many times for two hundred years after his death, but he was disinclined to overtax a lad of graceful good humour with needless skills of learning. The prince, living with a household of his own in his uncle Henry's old apartments at Richmond Palace, became a self-possessed young man at an age when other boys remained boorishly unresponsive to civilized courtesies. In Holy Week 1640 he was visited at Richmond by John Ferrar, whose brother Nicholas had established an Anglican religious community at Little Gidding in Huntingdonshire. John Ferrar, stuttering and ill at ease, brought with him a gift for the ten-year-old, a brightly bound volume wrapped with satin ribbons. 'Here's a gallant outside', Charles exclaimed excitedly as he untied the ribbons. Inside he found a bible, carefully illustrated by the holy ladies of the community. If the prince was disappointed that the work was not unknown to him, he mastered his feelings. 'Better and better', he beamed, turning the pages with real or feigned eagerness.[19] Newcastle and Duppa had given their young charge a polished education, sharpening an instinctive command of the social arts which was, in time, to make Charles the most accomplished and devious charmer of all English Princes of Wales.

Van Dyck's paintings and the etchings of Wenceslas Hollar – who was drawing master to the royal children – mirror the miniature court: lace cuffs and satins, velvet breeches, embroidered shoe-roses; Charles, 'Jamie', and the princesses grouped with their dogs before curtains at Windsor or Richmond, with the long loop of the Thames caught faintly behind the windows. The elegant domesticity of such scenes conveys no hint of the human predicament in the country as a whole, when defiance of unconstitutional taxation was breeding revolution. Yet the young prince was not cocooned within an isolated palace. He knew what was happening, although he could not begin to understand why (as the royalist Clarendon was to write) 'very many gentlemen of prime quality. . . were exceedingly incensed, and even indevoted to the Crown'. Just thirteen months after his boyishly polite acceptance of the bible from Little Gidding, Charles was sent on a grim mission by his father: on 11 May 1641 the prince entered the House of Lords with a letter from the king appealing for mercy for Thomas Wentworth, Earl of Strafford, condemned to death by bill of attainder for having bolstered royal autocracy through eleven years of non-parliamentary government. If the king thought that the appearance before the Lords of his ten-year-old son would soften the hearts of Strafford's enemies, he was mistaken. As the Venetian ambassador reported, the prince 'made the strongest representations' but was heard 'with scant civility'. The Earl was beheaded at noon next day.[20]

Civil war broke out in the summer of the following year. Charles was given command of a troop of horse known as 'The Prince of Wales's Own'. In September he was sent to Raglan Castle, where he made a good impression on the Welsh gentry. No Prince of Wales had visited their lands since Arthur's brief years at Ludlow: toasts were drunk to the king's 'ancient Britons'; young Charles swore always to be 'their own true Prince of Wales'; and in a rush of royalist sentiment the people of Monmouthshire and Glamorgan rallied to support their sovereign. Many Welshmen were killed in the first major battle, fought at Edgehill in southern Warwickshire on 23 October 1642, an engagement in which the prince narrowly escaped capture. But, despite their losses and despite the influence of individual parliamentarian landowners, the Welsh remained loyal to Charles throughout the war. The principality was, as a contemporary observed, 'the nursery of the king's infantry'.[21]

The prince did not go back to Wales. For most of 1643 and 1644 he was with his father at Oxford, where the king had established his court and the royal mint. Father and son participated in the abortive siege of Gloucester; they were together at Cropredy Bridge and in the second battle of Newbury. But the king wished his elder son to serve as nominal commander-in-chief of the armies in the field and to rally the royalist cause in the West Country. It was agreed that the prince would set up a court and council of his own at Bristol. He would be advised by soldiers like Ralph Hopton and by lawyers like Edward Hyde, the future Earl of Clarendon. The prince left Oxford for Bristol on 4 March 1645. He was never to see his father again.

The royalist army in the west continued resistance after the tide of war swung in favour of the parliamentarians. The prince's council had hopes of making Devon and Cornwall a royalist redoubt; and in the winter of 1645–6 the prince fell back from Exeter to Tavistock, Launceston and eventually to Pendennis Castle, above Falmouth harbour. He consistently ignored proposals from his father in Oxford to cross to France and join his mother in exile. When there was a risk that parliamentarians would kidnap him in Cornwall he escaped to the Scilly Isles, on the first anniversary of his departure from Oxford. St Mary's gave him sanctuary for six weeks but the parliamentarians concentrated a fleet of more than twenty vessels off the Scillies, and he was fortunate to get away to Jersey. He sailed in the converted merchantman, *Proud Black Eagle*, and was accompanied by the distinguished seaman, Sir Henry Mainwaring. The ship's master, Captain Baldwin Wake, had no objection to the prince taking the helm for a couple of hours as the *Proud Black Eagle* ran before the wind south to the Channel Islands. So pleased was Charles with this first experience of handling a vessel that he ordered a yacht from craftsmen in St Malo and celebrated his sixteenth birthday by learning to sail the waters around St Helier.[22]

While on Jersey the prince heard that fighting had ceased in England and that his father was an honourable prisoner of his Scottish subjects. He knew the king wished him to seek support from the French Court but his council thought he should remain in his father's realm as long as possible in order to defy the parliamentarians, who were far from united in their political objectives. The prince saw no merit in such a scheme. He landed in France on 26 June 1646 and joined Henrietta Maria at St Germain a week later. At first the French Court ignored his presence, for the situation in England was so confused that Cardinal Mazarin was afraid of burning his fingers by giving support to a hopeless cause. By the autumn, however, it was clear that the royalists were still influential and, as reports came of intrigues between the king and his captors, so the standing improved of the exiled Prince of Wales. That winter the prince was frequently entertained at Fontainebleau and the Louvre: and he was in the audience for every play presented at the Palais Royal. His mother was busy with marriage plans: Anne-Marie-Louise de Montpensier, Charles's first cousin, would make him an excellent wife, Henrietta Maria believed. She was just three years his senior. Dutifully Charles escorted the 'Grande Mademoiselle' to court entertainments. 'Whenever I visited the Queen he would be beside me in his coach; and no matter what the weather might be, he held his hat in his hand until he had left me. He showed courtesy to me in even the smallest things', she wrote in her memoirs. The cousins were not attracted to each other. She found him shy: he would not, or could not, speak French to her. At heart Mademoiselle pictured herself as consort to the sovereign in Vienna or Madrid. 'The prospect of the Empire so filled my mind that I no longer thought of the Prince of Wales save only as an object of pity', she confessed in later years, when she had resigned herself to a secret (and unhappy) marriage to a Gascon adventurer.[23] At the time, nobody except Henrietta Maria seems to have cared greatly when Anne-Marie-Louise spurned the dutiful courtship of the exiled heir to England.

Charles had other matters on his mind. Briefly he resumed his interrupted studies: while he waited on events in Paris he engaged that disturbingly original political philosopher, Thomas Hobbes, to teach him mathematics. But it was practical politics, not Hobbesian theory, that induced the prince to leave the French capital in June 1648 and head for Calais. There were rumours of mutiny in the parliamentarian fleet anchored off Deal, and Charles had hopes of assistance from the Prince of Orange, who had married his eldest sister. A Dutch warship carried him from Calais to Helvoetsluys, in the delta twenty miles south of Rotterdam. There eleven insurgent English ships placed themselves under his command. He sailed with them across the North Sea, although without any clearly defined objective. On two occasions late that summer a naval battle between rival English fleets seemed imminent, but a combination of natural hesitancy, changing weather conditions and Dutch concern to maintain nominal neutrality postponed the engagements. Charles, who was unwell that autumn, took up residence at The Hague, a guest of his brother-in-law William II who maintained a pleasantly entertaining court at the palace of Honselaersdijck. But while the prince was there he learnt that his father was to be put on trial for his life in Westminster Hall. Efforts to rally European support to save the rulers of England from the sin of regicide proved ineffective. Early in February an English chaplain at The Hague knelt before Charles, greeting him quietly as 'Your Majesty'; and thus he received the news of his father's execution. Now, officially, he reigned as King Charles II. Once again the principate of Wales passed into abeyance.[24]

A few weeks later – on 9 April 1649 – a little-known Welsh exile, Lucy Walter, gave birth to a boy in Holland whom Charles acknowledged as his son. Lucy was daughter of a former royalist governor of Roch Castle in Pembrokeshire and it is possible they may first have met in Wales during Charles's visit to Raglan in 1642, when they were both mere children of twelve; their romance, however, coincides with the high hopes he experienced at Helvoetsluys after the frustrations of his long stay in Paris. Legend recounts a secret marriage, but there is no evidence of any contract between Charles and Lucy, nor can he have seen much of her during the months following his father's execution. Yet for several years he thought affectionately of the Welsh girl, and the boy remained a favourite son, created Duke of Monmouth by Charles in 1663, five years after Lucy's death. Illegitimate fatherhood was followed by another scurry of marriage activity, the pace being set, once again, by Henrietta Maria in Paris. Charles was his mother's guest at midsummer 1649. She pressed him to renew his efforts to win the 'Grande Mademoiselle'; but Anne-Marie-Louise considered the role of exiled and uncrowned Queen of England no more rewarding than the role of exiled and uncoroneted Princess of Wales, and far more costly. Charles himself showed some interest in another cousin, Sophia, youngest daughter of his aunt Elizabeth, Electress Palatine and sometime 'winter queen' in Bohemia. Sophia, who was the same age as Charles (and Lucy Walter) enjoyed her cousin's company but gave no serious thought to a future in which as queen-consort in London she might mother a line of English kings. To be told by Charles she was prettier than his Welsh mistress seemed a doubtful compliment, and she began to look outside her immediate family for a husband.[25] In 1658 she married a Duke of Brunswick who had prospects of becoming Elector of Hanover. Sophia's staunch protestantism was to make her claim to the English throne a political question of major concern by the end of the century, but as yet no one rated her importance highly.

Charles did not marry until 1662, two years almost to the day after the Restoration of the monarchy. His bride was a Portuguese princess, Catherine of Braganza, who brought with her £800,000 in cash and cession to England of Bombay and Tangier. Such a dowry, and such a bride, would have been out of the question during Charles's years of exile. But by 1662 his stock had risen in the courts of Europe. The 'object of pity' of that first winter in Paris was now a legend incarnate, the hero of a great escape story, the six-week adventure of 1651 when, having failed to win his throne by arms, he was hunted as a fugitive from Worcester through the Midland shires to the Channel coast until he secretly took ship for Normandy from 'a creek near Brighthelmstone'. Nine more years of exile in Paris, Cologne, Bruges, and the Netherlands sharpened his qualities: the Restoration brought to London a king of wit, tact and common sense who was as shrewd as any man in political life and eager to check the fanaticism of religious extremists, catholic or protestant. But friendliness between crown and parliament could not last. Even before his marriage the Commons had rejected a declaration of indulgence which would have permitted a broad spread of religious toleration. The knowledge that his brother, James, was a practising Roman Catholic and the suspicion that the king was a crypto-catholic hardened the mood of the politicians. The hysterical accusations of the demagogue, Titus Oates, concerning an alleged 'Popish Plot' to murder the king and place James on the throne led, in the two years 1678-80, to more than thirty executions and to a sustained campaign by Whig politicians for 'Exclusion', the denial of the right of James or of any other non-Protestant to succeed to the throne. Charles fought tooth and nail against the Exclusion bills: in the end he was to govern without parliament, as did his father before him.

Had Charles become father to a Prince of Wales, tutored and advised by good Anglicans, there need have been no lasting heat in the controversies over papism. But, though Charles had eight illegitimate sons by five mistresses, his marriage to Catherine of Braganza remained childless. His brother, James, who secretly married Clarendon's daughter, Anne Hyde, in 1660, fathered four sons and four daughters but by 1671, when their mother died, only the two eldest princesses, Mary and Anne, were alive. Both were firm Protestants although their mother accepted conversion to the Roman Catholic Church some four years before her death. Their father then took as his second wife Mary of Modena, an Italian princess who had long felt she was called to 'another sort of life', in a convent. Mary of Modena's arrival in Whitehall in November 1673 fed new slanders to the Protestants. She was, they said, the Pope's daughter. So intense was the religious hatred that her brother, Duke Francesco d'Este, was convinced that the 'English Protestants' would poison any male child born to her. When in 1677 her firstborn son, Charles, Duke of Cambridge, died from smallpox on his twenty-sixth day of life, Duke Francesco believed his worst fears confirmed.[26]

Yet when Charles II died suddenly in February 1685, his brother succeeded peacefully to the throne and parliament voted the new king generous funds. Even when the Duke of Monmouth landed in the West Country and encouraged a Protestant revolt against his 'papist' uncle, public opinion supported the legitimate sovereign rather than the upstart claimant. The moderates were alienated by the cruelty of the Assizes which followed the suppression of Monmouth's rising and by James's folly in raising a standing army, placing his co-religionists in key military positions, and harassing the Anglican episcopate and the liberties of the ancient universities. Protestants, both moderate and extreme, consoled themselves with the thought that the heir to the throne was not Catholic. James's elder daughter, Mary, was married to her first cousin, William III of Orange, the strongest male claimant to the English throne.

On Christmas Eve 1687 it was announced that the queen was pregnant. She had already suffered four miscarriages, and on 29 December she was so ill that it was feared at court she might well lose this latest infant. Fantastic rumours filled the land, some of them circulated in broadsheets: the father was not the king but her confessor; the child did not exist, the queen being either ill with dropsy or padded with cushions; a babe would be smuggled into the royal bed at an appropriate moment. In the hope of combating these rumours James summoned some three dozen people to St James's Palace on 10 June 1688, when Mary of Modena went into labour. The Archbishop of Canterbury was unable to attend, being imprisoned in the Tower, but the Lord Chancellor was present, most of the Privy Council, and several Women of the Bedchamber, some of whom were Anglicans. The child was born about ten o'clock that morning, Trinity Sunday. Soon afterwards the infant was carried into an antechamber, the Earl of Feversham clearing a passage with the proud cry, 'Room for the Prince of Wales'.[27]

This was a solecism. Like Lord Dorchester in 1630, Feversham assumed the title was hereditary: Princes of Wales are made, not born.

Caernarfon, Edward I's imperial castle

Edward I and Queen Eleanor (Lincoln Cathedral)

The room in Berkeley Castle in which Edward II is believed to have met his death

The limestone and marble tomb of Edward II, erected by his eldest son at Gloucester Cathedral and for long serving as a pilgrim's shrine

opposite above: The Black Prince's introduction to warfare: the pillaging of Caen, June 1346

opposite below: The Black Prince, from the effigy in Canterbury Cathedral

opposite : A contemporary portrait of Richard of Bordeaux as king, Westminster Abbey

above : Richard II relinquishes his throne to Henry IV

Henry V, by an unknown contemporary artist

Tewkesbury Abbey, burial place of Edward, son of Henry VI. Lancastrians in flight from the Battle of Tewkesbury (1471) crossed this field to seek a last refuge in the Abbey

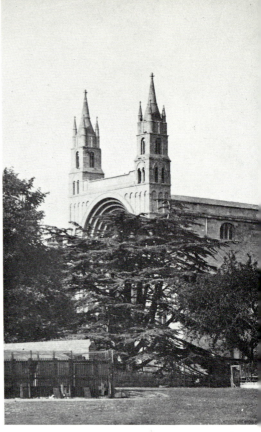

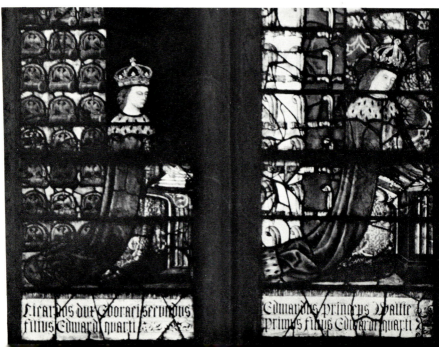

Ricarƥus ƥut Eƅorari ſecunƥus filius Eƥwarƥ quarti

Eƅuarƥus prinreps Ɯallie primus filius Eƥwarƥi quarti

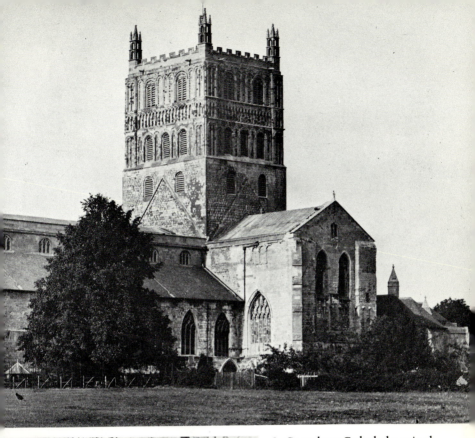

In Canterbury Cathedral a stained-glass window (dating from about 1482) contains portraits of the later 'princes in the Tower': Edward, Prince of Wales (*right*); and his brother, Richard of York

The presumed tomb of Edward of Middleham, 'Yorkshire's Prince of Wales', Sheriff Hutton Church

Henry VII, the king from Wales

Arthur Tudor, Prince of Wales

'Jack Smith' – Charles I when Prince of Wales

'Lace cuffs and satins'. The future Charles II

Henry Tudor, Prince of Wales (as a boy)

'The amiable majestic countenance' of
James I's eldest son, Henry

George Augustus of Wales and Hanover,
the future George II

Poor Fred

Frederick, Prince of Wales, and his sisters, based on
the painting by Nollekens (see page 130)

George III as heir to the throne

'The most elegant legs in London' – the
Earl of Bute

George IV when Prince of Wales in 1782, painted by Gainsborough

Albert Edward, Prince of Wales, at the age of twenty

The secret marriage of the Prince of Wales and Mrs Fitzherbert. A contemporary caricature in which Charles James Fox presents Mrs Fitzherbert to the Prince, while Lord North is sitting fast asleep

The sore, the rather awful visits of Albert Edward, Prince of Wales, to Windsor Castle

opposite: 'The rare, the rather awful visits of Albert Edward, Prince of Wales, to Windsor Castle', as recalled by Max Beerbohm

George V presents his son, 'in this preposterous rig', to the people of the Principality: Caernarfon, 13 July 1911

The twenty-year-old heir to the throne on the Western Front

David   *G.R.I.*   Bertie
July 6ᵗʰ 1935.

George V with his two eldest sons,
six months before his death and
shortly after 'David's' controversial
speeches at the Albert Hall
and Berkhamsted School

The Duke and Duchess of Windsor are received by Hitler at the Obersalzberg, October 1937

overleaf: Prince Charles

The investiture of the twenty-first Prince of Wales, Caernarfon Castle, 1 July 1969

Within twenty-four hours the heir to the throne was baptised James Francis Edward – the third name, new to Stuart usage, linking him with the Black Prince who was also born on a Trinity Sunday. Less than four weeks after his birth the boy was officially gazetted Prince of Wales: once again, as with his uncle, there was no formal creation by letters patent, and no investiture. Prayers were said for the prince, but there was scarcely any show of public rejoicing. Catholics believed the birth a miraculous dispensation of providence, protection for the king's majesty and the true faith. Dispassionate observers were convinced that the birth made certain the king's destruction: shortly a 'Protestant wind' would carry the Prince and Princess of Orange across the sea to protect the public rights of church and state. A satirical lullaby, long afterwards remembered totally out of context, caught the popular mood:

> *Rock-a-bye baby, in the tree top,*
> *When the wind blows the cradle will rock,*
> *When the bough breaks the cradle will fall,*
> *And down will come baby, cradle and all.*

Early in August the baby Prince of Wales nearly 'came down' without the blowing of any Protestant wind. Despite a diet of water-gruel, sweetened oatmeal, currants and 'canary wine', the prince did not flourish in his cradle at St James's Palace, and it was resolved that his governess-of-state, Lady Powis, should take him to Richmond. To her dismay the good country air of Surrey failed to stimulate the child and on 3 August she sent an urgent message to the king and queen. For Mary of Modena there followed a nightmare journey. Two days of heavy rain left the Thames valley flooded and the royal coach could make only slow progress. She feared any moment she would meet a courier bringing news of the miracle child's death. When she reached Richmond Palace he seemed scarcely alive. Instantly she ordered a search of Richmond for a healthy wet-nurse. One was found in the ample person of Frances Smith, wife of a brickmaker. Mrs Smith saved the Prince of Wales. Unwittingly she also became an object of scurrilous Protestant abuse: the prince, it was said, really died on 3/4 August and Mrs Smith was paid several hundred guineas to substitute a changeling of her own. Later that month the king summoned Sir Godfrey Kneller to paint the child as he reclined on draped velvet and ermine cushions. Kneller never doubted the Prince of Wales's parentage. The king and queen had sat for Kneller many times. 'The child is so like both that there is not a feature in his face but what belongs to either father or mother', he declared some years later; and he added with the authoritative precision of a craftsman, 'The nails of his fingers are his mother's.'[28]

Kneller was painting the king's portrait on the evening of 5 November when news reached Whitehall that William of Orange had landed that morning at Brixham. He had come in response to a secret appeal from the Bishop of London and five peers; and Latin streamers flying from the masts of the Dutch vessels proclaimed his intention of safeguarding 'The liberty of England and the Protestant religion'. James prepared to lead his army against the Dutch and their English supporters. Meanwhile he ordered Lady Powis to take the Prince of Wales to Portsmouth where she was to place herself under the protection of the Earl of Dartmouth, the commander of the fleet. If the situation grew desperate, she was to sail for France with the prince.

The king found support melting away as soon as his army marched westwards. By 27 November James knew he was a broken man, and he ordered Lady Powis to sail for France. She could not, however, obey him. Three mutinous ships were off Spithead ready to intercept her. After a hair-raising journey of twenty-four hours the Prince of Wales arrived back in Whitehall at three in the morning of Sunday, 9 December. Lady Powis and Mrs Smith had tales to recount of Orangist soldiery along the route, of finding a 'poor house' outside Guildford for the child to be fed, and of an angry anti-papist mob in Southwark. Yet through most of this ordeal the thirteenth Prince of Wales lay sleeping, scarcely rocked by the wind of revolution. That same night Mary of Modena with the child prince and the faithful Mrs Smith escaped from Whitehall, reached Greenwich with difficulty, and took ship for Calais where they arrived, after an exceptionally rough crossing, at nine o'clock on Tuesday, 11 December. The refugees owed their safety to the courage and resource of the Comte de Lauzun, the Gascon adventurer who had married the 'Grande Mademoiselle' and whose temperament was admirably suited to an enterprise of this nature. The queen sought protection for herself and the Prince of Wales from Louis XIV of France, who had authorized Lauzun to travel to London and offer James his services. The Prince of Wales, as the queen wrote to Louis, was 'still too young to join with her in the grateful acknowledgements that fill her heart'. In fact the prince landed at Calais in a healthily howling temper, for poor Mrs Smith was suffering far too much from the crossing to feed him.[29]

James II reached the French coast on Christmas Day. For another eighteen months he tried to recover his throne, raising a Catholic army in Ireland which was defeated by William's Orangemen at the battle of the Boyne. The remaining years of his life he spent in France, mainly at the château of St Germain-en-Laye, where he died in September 1701. His son was accorded all the dignities of a Prince of Wales by the French Court: on his father's death he was recognized as James III by Louis XIV. Traditionally he is remembered as 'the Old Pretender', hero of the muddled Scottish rising of 1715 and father of 'Bonnie Prince Charlie' who shook the Hanoverian hold on the English throne in 1745. For the most remarkable characteristic of the thirteenth Prince of Wales was his longevity: he lived until January 1766, thus surviving until the reign of George III. At St Germain he remained an object of interest to English visitors, a curiosity to be added if possible to a Grand Tour. 'His gait has great resemblance to his uncle, King Charles II, and the lines of his face grow daily more and more like him', wrote one such visitor while James Francis Edward was still a young man. 'He is always cheerful but seldom merry, thoughtful but not dejected, and bears his misfortunes with a visible magnanimity of spirit.'[30]

Neither as prince nor as claimant to the throne was he a person of major significance in European affairs. Yet negatively he casts a long shadow over British constitutional practice. The Bill of Rights of 1689 and the Act of Settlement of 1701 were measures 'declaring the rights and liberties of the subject and settling the succession of the crown'.[31] Both echoed the bitter controversies over 'exclusion' and the 'warming-pan baby' hysteria of 1688. 'Whereas it hath been found by experience that it is inconsistent with the safety and welfare of this Protestant kingdom to be governed by a popish prince, or by any king or queen marrying a papist', says the Bill of Rights, parliament enacted 'that all and every person and persons that is, or shall profess the popish religion, or shall marry a papist, shall be excluded and be for ever incapable to inherit, possess or enjoy the crown and government of this realm.' The veto on those 'who profess the popish religion or marry a papist' was repeated in the Act of Settlement twelve years later. Other outdated prohibitions have been repealed : this restraint on the freedom of British kings, queens and princes remains on the statute book, a legacy of Stuart folly.

CHAPTER SEVEN

Hanover

URING the quarter of a century which separates the crowning of William and Mary from the accession of George I there was little opportunity for any display of specifically Welsh dynastic sentiment. William and Mary remained without children: Anne was the mother of two sons and three daughters (as well as of nine stillborn babies) but none survived beyond the age of eleven and she, too, was left childless two years before her accession. There was accordingly no heir eligible to be created Prince of Wales. Unexpectedly, however, in the winter of 1695–6 a parliamentary storm blew up over the king's attitude to the principate of Wales. It revealed very clearly the strength of anti-foreign feeling at Westminster. Immediately after his coronation in 1689 William rewarded his principal Dutch companion-in-arms, Hans Willem Bentinck, by creating him Earl of Portland. Six years later the king wished to heap further honours on him: he proposed to grant Portland the estates and revenue of the lordships of Denbigh, Bromfield and Yale which together comprised almost five-sixths of 'the ancient demesnes' of the Princes of Wales. Welsh members of parliament protested vigorously at such a grant: they claimed that Portland would be made 'quasi-prince of Wales' and the principality transformed into 'a colony of the Dutch'. English MPs and peers sympathized with them. Robert Price, a Denbighshire man who sat for the Herefordshire constituency of Weobley, induced the Commons to carry unanimously a resolution declaring that these lands could be given away by the sovereign only through Act of Parliament. King William, though much peeved with the Welsh, knew when to bow before popular indignation, and the grant made to Portland was recalled.[1]

The whole episode lasted only a few weeks, but it was a portent: the Commons would not sanction royal gifts to a foreigner, 'a mighty Favourite and a great Courtier'. Price's speech in defence of Welsh rights was printed in pamphlet form as *Gloria Cambriae, or the Speech of a Bold*

Briton in Parliament against a Dutch Prince of Wales. It was on the streets shortly after passage of the Act of Settlement which held out the prospect of the crown passing to James I's granddaughter, the Electress Sophia, or her descendants from Hanover. The pamphlet sold well. Price had given a patriotic warning to other alien dynasties besides the House of Orange. Neither the English nor the Welsh wished to see Britain a dependency of Hanover although they were prepared to accept a German Protestant king or queen in order to keep at bay the bogey of popery.

Sophia missed being Queen of England by a mere eight weeks. The Electress died suddenly on 8 June 1714, while Queen Anne died on 1 August. Sophia's son, George, arrived at Greenwich on 18 September. He was accompanied by his son, George Augustus, Electoral Prince of Hanover and for the past eight years Duke of Cambridge in the peerage of the United Kingdom. Father and son moved into St James's Palace where, on 22 September at his first council, the king declared George Augustus to be created Prince of Wales, a dignity confirmed by Letters Patent on 27 September. A few months later a special act of Parliament granted the prince 'the regalities and lands now remaining to the Crown in North Wales and South Wales and the County of Chester'. This was the first time since the principate of Arthur Tudor that revenues were specifically assigned to a Prince of Wales and they were never again formally granted. From 1728 onwards income from the principality was merged in the crown, so that all later Princes of Wales have derived their principal revenue from the Duchy of Cornwall. George I regarded the dignity of 'Prince of Wales' as a customary appendage of the heir-apparent, the equivalent in England of the title 'Electoral Prince' in Hanover or of 'Crown Prince' in Prussia. Throughout the eighteenth century no Prince of Wales paid his principality the courtesy of a visit.

In 1714 George I was fifty-four years old, lazy, bad-tempered, unprepossessing in appearance and only capable of speaking a few words in the language of his new subjects. Once he had been a good soldier, respected for his courage and initiative. He had distinguished himself against the Turks at the siege of Vienna but that was more than thirty years ago and the only reminders of those days were two Muslim servants, Mustapha and Mahomet, who remained loyally in attendance on their master in England as in Hanover. The king was suspicious of his new subjects – 'All the king-killers are on my side', he remarked cryptically to his Hanoverian companions as the Londoners welcomed him for the first time – and he rapidly became a figure of scorn. He brought no queen with him; the English could not understand why, as Thackeray was later to write, 'he preferred two hideous mistresses to a beautiful and innocent wife'.[2] Many of his German companions roundly declared the king was a widower while others said his wife was mad and had been left, under care, in Hanover. The truth was that in 1694 he divorced 28-year-old Sophia Dorothea, who had planned to elope with a lover, the Swedish adventurer Count Philip von Konigsmarck, a colonel of Dragoons. Konigsmarck mysteriously disappeared; Sophia Dorothea was kept under house arrest in the castle of Ahlden where, apart from a four-month respite in 1700, she spent the remaining thirty-two years of her life. She was forbidden ever again to see her son, the new Prince of Wales, or her daughter (who was to become Queen of Prussia and mother to Frederick the Great). Her son, deprived of a mother to whom he was much attached at the age of eleven, is alleged on one occasion to have attempted to swim across the moat at Ahlden in order to see her. His father's vindictive persecution of the 'Duchess of Ahlden' left a bitter mark on George Augustus's character. He pledged himself to bring his mother to England and accord her the dignities of a Queen-Dowager as soon as he came to the throne, but she died eight months before his accession. The only gesture left to George II was to hang two portraits of his mother prominently in the audience chamber of his palace.

From his earliest days in England the Prince of Wales fitted easily enough into London society, although it was soon clear he lacked the grace and charm of the Stuart princes. He was a month short of his thirty-first birthday when he landed with his father at Greenwich. Already he was known and respected in military circles, for he had fought under Marlborough at Oudenarde in 1708, his horse being killed beneath him as he charged a position held by a French force which included, curiously enough, his predecessor as Prince of Wales, James II's exiled son. By 1714 George Augustus had been married for more than eight years to Caroline of Anspach, an amply proportioned blonde of high intelligence who was capable of discreetly managing her husband and even, from time to time, her irascible father-in-law as well. Their eldest son, Frederick Lewis, was born at Hanover in January 1707. The boy was left in Germany on his grandfather's orders so as to complete his education and did not come to England until he was twenty, but George I lavished high honours on him *in absentia*: he was made a Knight of the Garter in 1718 and created Baron of Snowdon and Duke of Edinburgh eight years later.These honours may have been intended as a rebuff to the Prince of Wales, who disliked Frederick as much as he was himself disliked by his own father. The king delighted in snubbing the prince, who fumed with rage at the slightest affront, real or imaginary, but repeatedly gave way to any bully, be it his father, his wife or – in later years – his ministers. English politicians and their womenfolk were titillated by the generation feud in the House of Hanover. Soon they learnt to exploit it.

In the summer of 1716 the king was anxious to leave England and spend some six or nine months in the Electorate where there was an accumulation of business for him to settle. Reluctantly he recognized that the Prince of Wales would have to serve as his deputy while he was in Hanover. George Augustus was told he could not enjoy the powers of a Regent: Edward III had appointed his eight-year-old son *Custos Angliae* when he went to Flanders in 1338, and this precedent was used by George I to justify the appointment of the thirty-year-old Prince as 'Guardian of the Realm' four centuries later. The 'Guardian' had no authority to fill vacancies in the government or the royal household, could not take decisions in foreign affairs, could not promote officers in any regiment above the rank of colonel or even commission a lieutenant in any of the Guard regiments. The king took with him to Hanover his principal minister, James Stanhope, leaving the Prince of Wales to deal with the First Commissioner of the Treasury, Robert Walpole, and his brother-in-law, Charles Townshend, Secretary of State for the North. Government under such a system was impossible. Each time the king heard that Walpole or Townshend had travelled to Hampton Court to see the Prince of Wales, he assumed there was a conspiracy. The prince, unlike the king, could speak English tolerably well; and reports reaching George in Hanover made it appear that the 'Guardian of the Realm' was collaborating more smoothly and easily with the English politicians than he had found possible during his twenty-one months in London. When the prince, Walpole and Townshend asked permission for parliament to be recalled in order to discuss the general situation in

Europe, the king was convinced he was being constitutionally upstaged by his son. Walpole and Townshend were forced into opposition, and the king returned from Hanover in March 1717 barely on speaking terms with the Prince of Wales.[3]

Eight months later there followed an absurd incident which was to have a decisive effect on the prince's political role. Caroline of Anspach gave birth to a second son. Her husband, with a show of filial courtesy, invited his royal father to be a godparent, proposing that his uncle (who was Bishop of Osnabruck) should serve as a second godfather. The king accepted the offer but insisted that English traditions required the Lord Chamberlain to be godfather of a newly-born prince. But the Lord Chamberlain was Thomas Pelham-Holles, a man ten years the Prince of Wales's junior, created Duke of Newcastle in 1715 by the king; and the prince, as Lord Hervey wrote, 'used always to speak of "Newcastle" as an impertinent fool'. After the christening of the child (who was, in fact, to live only a few weeks) the Prince of Wales gripped Newcastle fiercely by the arm and said to him, in heavily accented English, 'Rascal, I shall find you out'. This remark struck the easily confused Newcastle as so incomprehensible that he complained to the king: the prince, he said, was threatening his life by challenging him to a duel; 'I shall fight you out', he had declared. Now it was the king's turn to be angry. He at once placed the Prince of Wales under house arrest. Letters of explanation and even of apology from the prince were left unanswered. After four days of considerable embarrassment the king's ministers pointed out that detention without cause being shown was contrary to the Habeas Corpus Act: they advised the king to modify his treatment of the prince. George accordingly decided the Prince and Princess of Wales should be banished from St James's Palace; anyone who chose to pay court to his son and daughter-in-law would incur his displeasure.[4] The prince and princess duly established themselves at Leicester House, an impressive mansion standing on what is now the north side of Leicester Square, a little over half a mile from the king's apartments in St James's Palace. But the move to Leicester House, so far from inhibiting the prince's political activities, provided the setting for a rival and far livelier Court, frequented by men of tomorrow rather than by place-seekers of today. For George I, a choleric fifty-seven, was beginning to look unhealthily mortal.

No one benefited more from the move to Leicester House than the principal leaders of the political opposition, Walpole and Townshend. They found, largely through the mediation of Caroline, that it was possible for them to work with the prince who – as Duke of Cornwall – commanded considerable patronage and could muster influential support within the Commons. In April 1720 Caroline and Walpole between them succeeded in an outward reconciliation of the king and the prince. George, nearly choking with anger at the memory of past misdemeanours, heard his son express grief for the displeasure he had caused and hope that 'the rest of his life would be such as the king would never have cause to complain of'. In reply, the king could only speak in broken sentences: eyewitnesses heard him say, '*Votre conduite . . . votre conduite. . . .*', before he abruptly turned about and left the room.[5] Technically father and son were reconciled, Walpole and Townshend brought back into the government, and the king assured of parliamentary help to pay off debts on the civil list; but there was no real harmony at Court or in the government. King and Prince remained, as an observer wrote, 'gravely out of humour'.

George I lived longer than his son had anticipated when first he moved to Leicester House. The South Sea Bubble, which burst in September 1720, brought a collapse of the London stock market and financial ruin to many reputable figures who had allowed themselves to be tempted into seeking quick capital gains. Both the king, a considerable stock-holder himself, and his two mistresses were publicly criticized; the Prince of Wales much less so. Walpole, brilliantly managing the House of Commons, prevented an inquiry which would have damaged the monarchy, thereby making himself politically indispensable; and he served as First Lord of the Treasury – prime minister – continuously from April 1721 until February 1742. The king seemed to acquire a new strength from Walpole's rescue operation. He felt able to visit Hanover for long spells every other year, and his confidence in Walpole was shown when he made his chief minister a knight of the Bath in 1725 and a knight of the Garter a year later. These instances of kingly favour clouded relations between Walpole and the Prince of Wales who, as Hervey wrote in his *Memoirs*, 'in the latter years of his father's reign called Sir Robert "rogue and rascal" without much reserve to several people, upon several occasions'.[6] George I died suddenly at Osnabruck in his beloved Electorate on 11 June 1727. When a report of the king's death reached London three days later, the Prince of Wales refused to believe it. He seems to have suspected a trap, in which he would later be accused of assuming the crown of England while his father still lived; for when Sir Robert knelt before him at Richmond with news of his accession, he exclaimed, 'Dat is vun beeg lie'. Fortunately Caroline, better able than her husband to sift circumstantial evidence from mere rumour, held a higher opinion of Walpole's good sense in politics. By next morning all was ready for the proclamation of King George II at St James's Palace; and the new queen had persuaded her husband not to follow his natural instincts and dismiss Walpole. Sir Robert, who had found more funds for George I's civil list, might reasonably be expected to increase the civil list of the new sovereigns, too, in return for the favour of continued office. Caroline and Walpole appreciated the niceties of each other's worldly cynicism.

By now the king and queen's eldest son, Frederick, was twenty. He had not met father, mother or sisters since the autumn of 1714 and he had never seen his brother, William, who was born in 1721 and created Duke of Cumberland at the age of five. Not unnaturally, Frederick assumed he would be summoned to London for his father's coronation and created Prince of Wales. But when George was crowned in October, Frederick was still in Hanover: his three eldest sisters carried their mother's train the length of Westminster Abbey; his brother, Cumberland, was the spoilt pet of the coronation festivities; but Frederick might as well never have existed. More than a year went by without the king taking any notice of his son. Only the knowledge that he was planning to marry his cousin Wilhelmina of Prussia without his father's consent prompted the king at last to order him to London. Frederick arrived unheralded at Whitechapel on the evening of 7 December 1728 after a dangerous and tiring winter journey. He hailed a hackney coach which took him, with two attendants, to St James's Palace where he 'walked down to the Queen's backstairs whence he was conducted to Her Majesty's apartments'. Mother and son greeted each other for the first time in fourteen years. Even his father seemed pleased he had come to Court. Significantly the king remarked to Walpole, 'I think this is not a son I need be much afraid of'.[7]

Frederick was formally introduced to the privy council on 18 December, taking his rightful place at his father's side. Three weeks later he was created Prince of Wales, although there is no record of any ceremonial investiture. He was welcomed at a court ball that first Christmas, staying long after the retirement of his parents so as to enjoy the free and easy entertainment of a masquerade. There were no outward signs of tension between Frederick and his family. At first he remained in the 'schoolroom' at St James's Palace, on good terms with his sisters and young brother. A famous painting by J. F. Nollekens shows Frederick accompanying his two musical sisters, Anne and Caroline, on the cello while Princess Amelia sits behind them, not reading the book she is holding on her lap. But this delightfully composed picture of family concord is misleading. Frederick was neither a schoolboy nor a young innocent, and the role of dutiful brother to three spoilt sisters soon began to pall. In Hanover he had revelled in night adventures, outside and inside the palace, spending lavishly and running himself into debt. It was probably wise of the king to limit his son's funds when he arrived in London; but the prince found this restriction irksome, resenting it more than the largely ineffectual curbs on his freedom of movement. He was accustomed to living, with some show of state, in an establishment of his own. His pleas for a 'Prince of Wales's residence' were backed by the parliamentary Opposition, not least because a prince's rival court would become the natural homing ground of the politically dispossessed.

The prince was popular with the ordinary people in the capital. Once he found he could slip out from the palace, wander in St James's Park, or hail hackney carriages to take him to the Haymarket, Lincoln's Inn Fields and Covent Garden, he began to acquaint himself with the life of the city. Like so many contemporaries he threw himself into pleasure with animal zest. He sought his prey in the London fantasized by John Cleland in *Fanny Hill* and depicted with realistic savagery by William Hogarth. Frederick was a rake, but he paid well for his mistresses, and was not callously selfish. He took care of them when they became pregnant, although with due regard to their social rank: 'Fitz Frederick of Cornwall, natural son of the Prince of Wales by Anne Vane, daughter of Gilbert Lord Barnard' is buried near his father in Westminster Abbey; but no one knows the fate of the baby born a month after Fitz Frederick to Anne Vane's chambermaid. Nevertheless the Prince of Wales enjoyed a reputation for kindness. It was said that once, returning from the

Covent Garden area, he noticed a carelessly driven carriage knock a basket from the arm of an elderly woman. As he stooped to help recover her scattered oranges a porter recognized him, doffed his hat with a shout of 'Hooray for the Prince' and won in reply a slap on the back and a counter-cry, 'Hurrah for Liberty and Property'. This tale, and many similar stories, may well be apocryphal. But nobody bothered to invent fables about the king.

Society at Court found Frederick puzzling. 'He is the most agreeable young man it is possible to imagine, without being the least handsome', wrote the Countess of Bristol, one of the Ladies of the Bedchamber, when first she met the prince.[8] His appearance was, indeed, strange: a yellowish skin, thick lips, and a curved nose accentuated by a receding chin. Rumour said he was a changeling, or the offspring of one of Elector George's Muslim servants; and the king would say in moments of fury, 'the beast is no son of mine'. This was nonsense: Frederick had George II's nose, and his features so matched those of Princess Amelia that there could be no doubt they were brother and sister. In character, too, he was like the king. Both fought the family feud with malicious pinpricks; Frederick, however, showed more irresponsibility than his father, even seeking to humiliate the great Handel by a mischievous campaign which originated in a quarrel with his tiresomely haughty sister Anne. Frederick, again like his father, may have lacked self-confidence; but while George took refuge in gruff bluster his son affected contempt for the conventions of court life and delighted in practical jokes. The prince made enemies of the Walpoles, father and son, and of his earlier friend John Hervey, who was his mother's favourite gigolo and became a first-rate memoirist. The combined enmity of Horace Walpole and John Hervey have ensured for 'Poor Fred' a bad press from the historians. But against their rapier phrases may be set the generosity and kindliness which Frederick showed towards friends whom he trusted. His interests, too, were wider than Hervey was prepared to admit; he added two Van Dycks and two Rubens landscapes to the present royal collection; he knew a little science and more than a little about astronomy; he befriended and encouraged Alexander Pope; he championed religious toleration by showing an interest in Quakers and in the Calvinistic Methodism of Selina, Countess of Huntingdon; and he was virtually the founder of the Royal Botanical Gardens at Kew.

He took up cricket at the age of twenty-eight, and is known to have captained the Surrey Club against a team raised by the Duke of Marlborough in a match played at Moulsey Hurst in the summer of 1737 for stakes of £500 a side. The prince was patron of the first fully documented match, Kent against All-England, played at the Artillery Ground in Finsbury on 18 June 1744; he was also President of the London club which, in that same summer, printed the earliest version of the laws of cricket. His enthusiasm for cricket gave the Hanoverian-born prince sound roots in the home counties, where the sport was spreading fast during these years through the common interest of great landowners, the squirearchy and their tenants and dependants. The prince's father showed no understanding of such activities: to George II, as to James I, meadow and downland might be ridden over by huntsmen with their hounds, but not roped off for games with bat and ball.

Frederick's way of life was expensive, and the king was determined to keep him short of money. Here lies the basic reason for the intensive public quarrelling between the Prince of Wales and his parents during the years preceding Caroline's death in 1737. Although the king grudgingly allowed Frederick £24,000 a year from the revenue of the principality, the prince was sinking into serious debt within three years of his arrival in England. By March 1732, however, he had established a close friendship with the wealthy Whig eccentric Bubb Dodington, who lent the prince £6,000 without security in order to purchase for himself a London residence, Carlton House, which adjoined Dodington's own mansion in Pall Mall. Nor was this Dodington's only service. In that same year the Prince of Wales employed William Kent to assist naval architects and shipwrights in constructing the most graceful royal barge in the world, with a stateroom as delicately elegant as the interior of the finest country houses: such a gem – and it survives today in the National Maritime Museum at Greenwich – would not have been wrought without the generosity of the prince's rich friend. The king did not approve of Dodington: few people did. In private life he was a deplorable influence, a forty-year-old playboy seeking not to go seedy. He was also anathema to the king and Walpole as a political placehunter, closely linked to the parliamentary opposition. Through Dodington, and through the more respectable Lord Egmont, the prince made his entry into party politics, bringing with him the useful voting strength of pocket boroughs in the Duchy of Cornwall. By the beginning of 1735 the prince and the Opposition were working closely together, a partnership which continued through sixteen years of factious and often futile bickering. The Prince of Wales was not a sound or consistent political leader but he was a useful patron, with offices at his disposal in the household as well as some rewarding constituencies to offer.[9]

In March 1734 Frederick's sister, Anne, the Princess Royal, was married to Prince William of Orange, a distant cousin of his namesake, England's onetime Protestant Liberator. The Prince of Wales resented the king's concern at securing a bridegroom for the Princess Royal before arranging his own marriage, and the prince was also angry with Walpole for inducing parliament to approve a £80,000 settlement on his sister while he was himself denied his full income from the principality. He demanded marriage, and his father scoured Germany for an acceptable daughter-in-law. The king, still opposed to any link with Hanover's neighbour, Prussia, turned to the smaller Lutheran dynasties and thought he had found a suitable bride in Saxe-Coburg. Princess Augusta was seventeen, twelve years younger than Frederick, when they were married in the chapel royal of St James's Palace in April 1736. To the anger of the king there was widespread public rejoicing in London over the royal marriage, and fulsome addresses in the House of Commons, especially from the group of 'Boy Patriots' opposed to Walpole. Among the members who congratulated Frederick and Augusta was a young cavalry officer making his maiden speech, William Pitt. The prince replied to these gestures of goodwill by entertaining a thousand Londoners to a giant banquet in Carlton House. 'The city was exceedingly pleased and people said to one another, "Now we have a Prince of Wales of our own",' noted Egmont. Queen Caroline, full of contempt for Augusta, remarked sourly that her son's popularity 'makes me vomit'.

Marriage brought the prince £50,000 a year from Wales rather than the previous £24,000. Another £50,000 of the principality's revenues was still retained by his father. As soon as parliament met in February 1737 the 'Patriots' resolved to raise the question of the prince's income in the Commons – although the Opposition leader, Pulteney, and Dodington both thought Frederick would weaken his standing in the country by bringing the monarchy into public debate. The Commons supported the king by thirty votes, after feverish canvassing by Walpole and his managers; while in the Lords the king had a substantial majority. The royal family were furious with Frederick, his sister Caroline declaring she grudged him every hour he continued to breathe. His mother, too, was all fire and venom. On the day of the Commons debate, Lord Hervey recorded how, that morning, he had been talking to the queen when she saw her son walking across the court beneath her window: 'Look, there he goes', Caroline exclaimed, reddening with rage, 'That wretch! That villain! I wish the ground would open this moment and sink the monster to the lowest hole in hell.'[10]

Five months later the prince, in formal but polite letters, let his mother and father know independently that Augusta was pregnant. The king ordered the Prince and Princess of Wales to join the royal family at Hampton Court, even though no spoken words had been exchanged between Frederick and his mother and sisters since the parliamentary debates of the previous February. Caroline was determined to be present when Augusta's child was born, wishing to verify for herself that the child, who would be second in line of succession, was not a changeling. On Sunday evening, 31 July 1737, Augusta unexpectedly went into labour. Frederick hustled her out of Hampton Court, while the rest of the family were playing cards, and conveyed her to his old apartments at St James's Palace, for he was obstinately set against the presence of his mother at such a time. Remarkably Augusta and her baby survived the twelve-mile journey to St James's, the birth starting as the coach rattled into the courtyard: even more remarkably the baby – a girl named after her mother – lived to marry a Duke of Brunswick, give birth to a future Princess of Wales, and die in Regency England at the age of seventy-five. Nothing in her long life was so dramatic as its beginning.

The king was furious at what he regarded as outright rebellion by his son. Exchanges of angry letters culminated in a formal order of expulsion from St James's Palace, read by the Lord Chamberlain to the Prince of Wales on 10 September. 'Peers, peeresses, privy counsellors and other persons of standing' were informed that 'whoever goes to pay their court to the Prince and Princess of Wales will not be admitted into His Majesty's presence': the prince's bodyguard was withdrawn; the king's guards ordered not to present arms or even salute if the Prince of Wales passed by. Two days later the evicted couple and their six-week-old baby left the palace for the peace of thirteen acres at Kew.

'I hope in God I shall never see him again', Caroline said after her son's departure. She never did. Some of her strange behaviour in that summer of 1737 may well have sprung from the suspicion, which she concealed from her husband, that she was mortally ill; a ruptured womb turned malignant, and she died with great fortitude on 20 November, still refusing on her deathbed to receive the Prince of Wales. Her death intensified, rather than lessened, the hatred felt by the king for his elder son; for George claimed that the unfeeling conduct of Frederick and Augusta clouded the last months of Caroline's life. The Court continued to ostracize the Prince. He declined to live in Carlton House, which would have brought him too closely in contact with others in the family. Instead, Frederick leased the Duke of Norfolk's town residence in St James's Square. Gradually society defied the king's displeasure and began to call once more on the Prince and Princess. The formidable Dowager Duchess of Marlborough, who had known personally every British sovereign since Charles II, made it clear she approved of Frederick and Augusta. If Duchess Sarah's coach was seen to visit Norfolk House, lesser worthies might with no affront to their dignity exchange courtesies at the rival court. And the Prince and Princess could count on public applause every time they went to a play or an opera.

It was at Norfolk House, on 24 May 1738, that Augusta gave premature birth to the sickly boy who was to become King George III (celebrating his birthday on 4 June from 1753 onwards when Great Britain adopted the Gregorian calendar). The king acknowledged the birth of his grandson by ordering the firing of official salutes, but the first widespread celebrations fell outside the capital, at Bath when the Prince and Princess paid an extended visit to the city in the autumn, ostensibly to take the waters. While at Bath the prince was able to discuss political questions with Pulteney, Lord Chesterfield and other 'Boy Patriots' fretting at Walpole's seemingly endless premiership. Walpole had strengthened the national economy and helped the British develop world trade by keeping the country at peace. Public feeling, however, resented a series of insults from the Spanish colonial authorities who wished to keep in check the smuggling operations of English merchants in the West Indies. The Boy Patriots, and the Prince of Wales with them, scoffed at Walpole's attempts to negotiate with Spain. The king had never forgotten the thrills of the Oudenarde campaign: his peppery character made him impatient with Walpole, even though he distrusted the 'boobies and fools and madmen' in the Opposition who befriended the Prince of Wales. In 1739 public feeling stampeded Walpole into a conflict with Spain over trading rights. Soon the war spread to England's old enemy, France. By the beginning of 1742 it was clear Walpole was no war leader and his days seemed numbered. When he resigned in February the prince hoped his 'Patriot' friends would come to power, securing for him both responsibility and political influence. So, though Frederick did not know the precedent, had Henry of Monmouth believed in the winter of 1409–10.

The Prince of Wales was disappointed. Pulteney, weakly, declined to take office in a ministry likely to be concerned with European affairs, about which he knew nothing. Pitt and most of the 'Patriots' were passed over as too young and irresponsible. Carteret, who dominated the new Ministry, had spoken up for Frederick in the House of Lords during the revenue debate of 1737 but he was not one of the prince's close circle. His great linguistic gifts and deep understanding of European complexities won him the king's warm support; and he disdained to strike political bargains over what now seemed to him the trivial grievances of the Prince of Wales. All the same, the coming of the new ministry (of which the Earl of Wilmington was technically the head) gave the prince the chance of settling his disputes with the king. There was a formal reconciliation at St James's Palace on 18 February 1742, after four and a half years of ostracism. The prince's footguards were restored to him; and the king suggested he might move to Leicester House, where there was better accommodation for a growing family than at Norfolk House or at Carlton House. No promise was made of any improved grant for the prince.[11]

The Lord Mayor of London welcomed the reconciliation with decorated streets and a reception for Frederick and Augusta. Tactfully the City of London remembered also to send a loyal message to His Majesty. But it was for the Prince and Princess that the crowds turned out, cheering them in the streets and from the river bank as they were rowed in Frederick's magnificent state barge down to Greenwich. For the Prince of Wales it was a day of triumph. Yet, in reality, nothing had been achieved and there was little to celebrate beyond the exchange of spoken civilities between father and son. Soon Frederick began to sense he was doomed to political impotence. The war in Europe boosted the king's standing among his subjects: he crossed to Germany and, at Dettingen on 15 June 1743 led a motley army of British, Hanoverian, Hessian, Dutch and Austrian troops to victory over the French. The prince's brother, Cumberland, also distinguished himself in the campaign. Frederick, however, was forced to remain in England. He had sought an army command, but since he was totally without military training and regarded by his father as naturally undisciplined, his request was turned down. More and more of his 'Patriot' friends gained minor office either in the government of Wilmington or that of his successor, Henry Pelham; Frederick found himself left as head of a petty-minded faction rather than as leader of a powerful, responsible pressure group. The Jacobite fiasco of 1745 gave another fillip to the king's prestige, while the public mood in London accorded more closely with 'Butcher' Cumberland's callousness than with the Prince of Wales's pleas for humane treatment towards the captured rebels. He never again savoured the popularity of that third week in February 1742.

Unexpectedly the prince met the frustration of these war years with more serenity than his temperament had commanded while his mother was alive. He was content that time should be on his side. From 1747 onwards he began to hold discussions with new and old friends, planning ahead rather than seeking immediate political advantage. His ideas included a sharing of dynastic responsibilities: he proposed, on his accession, to separate Britain and Hanover, sending his second son to Germany to rule the Electorate; and he thought he might find 'an island near Antigua' for his fourth son, where Prince Henry would be established as Duke of Virginia, a viceroy for the colonies in the West Indies and mainland America.[12] It is not surprising Frederick placed such emphasis on the future of his children, for much of his newly found calmness sprang from the happiness of his home life. In 1739 he had rented Cliveden House in Buckinghamshire from the Countess of Orkney and it soon became a favourite residence for both Frederick and Augusta. Essentially Cliveden was a private retreat, only ten miles upstream from Windsor but tucked away on a wooded bluff. Occasionally selected guests were entertained at Cliveden: the first performance of Arne's *Rule Britannia* took place in the rustic amphitheatre there, as part of a mask on Alfred the Great performed in the summer of 1740. But such public moments were rare. Cliveden was a home for

Frederick's family – four boys and four girls born within thirteen years. The prince was 'a tender and obliging husband' and 'a fond parent' according to the novelist Smollett, who knew him. Surviving letters between Frederick and his eldest son certainly show none of the customary generation feud of the Hanoverians, perhaps because in this instance the father was not yet a ruling sovereign. He was sympathetic to his children, helpful to them in their studies, generous in his praise, and ready to join in games with them. At Cliveden, as at Kew, he delighted in the trees and shrubs: a grove of ilex survives as testimony to his interests.

While playing cricket at Cliveden in the summer of 1748 Frederick appears to have been hit hard 'on the side of the chest' by a ball. This mischance may have shortened his life. According to Bubb Dodington the bruising caused an abscess which broke three years later and 'suffocated the prince'. His death at Leicester House on 20 March 1751 was certainly unexpected. He had, however, been ill for four weeks, suffering originally from pleurisy contracted through supervising work in his gardens at Kew during bitterly icy weather. Impatience induced him to go to the House of Lords before he was fully fit and he suffered a major relapse when he eventually arrived back at Leicester House. Within a week he was fit enough to receive friends in his room but, on that same evening, he suddenly succumbed to a severe fit of coughing. Probably he died from pneumonia, but the abscess may well have aggravated his breathing.[13] He was only forty-four years old.

The king was shocked, came to Leicester House, and wept with his daughter-in-law (who was expecting yet another child) and with his grandson. But he was too honest with himself to remain in genuine grief for more than a few hours. He declined to settle the prince's debts and trimmed all funeral expenses; but as soon as the decencies of mourning permitted, he was determined his subjects should see His Majesty honouring his dead son's heir. Exactly a month after Frederick's death, Prince George William Frederick was created Prince of Wales, a few weeks short of his thirteenth birthday.

Only once before – in 1376 – had a king created his grandson Prince of Wales; and there is no parallel between the two occasions. Edward III was then in his dotage, Richard's principate lasting a mere seven months: in 1751 George II was a robust sixty-seven, with more than nine years of life ahead of him. The new Prince of Wales showed few signs of personality: his father had believed his second son, Edward, more intelligent; and his mother, although fondly possessive, thought him backward for his age. The king was convinced it would be good for the boy to become less dependent on his mother and on the Leicester House set. Augusta, however, was resolved to keep her hold on the prince, partly because of her aversion for her father-in-law and partly because she did not wish her God-fearing son corrupted at a court of such casual virtue. She had no respect whatsoever for the king, believing – as Frederick had taught her – that he was a pliable creature in the hands of unscrupulous ministers. In January 1753 she told Bubb Dodington 'with much warmth' that whenever government ministers 'talked to her of the King she lost all patience; that she knew it was nothing; that in their great points she reckoned the King no more than one of the trees we walked by'.[14] It appears she was accustomed to speaking of his grandfather in these terms to the young Prince of Wales. Not surprisingly, he soon learnt to despise the king.

One of Frederick's last acts had been the appointment of George Lewis Scott, a mathematician, Fellow of the Royal Society and scientist, as his son's tutor. Scott, the friend of Samuel Johnson and of Gibbon, was a good teacher. Unfortunately he was suspected of Jacobite sympathies, a suspicion which even so staunch a Whig as the Duke of Newcastle regarded as ridiculous; but Scott had to go. Earl Waldegrave, who became the prince's Governor in 1752, was sober and sensible. He was, however, hampered by the prince's dislike of book learning, and by his mother. For Augusta was determined to insulate her son, keeping him out of the company of other young people and (as she told Dodington in December 1753) 'away from the excessive bad education they had, and from the bad examples they gave'. He became lonely and moody. Sometimes he was silent; sometimes his conversation would ramble on inconsequentially. His 'real good sense, innate rectitude, unspeakably kind heart, and genuine manliness of spirit, were overlooked in his youth', later wrote one of the few young people who had known him in boyhood.[15]

Greatest influence of all upon the Prince of Wales was James Stuart, third Earl of Bute, his tutor during the most formative years of his life. Bute rose from backwoods obscurity to backstairs eminence in the twinkling of a shower at Egham races during the summer of 1747. Frederick, Prince of Wales, who had travelled to the races from Cliveden, needed a fourth hand at whist and invited the unknown earl into his tent until the weather cleared. The two men became friends. They had much in common as well as a liking for cards and horse-racing: both enjoyed amateur theatricals; both appreciated music; both were interested in landscape gardening. Bute was invited to Cliveden, and Augusta found him an agreeable companion. He was indeed pleasant, polite and good-looking: people seeing him in knee-breeches maintained that he possessed 'the most elegant legs in London'. Frederick saw his limitations more clearly than did his wife or his eldest son: 'Bute', Frederick once remarked, 'you would make an excellent ambassador in some proud little Court where there is nothing to do'.[16] But by 1756 he had become, not an envoy in deepest Germany, but 'dearest friend' to a young and impressionable Prince of Wales. Bute was a most conscientious tutor. Politically, however, he was a backbench isolationist who thought the system corrupted by patronage, from which he had never benefited. There was nothing Whiggishly wrong or radically Tory in his principles and ideals, but they bore little relationship to constitutional realities. His ragbag of ideas confused a young man who had never been trained to think deeply. It was easier to talk, as George did, of 'the independence of the Crown', of 'restoring liberty and virtue', of a mission 'to make this great nation happy' than to analyse what these fine phrases meant. The Prince of Wales, dutifully writing page after page of essays for this substitute father, spent too many years in a comfortably regulated schoolroom to notice the nation around him.

Shortly after his twentieth birthday Lord Waldegrave wrote a general report on the young man who had been in his charge for over four years. He praised the prince's honesty, his sense of religion, and his spirit; but it is Waldegrave's criticisms that are of greatest interest. The prince's piety, he said, 'is not of the most charitable sort, he has too much attention to the sins of his neighbour'. 'He has great command of his passions, and will seldom do wrong, except when he mistakes wrong for right, but as often as this shall happen, it will be difficult to undeceive him, because he is uncommonly indolent and has strong prejudices.' Waldegrave hoped that, as the prince was still so young, there remained 'much time for improvement'.[17] But could he shake off these 'strong prejudices' before he came to the throne? Bute as friend and tutor was not the man to rid him of them.

Although George II was as rude and short-tempered as ever, he treated his grandson generously. In 1756, under pressure from Pitt, the king proposed to allow the prince to have £40,000 a year and his own establishment within St James's Palace. The prince accepted the money, secured the post of Groom of the Stole for Bute in his household, but declined to change his place of residence. He preferred, so he said, to remain 'with the Princess, my mother' although, in fact, he was living when in London at Savile House next door to her residence, Leicester House. Yet in his letters to Bute during the Seven Years War the prince roundly abused his grandfather's ministers. Pitt, once a familiar figure at Leicester House but now the great war leader, was 'the most dishonourable of men', 'the blackest of hearts', one who by joining Newcastle in the government was playing 'an infamous and ungrateful part'. When, in December 1758, Pitt failed to notify Bute and the Prince of Wales of a forthcoming change in foreign policy, the prince wrote indignantly to Bute, 'Indeed, my dearest friend, he treats both you and me with no more regard than he would do a parcel of children.' Other friends of the prince's father who had moved with the times and into office fare no better: they became 'vermin', 'void of principles'. Nor was his grandfather spared: when in 1759, 'the Year of Victories', the king with studied tact turned aside the Prince of Wales's request for a military command, his grandson complained to Bute of 'H.M.'s . . . shuffling and unworthy letter'. 'The conduct of this old King makes me ashamed of being his grandson', the prince wrote, while the old king's redcoats were besieging Quebec and six of the old king's infantry regiments were about to add 'Minden' to their battle honours.[18]

From his mother the prince inherited Frederick's grievances and prejudices, even his phrases. But Frederick appreciated there was always an element of make-believe in the game of Government and Opposition. His son was in earnest. A wiser man than Bute could have imposed on the receptive prince greater sophistication of judgment. Perhaps, in his clumsy way, Bute did belatedly attempt to show him that ministerial actions were not determined by simple questions of 'right' or 'wrong' and that his grandfather's war ministers were not 'knaves and rascals' beyond redemption. But, if this was the intention of some of Bute's advice, the prince misunderstood him. When the prince examined the supposed virtues of other political figures, he saw only the superior merit of his friend and tutor: 'As to honesty', wrote the prince on St George's Day 1760, 'I have already lived long enough to know you are the only man who possesses that quality'.[19] He was twenty-two when he paid Bute this sweeping compliment, and a mere twenty-six weeks away from the throne.

CHAPTER EIGHT

Farmer George and Prinny

GEORGE II, who had defied death in battle at Oudenarde and at Dettingen, finally collapsed while seated on his commode at half-past seven in the morning of 25 October 1760. The Prince of Wales was proclaimed King George III later that same day. The country welcomed the accession of a monarch born and educated in England, reasonably good-looking, young, and 'full of dignity', as Horace Walpole noted. Yet the ministers whom he inherited from his grandfather's reign were ill-at-ease. Who really ruled? When the prime minister, Newcastle, waited on the king immediately after his accession, he asked if George had any general wishes over policy: 'My Lord Bute is your good friend', the king replied, 'He will tell you my thoughts at large'. The remark confirmed Newcastle's worst fears. Bute was sworn of the Privy Council on that same day.

Throughout the early months of the reign George consulted Bute daily over 'what must be done'. 'I have put that off till I hear my Dear Friend's opinion', he would write in a letter reporting his ministers' efforts to secure decisions over proposed measures or appointments. By the spring of 1761 Bute had been brought into the government. A year later (26 May 1762) the king fulfilled the one political ambition he had consistently shown as Prince of Wales by inviting Bute to succeed Newcastle as prime minister. He remained in office for only eleven months, long enough to show the king the folly of promoting a favourite with little political experience or gifts of parliamentary management. Technically Bute's ministry was responsible for the Peace of Paris, which enabled Britain to retain enough overseas conquests to create a colonial empire. Public opinion, however, blamed Bute for taxes which remained at war level even though hostilities had ended. This unfamiliar Scotsman, suddenly thrust forward as spokesman for the king, was loathed by rich and poor in the capital: sometimes in London he travelled incognito, fearing physical assault and perhaps even death.

Within the cabinet he was faced with repeated intrigues by veteran schemers. Bute was forced to strike bargains with the 'bad men' whom the Prince of Wales had so scorned in the letters of their innocence. By January 1763 the Earl of Bute was losing his nerve for politics. He began to look for an excuse to resign. Riots against a proposed cider tax enabled him to retreat with dignity. He left office on 7 April 1763: 'I shall never meet with a friend in business again', the king wrote wretchedly to him after his fall. The partnership of young sovereign and court favourite had been an odd constitutional experiment, out of step with the times and the mood of the nation. Unfortunately the experiment cost George much of the goodwill which had greeted his accession.[1]

By 1765–6 George had freed himself entirely from dependence on Bute, who nevertheless remained a bogey-man to the gutter press until well into the next decade. Emotionally the king overcame his adolescent enthusiasm: the 'dearest friend' of earlier letters became the 'dear friend' of 1762 and the 'friend' of 1763. For by 1762 the king, like his father twenty years before, was finding contentment in family life. George had wished to marry in 1759, when he fell in love with the fifteen-year-old Sarah Lennox, daughter of the Duke of Richmond and a descendant of Charles II; but Bute, on being asked for 'consent to my raising her to the throne', advised him not to marry one of his own subjects; and George dutifully settled down (as he wrote) to the task 'of looking in the New Berlin Almanack for Princesses'. He found an acceptable bride in Charlotte Sophia, the plain and wholesome younger daughter of the late Duke of Mecklenburg-Strelitz: the royal wedding was celebrated in the chapel of St James's Palace on 8 September 1761. Eight children were born to them in their first ten years of married life, to be followed by seven more in the following thirteen years. At a time when there was a high incidence of infant mortality, it is remarkable that only the two youngest boys should have died in childhood. Queen Charlotte, who was six years younger than her husband, lived to the age of seventy-four. George, a model of Protestant piety throughout his reign, remained scrupulously loyal to his marriage vows.[2]

Their first child was born during Bute's brief premiership, in the evening of 12 August 1762 at St James's Palace. The boy was named George Augustus Frederick. With a curious sense of priorities he was formally created Prince of Wales by Letters Patent when he was five days old but not christened until 16 September. Genteel visitors were allowed into the palace on Thursday afternoons between one and three when they might, from a respectful distance, view the baby in his cradle. Others among his father's subjects saw the prince occasionally filling his lungs with the clean air of Hyde Park, but most of his infancy was spent at Kew or within the privacy of Buckingham House, the home which the king was making for Queen Charlotte's comfort in the year of the prince's birth. The boy seems to have been precociously intelligent: before the age of four he pleased the spokesmen of a Welsh charitable institution, the Society of Ancient Britons, by carefully chosen words – and a gift of £100 – when they paid a formal visit to their prince in London; and he could read and write by his fifth birthday. 'The king has made his brat the proudest little imp you ever saw', remarked Sarah Lennox at that time. The formal portraits by Zoffany and Gainsborough seem to catch this mixture of mischief and arrogance; although Lady Sarah's comments on Charlotte's growing family may not have been entirely impartial.[3]

The prince was brought up strictly, but ill-advisedly. He saw no companions of his age apart from his brother, Frederick Duke of York, who was less than a year his junior. A rigid routine set out the hours in which George was to learn his Latin, Greek, French, German and Italian, acquire his smattering of mathematics and natural philosophy, study 'polite literature' not too deeply, and play the cello. The king, now painstakingly conscientious and disinclined to recall his own hours of indolence, constantly complained that his son was not working hard enough, although he was probably as accomplished as any contemporary prince on the continent. Young George and Frederick were expected to cultivate a strip of soil at Kew because their father was deeply interested in farming and particularly in improved agricultural techniques. If the prince allowed his sense of humour or his gift of mimicry to relax the solemnities of the schoolroom, he was soundly rebuked. Lapses of work, fits of temper, boyish escapades, were all punished with beatings, as in the best schools of the land: one of his sisters later recalled seeing her two eldest brothers 'flogged like dogs with a long whip' by their tutors. It must have seemed to the boy that there was little he could do to satisfy his elders. By his eighth birthday he was accustomed to receiving heavily phrased letters of moral guidance from both his mother and his father.

That year the princes' governor, the Earl of Holderness, began to send earnest advice in written notes to his charges; and soon there came, too, well-meant strictures from the prince's Preceptor, Bishop William Markham, ex-headmaster of Westminster and shortly to become Archbishop of York. The prince liked Markham, respecting him as a good teacher, but in 1776 he was succeeded by Bishop Hurd of Lichfield, a stiff, correct and coldly unsympathetic supervisor although as eager as his predecessors to help mould the character of a future sovereign. No Prince of Wales ever received such fine, uplifting sentiments from so many stern and righteous worthies. They set him impossible standards. Before he reached manhood the prince learnt to take refuge in sly evasions and compromises with the truth. This reputation for duplicity he could never quite shake off in later life.

By the spring of 1780 the prince was gaining some notoriety for his extravagance in love. Mrs Mary Robinson, a beautiful actress four years older than himself, won his heart by her performance as Perdita in Garrick's hotted-up version of *The Winter's Tale*. Secret meetings at Kew were followed by gifts of jewelry and trinkets: there were rash promises of a rosy future for the girl. But by the following year the prince began to tire of the romance, his eyes roving elsewhere. Perdita Robinson would not, however, make a quiet exit: she held on to the prince's letters, and to a bond promising her £20,000 when he should come of age. His father was shocked to learn of this 'shameful scrape' and his representatives had some difficulty in reaching a settlement with Mrs Robinson.[4] Lord North, the prime minister, had to help the king with funds to rescue the prince from his embarrassments: Mrs Robinson received an outright payment of £5,000, an annuity of £500 for life, and the promise of £250 a year for her daughter after her death. To the king's indignation, satirical cartoons of Perdita and her 'Prince Florizel' were soon on sale in London. Society took malicious glee in the discomfiture of a censorious court.

George himself still thought it possible to keep the Prince of Wales under his personal surveillance, expecting him to reside at Buckingham House and observe strict rules of conduct. He might have dinner parties twice a week and go to a play or an opera, provided he gave the king personal notice of his plans in advance; but he was forbidden to attend dances or assemblies in private houses. He was told that it was his duty to be with the king at court levées and to accompany his father to church on Sundays as well as joining him on his morning rides. This code, which seemed enlightened to his father, provoked the eighteen-year-old prince to open rebellion. More and more he slipped out to private celebrations. There was gossip of madcap horse-riding in Hyde Park, of 'indisposition' following a party at Lord Chesterfield's house at Blackheath, of drunken brawling in the pleasure gardens at Vauxhall. Wearily George sent his son a note one morning complaining that when he picked up his newspapers each day he felt 'almost certain that some unpleasant mention' of the prince would be inside them.[5]

The king was disturbed, too, when he saw the names of the prince's boon companions. They were, for the most part, clubbable men of impeccably Whig sympathies, bitterly hostile to the muddled Toryism of the king's 'good friend', Lord North. Some, like Anthony St Leger and Charles Wyndham, were mere rakes about town, but they had contacts with the political opposition. So, too, did the prince's favourite uncle, George III's exasperating brother Henry, Duke of Cumberland. By the winter of 1781–2 the Prince of Wales had become a friend of Charles James Fox, castigator in chief of the government over the past seven years and a confirmed personal enemy of his sovereign. The prince responded naturally and contentedly to the charm and good talk of Fox, finding the company of the young Whigs agreeable. This spontaneous friendship gave a new twist to political life. The 'reversionary interest', in which out-of-office politicians cultivated their future king in expectation of good rewards in years to come, had plagued politics during the reign of George I and in the heyday of 'Poor Fred'. Now once again a Prince of Wales became honorary patron of the Opposition. It was a position he maintained for almost thirty years, without ever acquiring a real understanding of politics or of party management.

'The Prince of Wales had of late', wrote Horace Walpole a few years later,

thrown himself into the arms of Charles Fox, and this in the most undisguised manner. Fox lodged in St James's Street, and as soon as he rose, which was very late, had a levée of his followers, and of the members of the gaming club at Brook's – all his disciples. His bristly, black person, and shagged breast, quite open and rarely purified by any ablutions, was wrapped in a foul night-gown, and his bushy hair dishevelled. In these Cynic weeds and with Epicurean good humour, did he dictate his politics, and in this school did the heir to the throne attend his lessons and imbibe them.[6]

The prince's closest friends – notably Colonel St Leger – could see that, though the 'heir to the throne' might be fascinated by Fox's personality, he could never follow his full range of ideas nor accept every one of his judgments. But this was no comfort to the king. He only knew his son was consorting with politicians who (to quote Walpole again) 'were strangely licentious in their conversation about the King' – and all this at a time when George believed the monarchical constitution of the country to be reeling under the impact of defeat in America by rebels against the Crown.

For four years, ever since December 1777 when news came of Burgoyne's capitulation to 'the colonists' at Saratoga, Lord North had begged the king to receive his resignation. But George was remarkably obstinate. Only in March 1782, when everyone of consequence in Westminster and London was urging the king to accept the end of the war, did he reluctantly agree to ask the Marquis of Rockingham to form a Whig Government and entrust Fox, as foreign secretary, with the making of peace. So saddened was the king that he drafted a message of abdication and, as he wrote, contemplated 'the painful step of quitting . . . for ever . . . his native country'. But the act of abdication was never signed nor sealed. He stayed on and watched, with amazement and some disillusionment, the political squabbles of the following three years. He had been sad to lose Lord North, but he was even sadder to see North back in the spring of 1783 serving in coalition with Fox under the Whig Duke of Portland. 'I am sorry it has been my lot to reign in the most profligate age', the king wrote as he observed this 'most unnatural coalition' coming into being. Fox tried hard to charm the king when he was received in audience but George remained suspicious, delighting to snipe at the new government and looking for an opportunity to bring it down. 'Religion and public spirit', the king complained, were now 'quite absorbed by vice and dissipation' and 'the downfall of the lustre of this Empire' complete.[7]

The Prince of Wales shared none of his father's gloom. His Whig friends, once in office, were prepared to secure for him a generous settlement when he came of age. Fox proposed, and Portland rashly agreed, that the king should be asked to allow his son £100,000 a year as well as a lump sum to settle his debts. The king realized that the Whigs were making a major error. 'It is impossible for me to find words expressive enough of my utter indignation and astonishment', he wrote to the Duke of Portland, threatening 'to let the public know . . . my opinion of the whole transaction' and accusing the government of neglecting the true interests of the realm in order 'to gratify the passions of an ill advised young man'. The most Portland and Fox could obtain for the Prince was £50,000 a year and a capital sum from parliament to pay off his debts and allow the prince to modernize Carlton House as a London residence for the heir to the throne. On 22 June 1783 the Prince of Wales accepted this settlement. He took his seat in the House of Lords that November and proceeded to vote for Fox's India Bill even though his father declared he would look upon any supporter of the Bill in the Lords 'as an enemy'. A week before Christmas the king summoned up his courage and dismissed Portland, North and Fox, inviting the 24-year-old William Pitt 'the Younger' to form a basically Tory administration. The prince and his friends expected this minority government, in which every member of the cabinet except the prime minister was a peer, to fall within weeks. They miscalculated. North's followers, tired of a topsy-turvy world in which they were required to hunt with the Fox, rallied behind Pitt. A general election in the spring of 1784 showed that the voters, like the king, wished to play safe: Pitt gained a massive electoral triumph. He remained prime minister without a break for seventeen years.

For the Whigs, Fox's championship of the Prince of Wales was a liability rather than an asset. 'Poor Fred' had been popular: his grandson was not. The press published salacious titbits about his private life. He seemed to spend long hours in drinking and debauchery, his days occupied with endless trivialities. In fact, he was a shrewd connoisseur of the visual arts, a patron of Gainsborough, Romney, Hoppner and Stubbs. He possessed architectural imagination, too; he could sense the impact on distant observers of porticos, colonnades and balustraded wings set in disciplined lawns stretching beyond avenues of elm or chestnut trees. Later, when he was turning sleepy, cobbled Brighthelmstone into Brighton, his inspiration rejected classical austerity and he brought the exoticism of the East to Sussex by the sea.

Whatever London society may have felt about him, Brighton liked its prince; and the prince liked Brighton. Some who met him, at Carlton House or from 1784 onwards in Sussex, were impressed by his quality of mind. The great musicologist, Charles Burney, told his daughter, Fanny: 'I was astonished to find him amidst such constant dissipation possessed of so much learning, wit, knowledge of books in general, discrimination of character as well as original humour. H.R.H. took me aside and talked exclusively about music near half an hour.'[8] But few people thought of the heir to the throne as an intelligent and cultivated man. His father made no effort to find him any post of responsibility. Although the king continued to correspond with his son, avoiding any complete rupture, he still regarded him as a dissolute wastrel unworthy to hold a position of power in civil government or a high rank in the army. There seemed little left for the prince to do, except live as elegantly as possible, talking, racing, gaming, seeking pleasure and amusement while speculating on his father's continued good health.

On Saturday, 20 March 1784, the *Morning Herald* announced 'Mrs Fitzherbert is arrived in London for the season.' Since the country was preparing for a general election it was a little strange for a respected newspaper to comment on the movements of a twice-widowed Roman Catholic, wealthy but untitled and to most readers unknown. But the *Morning Herald* had a sure instinct for royal gossip. In mid-February the Prince of Wales had seen her one evening in a box at the opera and, as he later told his friends, became 'really mad for love' of her. It is difficult to understand why the prince should have been so attracted by a commoner six years his senior who had golden hair and a fine presence but was by no means pretty. She was also chaste, virtuous and devout and had no intention of becoming the prince's latest mistress. Yet by midsummer the prince was talking of marrying her, renouncing the succession, and settling down to a new life in the freedom of America. Mrs Fitzherbert, alarmed by his infatuation, announced her intention of going to the continent but, on 8 July 1784, she was brought hurriedly to Carlton House by news that the Prince of Wales had apparently stabbed himself in despair. In a dramatic scene she allowed him to place a ring on her finger as a sign of betrothal (an act which seems magically to have healed his wound); she then crossed to France from Southampton, with assurances that the prince would seek permission to live abroad. He did indeed suggest to the king that, if he settled on the continent, it would be possible for him to cut down his expenditure and so avoid running into debt; but George was not impressed by this argument. Letters to 'Maria, the best and most adored of women' induced her to return to London after seventeen months abroad. They were secretly married on the evening of 15 December 1785 in Maria Fitzherbert's Park Street home by an impecunious Anglican curate.[9] There was no doubt that the Prince of Wales and Maria were husband and wife. In the eyes of the Lord Chancellor, however, their marriage could never be recognized as legal: the Royal Marriage Act of 1772 required the sovereign's consent for any union contracted by a prince or princess under the age of twenty-five; the Act of Settlement of 1701 excluded from the succession any claimant who married a 'papist'. But there was no question of the Lord Chancellor or the king learning of the marriage. Not even Fox was let into the secret.

At midsummer 1786 the prince closed down Carlton House because of his debts and settled in economic domesticity at Brighton. So did Maria Fitzherbert, taking a small villa close to the converted farmhouse which was the prince's first 'pavilion'. Some gossips believed she was the prince's mistress: others claimed to know that the couple were secretly married by a Roman priest. The caricaturist James Gillray mocked the alleged Catholic marriage in savage cartoons; and in the following spring the prince's friends leapt to their patron's defence in parliament. Fox, relying on the prince's word, formally declared that such a marriage 'could have never happened legally' and 'never did happen in any way whatsoever'; and the playwright Sheridan asked the Commons to respect a lady 'on whose conduct truth could fix no just reproach'. It was embarrassing for Fox to learn soon afterwards from her uncle that he had been present at an Anglican marriage ceremony, and that the couple were indeed man and wife. Relations between Fox and the prince were never again so cordial, although there was no complete break in their friendship. Pitt, ignorant of the marriage but fearing revelations which might provoke anti-papist demonstrations, induced parliament to help the prince pay off his debts. Carlton House was re-opened; the king and the Prince of Wales were seen together in apparent amity; and the prince sent his father a letter promising 'never to incur future debts, which must undoubtedly be as disagreeable to the King as painful to himself'.[10]

In October 1788 George III began to talk rapidly and incoherently. He was feverish, with stiffness in his limbs. By the first week in November his doctors believed the balance of his mind disturbed. The Prince of Wales and the Duke of York were summoned to Windsor. Rumour said the king was dying; and there was widespread sorrow, especially at Kew and Windsor where 'Farmer George' was loved as an amiable country squire who 'knew everyone'. But the king was physically strong. He was out of danger by the end of November, although incapable of attending to the affairs of government. Fox and the Whigs pressed for an Act of Regency, confident the Prince of Wales would then use a sovereign's right to change the ministers of the crown. Pitt, however, astutely played for time. He inserted so many restraints on the powers of a Regent that debate on the Regency Bill was protracted. By February 1789 it was so much waste paper. Everyone could see that George was well on the way to recovery. A service of thanksgiving for the restoration of his health was held, appropriately, on 23 April. Yet he was never again fully in control of all his senses, for the illness aged him considerably. His letters show he no longer bothered to weary himself with the detailed day-to-day conduct of government. But over some topics he remained adamant; and among them was the assumption that his eldest son should not be trusted with responsibility.

The Prince of Wales, declared *The Times* that spring, 'is like a hard-drinking, swearing man who at all times would prefer a girl and a bottle to politics and a sermon'.[11] That was an unfair jibe. He was belatedly shaking off the peevish desire to spite his father's wishes. By his twenty-ninth birthday, in the summer of 1791, he was sufficiently poised in the social graces to receive a compliment from the press: 'Perhaps no heir to the Crown since the days of Edward the Black Prince has been more generously admired for his amiable manners than the Prince of Wales', *The Times* now said. He still enjoyed himself, at York races or at Newmarket; he had discovered a new enthusiasm for the 'manly exercise' of cricket; but he was also aware of what he called 'the damnable doctrines of the hell-begotten Jacobins' across the Channel. On 31 May 1792 he delivered his maiden speech in the House of Lords, dutifully affirming the 'glory' with which he professed Britain's 'great and sacred Constitution'. The king relented sufficiently to commission the Prince of Wales as colonel-in-chief of the Tenth Light Dragoons. For a month that summer he was in camp with the regiment at Lewes, observing exercises on the South Downs. With the monarchies of Europe united against republican France, the prince held hopes of a command in the field. His father had vainly wished to see action in 1759, his grandfather in 1743; and so now the king had no hesitation in refusing to allow the Prince of Wales to participate in any campaign on the continent. Nor did he think four weeks under the canvas of a comfortably furnished marquee in Sussex justified the prince's expectation that he should be promoted to the rank of General.[12]

No doubt it was disappointing and frustrating for the not-so-young man. His private life deteriorated. Once more he started to drink heavily and run up fresh debts. By the winter of 1793–4 Maria Fitzherbert began to suspect that he was tiring of her company. She blamed the Countess of Jersey, a vivacious grandmother of forty, whom the prince had long known but whose habitual coquetry he had hitherto resisted. Yet there were other reasons for the prince's changed attitude towards Mrs Fitzherbert. He wished to end the illicit union in order to conclude a dynastic marriage. A good Protestant bride, he reckoned, was worth another £50,000 a year from parliament, together with settlement of his latest debts. In August 1794 the prince travelled to Weymouth where he told his father he had severed all links with Mrs Fitzherbert and was prepared to take a German bride. The most natural choice for a wife, he thought, was Princess Caroline of Brunswick, daughter of his father's sole surviving sister, Augusta, whose birth provoked that great family quarrel back in 1737. The king – although not the queen – approved: the prince, who had never met his first cousin, showed little real interest in the matter. Lord Malmesbury, an experienced diplomat, made the dangerous wartime journey to Brunswick to escort Caroline to England. She landed at Gravesend on 5 April 1795. The prince, awaiting her at St James's Palace, found Caroline physically repugnant. He withdrew to a corner of the room, turned to Malmesbury (James Harris, before he became a peer), and remarked, 'Harris, I am not well. Pray get me a glass of brandy.' But no change was made in the marriage plans. The wedding took place three days later in the Chapel Royal of the palace. The bride nearly fell over because of the weight of her dress: the bridegroom could scarcely remain upright because he had drunk so much brandy. On his way to the Chapel Royal he asked his brother William to make certain that he let Mrs Fitzherbert know 'she is the only woman I shall ever love'.[13]

The marriage was a disaster. Even the prince's hope of increased revenue remained unfulfilled. After a public debate, emphasizing his personal extravagance, parliament appointed a commission to study his debts. By the time the commissioners had completed their task, he was left with an annual income lower than he had received ten years before. A child – Princess Charlotte – was born on Tuesday, 7 January 1796; but by then the Prince of Wales was in a state of complete nervous depression. On the following Sunday (12 January) he wrote in his own hand an extraordinarily long 'last will and testament'. It safeguarded 'my infant daughter'; but it was mainly concerned with his love for 'my Maria Fitzherbert who is my wife in the eyes of God, and who is and ever will be such in mine'. The testament requested that when he died 'the picture of my beloved wife, my Maria Fitzherbert, may be interred with me'. Beneath his signature, added as an afterthought, the prince wrote, 'I forgot to mention that the jewels which she who is called the Princess of Wales wears are mine, having been bought with my own money. . . . These I bequeath to my infant daughter as her own property, and to her who is called Princess of Wales I leave one shilling'.[14] Six months later he told the queen that his wife was 'the vilest wretch this world was ever cursed with, who I cannot feel more disgust for from her personal nastiness than I do from her entire want of Principle'. There was no hope for such a marriage, despite efforts by the king and by the Duke of Clarence (the future King William IV) to heal the rift. By the end of May 1796 *The Times* was attacking the prince for seeking a separation. Public opinion was resolutely on the side of Caroline. No Prince of Wales had ever been so unpopular in London. He was spending money on an unprecedented scale and by the autumn of 1796 had accumulated debts of more than £600,000. His personal life was ostentatious and his amorous adventures made salacious gossip. Now, at a time when he was already being attacked by the cartoonists and castigated by the more responsible newspaper editors for his trivial style of life, came the revelation of a breakdown in his marriage. Caroline was cheered whenever she went to the theatre or opera while the prince was hissed, like the villain in a melodrama. The king, judiciously trying to examine the behaviour of both his eldest son and the daughter-in-law who was his niece, admitted Caroline had not been 'happy in the choice of conduct she had adopted': but he refused to allow any formal separation. They did, in fact, live apart – as James I and Anne of Denmark had done in his later years. But officially they were still husband and wife, and father and mother to the king's firstborn grandchild.

'The behaviour of royalty should be the exemplar for the nation', the king told his son in June 1796, echoing sentiments he had expressed many times before.[15] Judged by such a standard, the Prince of Wales was a failure. And yet he was a man of great qualities, cultured, witty, artistically sensitive. Most of his debts came from his desire to accumulate a collection of paintings which, in time, would prove to be a monetary investment as well as a treasured addition to the nation's cultural heritage. Moreover, although his public marriage set no example, there were moments when he sought and found a contented domesticity with his 'wife in the eyes of God', drawing strength from her homely affection. In the summer of 1800 Maria Fitzherbert, having sought advice in Rome, received an assurance from Pope Pius VII that, if the Prince of Wales was penitent and sincerely resolved to mend his ways, Maria Fitzherbert might resume with him the married state which was hers by right. The Prince of Wales was delighted. On 16 June 1800 Mrs Fitzherbert entertained four hundred guests in three marquees in the gardens of her London home, where they were invited 'to meet His Royal Highness'. Inevitably this proud gesture reminded her guests of a wedding reception.

'The next eight years were the happiest ones in my connection with the prince', Maria Fitzherbert remarked long afterwards. She purchased a house at Brighton, just across the Steyne from the Royal Pavilion. There the prince and his true wife lived, with little of the flamboyance associated with the later Regency era. The Whig MP, Thomas Creevey, visiting Brighton, described Maria as 'the best-hearted and most discreet human being that ever was to be without a particle of talent'; while he remembered the prince as 'always merry and full of jokes . . . a really happy man'. The caricaturists, fanning anti-papist embers, made mischief. Maria Fitzherbert, unpretentious and motherly though she was, appeared in their cartoons as a Jesuit schemer, eagerly seeking converts for a life which (so Gillray wrote) was full of 'indulgences, absolutions, luxuries and dissipations'. The people of Brighton saw Mrs Fitzherbert in a different light. They respected her good works and her kindliness. She was indeed a virtuous woman: she enjoyed playing whist and listening to music; she nursed and cosseted the prince, inducing him to cut down his drinking; she showed no interest in politics, but she appreciated good talk, and the Whigs were the liveliest conversationalists. Luxuries were few: 'dissipations' alien to her character.[16]

Visitors to Brighton were puzzled by the presence in Maria Fitzherbert's household of young Minny Seymour, whom the scandalmongers maintained was a daughter of the Prince of Wales. So, indeed, on occasions did the prince himself: but there was never any real doubt that the mother of Minny – Mary, as she was christened – was Lady Horatia Seymour, a daughter of George III's one-time governor, the Earl of Waldegrave; and it is more probable that Minny's father was Lord Hugh Seymour than the Prince of Wales. Minny was entrusted to Mrs Fitzherbert in 1799 when she was less than a year old because Lord Hugh and Lady Horatia (a close friend of Maria) had to travel to Jamaica. Both Minny's parents died in the summer of 1801; and, after a long legal battle in which the prince actively supported Maria, she was recognized as the child's guardian. The prince consistently treated Minny with a generous indulgence, showing her more affection than he gave his own daughter, Princess Charlotte. Probably he spoilt Minny. He delighted in the company of this pretty, high-spirited and intelligent child: she was, apparently, the first person to call him 'Prinny', sending him charmingly phrased letters as soon as she learnt to hold a pen and slightly more sophisticated ones as she grew older ('What a naughty personage you are dear Prinny to send me such new years gifts', she could write at the age of twelve).[17] The local Sussex newspaper – which described Minny Seymour as 'the interesting protégée of Mrs Fitzherbert' – dutifully chronicled a succession of entertainments and parties for th 'juvenile nobility' at Brighton each summer the Prince of Wales was in idence.

This eight-year idyll of the prince and Maria coincided with the climax in the naval war against Napoleon. Throughout three of the Brighton summers – 1803, 1804, 1805 – there seemed a real risk of invasion, if the French could only 'be masters of the Straits for six hours'. Once again the Prince of Wales chafed at his enforced inactivity. Were the king to give him a military command, so he argued, this show of confidence would 'excite the loyal energies of the nation'; and on 6 August 1803 he wrote to his father offering 'to shed the last drop of my blood in support of Your Majesty's person, crown and dignity'. The king was much gratified by this show of patriotism; he promised the prince that, when the French invaders landed, father and son would meet them in battle together, as had Edward III and the second Prince of Wales at Crécy; but, for the moment, he declined to promote him to the rank of General or allow him to see active military service in the field. At times the king's strict rules of conduct puzzled and exasperated his son. The king saw no reason why the Prince of Wales should not attend Nelson's funeral in a private capacity, but felt it was inappropriate for him to follow the cortège to St Paul's Cathedral as a principal mourner, representing his sovereign. Since the London crowd was deeply moved by the sight of *Victory*'s crew tramping through the January streets behind their admiral's funeral car, it is probable the king was right in his judgment; but the prince resented the royal veto. Once more he was excluded from any public share in the nation's triumphs and tragedies. There remained for him only social trivialities, a circuit of the great houses, staying sometimes in Gloucestershire, sometimes in Warwickshire or Derbyshire, Shropshire or Durham or Yorkshire. Occasionally a hostess would complain, in private letters, that the prince was a peevishly restless guest. None handled him so well as 'dearest Mrs Fitzherbert'.

In the second week of September 1806 the prince, with his brother the Duke of Clarence, arrived at Lotton Park in Shropshire as a guest of Sir Robert Leighton. Lotton Park, some eight miles west of Shrewsbury, was close to the Montgomeryshire border, and on the following morning the prince agreed to cross into Wales, being 'introduced' to the principality by a Welsh friend, Sir Richard Puleston. Years later Lady Puleston described this 'friendly but flying visit': the prince planted 'a young oak on the spot where he and his royal brother first trod upon Welsh ground . . . about a mile from Lotton, on the road to Llandrinio, where they were received with loud acclamation of the gentry . . . Sir Richard, in a very appropriate speech, addressed the Prince . . . at the same time presenting his Royal Highness with a sprig of an Oak Tree, which the Prince most graciously accepted, and said it was the proudest ornament he had ever worn.'[18] The tree was enclosed with a railing and marked by a plaque; and the visit is commemorated by the place-name 'Prince's Oak' which greets any traveller entering the present county of Powys along the B4393 road. It is a significant commentary on the neglect of Wales shown by successive heirs to the throne that such notice should have been taken of so brief an incident. These few minutes on Tuesday 9 September, 1806, were the first visit made by a Prince of Wales to the land from which he derived his title since the future Charles II stayed at Raglan in September 1642.

From Lotton Park the prince moved on some sixty miles across country to Trentham, Lord Stafford's fine park near Stoke. There he learnt of the death of Charles James Fox, on 13 September. Although their friendship became less intensive with the passing of the years, the prince still believed himself to be a Foxite, and he grieved for 'dear Charles'. He continued his planned autumn circuit as far as Wentworth Woodhouse in Yorkshire, but then hurried back to London for Fox's funeral. To his dismay he found that the king would not permit the heir to the throne to attend the service in Westminster Abbey or make any public show of his admiration for the dead statesman. The prince contributed £500 to the expenses of Fox's funeral, and then returned to Yorkshire. His host found him a sick man, greatly agitated over public and private affairs. The new Whig leaders, Grenville and Grey, did not bother to discuss political tactics with him: Fox had flattered him by asking his advice, even if he rarely acted upon it. Those days were over. With Fox's death the Prince of Wales ceased to be, in any sense, a man of party.[19]

He seems in that winter of 1806–7 to have come close to a nervous breakdown, and was himself painfully aware that at times he was seized with excessive loquacity, as his father had been on the eve of his illness in 1788. Apart from his genuine grief for Fox, the prince was troubled by the conduct of Princess Caroline, about whose private affairs such scandalous tales had reached other members of the royal family that they supported the prince's request to the king for an official inquiry to be made into her behaviour. The king duly asked the prime minister, the Lord Chancellor, the Lord Chief Justice and the Home Secretary to serve as Commissioners for a 'Delicate Investigation', establishing in particular whether the Princess of Wales was mother to an infant boy who was known to sleep in the Princess's room at her home in Blackheath. The Commissioners accepted Caroline's assurance that the boy was a labourer's child taken into her household as an act of charity, but they found her conduct liable to 'very unfavourable interpretations'.[20] The king was shocked to learn that she had romped immodestly with a number of naval officers, and duly drafted a royal reprimand. But the Prince of Wales had hoped the evidence would allow him to free himself for ever from 'the fiend' (as he called Caroline). In this hope he was disappointed. To his dismay the general public still sympathized with her as a 'discarded wife'. At the same time the prince began to find Maria Fitzherbert less understanding. Brighton, the prince complained, was 'too cold' for him. He liked the climate of Cheltenham, which was not much more than thirty miles from Lord Hertford's country seat, Ragley Hall in Warwickshire. And by the summer of 1807 it was clear that the prince was infatuated by that haughty, staunch Tory grandmother, the Marchioness of Hertford. There was no sudden break with Mrs Fitzherbert: he continued to favour her with letters and courtesies. But she was not prepared to share her husband with Lady Hertford or any other formidable grandmother; and she stayed in queenly dignity as the most respected resident of Brighton, while the Prince of Wales, hearing tales of his father's disconcerting habits, waited impatiently for a summons to the throne, or at least to the cares of a regency.

Yet it was not until the closing weeks of the year 1810 that George III's mental derangement manifested itself so markedly that the prime minister (Spencer Perceval) decided to introduce a bill of regency. At Christmas the king, now seventy-two, seemed at the point of death, but his physical constitution was remarkably tough and by the second week in January he was walking on the terrace at Windsor. It was thought possible that, sooner or later, the king would recover his mental stability, and the Prince of Wales sought to reassure public opinion by declaring that, were he made Regent, he would not change the government so long as there were prospects of a restoration of his father's 'good health'. A Privy Council was convened at Carlton House on 5 February 1811 and the Prince of Wales was sworn in as Regent of the United Kingdom before the Archbishops of Canterbury and York, the Lord Chancellor and nearly a hundred other members of the council. At the head of the room, as though surveying the scene, was a marble bust of Fox, specially removed to the grand saloon from the prince's private apartments as a token of past loyalties.[21]

The Whigs still hoped a Regency would bring them to office at last.

But after a probationary year the prince decided that, with military affairs going well in the Spanish Peninsula, it would be a mistake to throw out the Tories. He invited Grey and Grenville to serve in a broad-based coalition, resolved on winning the war against the French, but Grey favoured a negotiated peace, and only Sheridan's handful of supporters in the Commons were prepared to back the Regent. Soon two of the most vociferous Whigs, Brougham and Whitbread, were championing the wrongs of the Princess of Wales, thereby ensuring the lasting enmity of her husband. The parliamentary Opposition made the great error of concentrating on personalities, thinking in terms of heroines and villains, rather than voicing the discontent caused by economic distress in Lancashire, Cheshire, Yorkshire and the Midlands. The Regent, too, knew nothing of the new, harsh world of industrialism and when, in May 1812, the prime minister was assassinated at Westminster by a bankrupt commercial agent, the prince was deeply shocked. But at least he refused to panic. In seven weeks of careful negotiation, conducted shrewdly and responsibly, he found a successor to Spencer Perceval in an admirable chairman of committees, the Earl of Liverpool, who had been Home Secretary and Secretary at War. The new government was defeated on a 'no confidence' motion as soon as the prime minister met parliament; but the prince insisted that he should try again. This time he was more successful. The Liverpool ministry remained in power for almost fifteen years, a span unmatched by any of its successors.

As soon as he became regent the Prince of Wales promoted himself to the rank of Field-Marshal, personally designing his uniform. He enjoyed the trappings of soldiery and all his life resented his exclusion from active campaigning. From 1812 to 1814 he basked in the reflected lustre of Wellington's victories in the Peninsular War. His private letters to his mother show that he identified himself with the fortunes of Allied arms on the continent as a whole, believing he was present 'in spirit' at each great encounter from the Berezina to the hills around Paris. To celebrate final victory he invited his allies to London in June 1814. He found little difficulty in dominating King Frederick William of Prussia and he struck up a lasting friendship with the Emperor of Austria's representative, his foreign minister, Prince Metternich, whom he had first met as a young man. But he was exasperated by the behaviour of the Russians, Tsar

Alexander I and his sister, Grand Duchess Catherine Pavlovna. They befriended the Whig Opposition, asked awkward questions concerning the absence from court of the Princess of Wales, tendered unsolicited advice on the upbringing of Princess Charlotte, and courted popularity with the London crowd. Moreover it was galling for the prince to find himself upstaged by an emperor who had, in person and not in spirit, accompanied his army from Poland to Paris. The Prince Regent mounted a series of magnificent reviews and banquets for his guests, showing talent and ingenuity as an impresario of monarchy. He believed his very real sense of dignity and occasion would allow him to personify in appropriate style a triumphant Great Britain. But, except during the visit of the allied sovereigns to Oxford University, he won few cheers. The Princess of Wales, on the other hand, was applauded in the streets and in the theatre any evening she chose to seek public entertainment in London. Nothing could shake the conviction of his father's subjects that their regent was a reckless, extravagant hedonist.[22]

In those first years after the long war foreign observers feared that 'the Jacobins have crossed the Channel'. Blood was shed in rioting at Manchester and there was a flutter of tricolor flags and caps of liberty in the demonstrations at Spa Fields, London. At the end of January 1817 a shot was fired at the prince's carriage as he was returning from the opening of parliament; and prayers were offered on the following Sunday for 'protection of the Royal Person'. Yet the public mood was fickle. He was cheered when he opened Waterloo Bridge the following June. No doubt much of the warmth in this reception was a tribute to the Duke of Wellington, who sat beside the Regent in his carriage, but Londoners were also glad to see a fifth bridge spanning the Thames. John Rennie's nine semi-elliptical arches and Doric columns gave the new bridge a dignified grandeur well suited to Regency London. Other building projects patronized by the prince provoked a more critical reaction. John Nash's plan for London's West End, in which colonnades and crescented terraces were to stretch for three miles from the Regent's canal to Carlton House, was never completed. And the prince's own projects for expanding and adorning Buckingham Palace, for building a Royal Lodge in Windsor Great Park and eventually for transforming Windsor Castle, aroused as much hostility as had what *The Times* called his 'unbounded prodigality' at Brighton. The prince, as regent and later as king, contributed more to the splendour of the English scene than any other British sovereign; but the magnificence of his achievement was totally lost on his contemporaries, except perhaps the Duke of Wellington.

In November 1817 the prince was overwhelmed with grief at the death in childbirth of his only daughter. Princess Charlotte, a problem teenager in the early days of the Regency, was in May 1816 married at Carlton House to Prince Leopold of Saxe-Coburg-Saalfeld: it was a happy occasion, and the young couple settled at Claremont Park, near Esher, Surrey. Her tragic death shocked the nation. Yet so bitter was feeling against the Regent that, even in his deep distress, there were rumours the princess had died from his neglect; it was asked why he had gone shooting in Suffolk with the Hertfords when his daughter was expecting the birth of an heir to the throne. People said he should have been with Charlotte and her husband at such a time or at least near to Claremont. It was left to the septuagenarian queen, Charlotte of Mecklenburg, to reassure the prince: he had, she told him, made his daughter 'completely happy by granting her to marry the man she liked and wished to be united to' and by giving her Claremont where she enjoyed 'to the very last almost complete felicity'.[23]

Queen Charlotte died a year later, her eldest son in tears at her bedside. The king, existing in a world of his own at Windsor, survived her by fourteen months. The Prince of Wales was proclaimed King George IV by Garter King of Arms in the forecourt of Carlton House at noon on 31 January 1820. He was grossly overweight – 'Prinny has let loose his belly which now reaches to his knees', a guest at Brighton had written two years before – and easily susceptible to rheumatism. The cold ceremony of proclamation almost killed him. By the following evening medical bulletins indicated that the new king was suffering from congestion on the lungs. The longest reign of a British king was nearly followed by the shortest. Indeed, in Vienna, Prince Metternich (whose intelligence service was occasionally over zealous) was amazed to learn that there were now two kings awaiting burial in England. George was too ill to attend his father's funeral, and his doctors thought his general condition poor. They recommended him to be abstinent and take some rest; and as soon as spring began to warm the Sussex countryside he set out for two months at Brighton. A spell of residence in the Royal Pavilion was not, perhaps, an ideal setting for convalescence owing to the excellent standard of the cuisine. But he recovered speedily enough: the place was full of happy memories for him. He no longer called on Mrs Fitzherbert, who discreetly absented herself from Brighton on such occasions, but he was deeply attached to the idea of their old companionship; and in 1823 he increased her annual pension, on his own initiative, from £6,000 to £10,000, a sum she received each year until her death in 1837. Maria Fitzherbert knew she could never shine in the slightly tawdry flamboyance of the Regency. At sixty-four she, too, was content with the past.

There was no blissful glow of dawn about the new reign, only evening storms followed by a clouded sunset. George had been Prince of Wales for fifty-seven years and five months, much longer than any of his sixteen predecessors; and the problems of his principate continued to nag at him after his accession. Chief among them was the woman whom the king had recently called 'the vilest wretch this world ever was cursed with'. For in June 1820 Caroline, a voluntary exile in Italy since August 1814, returned to Dover claiming her rightful status as Queen Consort. Already in 1818 the Regent had consulted Liverpool over the possibility of starting proceedings for a divorce. Caroline's tempestuously vulgar way of life in Italy, and her adulterous association with her chamberlain, Bartolomeo Pergami, were well known. But the prime minister shirked the responsibility of seeking to end the Regent's marriage so long as Caroline remained abroad, not least because he suspected that a wave of sympathy for her would sweep through London and rock the government. Her arrival in England released just such a wave as Lord Liverpool had feared. Reluctantly the government introduced a bill which would have annulled the marriage and deprived her of the title of queen. For six weeks her private life was debated at Westminster, in what was wrongly termed the 'Queen's Trial'. Eventually, in the second week of November, Liverpool decided to drop the bill rather than face defeat in the House of Commons. The king was so indignant that he spoke, briefly, of retiring to Hanover.[24]

Caroline enjoyed a fortnight of hysterical adulation in London, but by the beginning of the new year she had become yesterday's sensation. To his surprise the king found himself cheered and applauded when he went to Drury Lane and to Covent Garden in the first week of February. He decided to risk an unpopular demonstration, and planned an elaborate coronation in which there would be no provision for a queen. When, on 19 July 1821, Caroline came to the abbey and sought admission to see her husband crowned king, she was turned away. Some of the crowd hissed her: for, whatever their feelings a few months previously, they were certain that the ritual pageant of coronation deserved a display of dignified loyalty. Although neither they nor the king knew it, Caroline was already a sick woman. Within three weeks she was dead, having been seized with abdominal pains while at the theatre. She was buried in Brunswick.

The king was not deeply affected. Caroline's death relieved him of the tragic burden he had assumed in his years of folly. He was, at the time, in Anglesey, about to undertake the first state visit made by a king to Dublin. He was greeted enthusiastically in Wales and in Leinster. So successful was this royal progress that he planned further state visits. At the end of September 1821 he set out for Hanover, stopping briefly at Brussels so that the Duke of Wellington could escort him round the battlefield of Waterloo. The king had a sound understanding of Europe's problems and his judgment was respected by continental statesmen. Next year he planned a trip to Vienna and possibly to the diplomatic Congress at Verona, but his ministers distrusted his friendship with Metternich. They persuaded him reluctantly to avoid foreign entanglements. Instead of Vienna, he sailed up to Edinburgh, where his state visit was as great a personal triumph as his journey to Dublin twelve months previously. Instinctively he saw the need to reconcile outlying regions of the United Kingdom to a dynasty which appeared to have neglected them. It was for this reason that towards the end of his reign he proposed to institute the 'Order of St David' for his former principality, giving Wales a form of knightly chivalry comparable to Scotland's Order of the Thistle or Ireland's 'Most Illustrious Order of St Patrick', which his father had created in 1783. He drew up a list of fifteen Welshmen worthy of the honour but his final illness postponed institution of the Order. His successor, William IV, did not share his brother's liking for what William regarded as costly flummery; and Wales remained without its order of knighthood.[25]

It is remarkable that George IV reigned for as long as nine years. His doctors diagnosed 'an organic disease of the heart' soon after his accession. By 1826 he was almost as much a recluse at Windsor as his father had been, his movements hampered by dropsy and by the effort of propelling his massive body from his rooms into a carriage. Frequently he was bored. Sometimes, in his conversation, he allowed imagination to confuse past facts with private fantasy: thus he convinced himself that he had been present with the 'Prince Regent's Own Royal Hussars' when the officers whom he knew so well led the charge against Napoleon's Old Guard at Waterloo on that evening in June 1815. He was not mad; strictly speaking, he was not a liar; he merely described what had long remained a romantic image in his mind. The bitterness of those years when, as Prince of Wales, he vainly begged his father for a military command left as deep a mark on his character as the frustrations of his marital life.

He died at last on 26 June 1830, a prematurely old sixty-seven. During his final days he made a request to his executor, Wellington, which puzzled the duke. He asked that he should be buried in night clothes 'with whatever ornaments might be upon his person at the time of his death'. Wellington found one diamond locket around his neck during his illness, and it accompanied him to the grave. Within the locket was a miniature of Maria Fitzherbert.[26]

CHAPTER NINE

Albert Edward and Son

QUEEN VICTORIA's eldest son and second child was born at Buckingham Palace on 9 November 1841. Once again, as in 1762, the boy was given status before baptism, becoming Prince of Wales on 4 December. It was not until the last week in January that he was brought to St George's Chapel, Windsor, where he was christened Albert Edward by the Archbishop of Canterbury. The christening followed a special ceremonial devised by the baby's father, Prince Albert, in order to add regal dignity to a simple service.[1] The primate was assisted by the Archbishop of York and by four diocesan bishops; the Duke of Wellington bore the Sword of State; and one of the godparents, King Frederick William IV of Prussia, had made a wintry journey from Berlin specially for the occasion. For the first time representatives of the press were admitted to a royal christening, which they reported with due reverence and appropriate length: 'The little gentleman', fawned *The Times* next day, 'behaved with a truly princely decorum.' The last Prince of Wales had been baptised privately in the queen's drawing-room of St James's Palace: the new ceremony at Windsor was intended as a public act of dedication, associating the sovereign's heir with service to her people. It was one aspect of Prince Albert's determination to rescue the British royal family from some thirty years of ridicule and contempt. Victoria and Albert were resolved that 'Bertie', as they were soon calling the boy, should not become a second Prinny.

As a seven-year-old child, Victoria had found George IV – 'Uncle King' – great fun. She remembered him at Royal Lodge, Windsor, 'large and gouty but with a wonderful dignity and charm of manner': 'Give me your little paw', he said as he stooped to take her hand; and a few days later he disconcerted 'Mamma' by a hearty 'Pop her in' as he set off in his phaeton for Virginia Water.[2] But as she grew older Victoria heard more and more tales of dissipation and extravagance. The harshest judgments on George IV came from her mother's brother, Leopold of Saxe-Coburg-Saalfeld, who, after his eighteen months of married life with Princess Charlotte, remained in England until he became King of the Belgians in 1831. Leopold, a great favourite of his niece, fostered the marriage project by which Victoria took as her husband his nephew and her own first cousin, Albert, a handsome and talented young man with whom she had fallen in love. In this closely knit family circle Albert heard similar criticisms of George III's sons from the same source; and they were amplified by the memories of Baron von Stockmar, who accompanied Leopold to England in 1816 and remained a counsellor to the Saxe-Coburgs for more than forty years. There were, of course, many English public figures capable of bringing warmth to the Regency ghosts for the benefit of the young queen and her husband. Wellington, who had always disliked Brighton extravagance, was reticent; but the queen's first prime minister, Lord Melbourne, had known Prinny since boyhood and remembered him with fairness and generosity. Only three weeks after Albert Edward's birth, Lord Melbourne offered the queen sound advice on the upbringing of her son: 'Be not over solicitous about education', he wrote,

It may be able to do much, but it does not do so much as is expected from it. It may mould and direct the character, but it rarely alters it. George IV and the Duke of York were educated quite like English boys, by English schoolmasters, and in the manner and upon the system of English schools. The consequence was that, whatever were their faults, they were quite English men. The others [i.e. the younger sons of George III], who were sent earlier abroad . . . were not quite so much so.

But in case this plea for the English system offended the queen by its insularity, Lord Melbourne remarked that 'Your Majesty cannot offer up for the young Prince a more safe and judicious prayer than that he may resemble his father.' That was, indeed, Victoria's wish: 'I *hope* and *pray* he may be like his dearest Papa', she wrote to Uncle Leopold in Brussels. She was not sure that 'quite English' was a desirable quality.[3]

Baron Stockmar, pious Lutheran though he remained, was disinclined to leave such matters to the will of the Almighty. If Bertie was to be shaped in the image of his dearest Papa, then he should be trained in moral leadership so as to become 'a man of calm, profound, comprehensive understanding'. The 'glaring iniquities' in the lives of George III's sons had sprung from fundamental errors in their upbringing, Stockmar argued. He recommended a rigid system of education from the age of seven onwards: no long holidays; state occasions and family celebrations might merit a break in routine; but ideally tuition should continue for at least five hours of intensive coaching six days a week. Stockmar's scheme was warmly welcomed by Prince Albert as a means of making the Prince of Wales worthy of the responsibilities which would fall to him in later life. For poor Bertie suffered the disadvantage, unknown to his predecessors, of having a father whose own status was undefined. There are moments when Albert's excessive supervision of his son seems to reflect, if not parental jealousy, at least resentment over his position at the English court: it was frustrating for him to stand almost, but not quite, at the side of his wife and sovereign. Victoria was impressed by the solicitude of Albert and 'dear old Stockmar' for her son's upbringing. She approved of the educational scheme, adding a directive of her own: the royal children 'should be brought up as simply as possible', she said, 'they should be as often as possible with their parents (without interfering with their lessons) and place their greatest confidence in them in all things'. Her uncles had been individualistic: her son would conform to the dull, dignified domesticity which enveloped Windsor and Buckingham Palace with the coming of Albert the Good.[4]

Had Bertie inherited his father's scholarly conscientiousness, the Stockmar plan might have produced the paragon prince of Albert's imagination. The boy was intelligent but never bookish. His later life showed he possessed a good aural memory for, while he hated having to read through a detailed memorandum, he could readily grasp the essentials of a problem from a succinct verbal briefing. As a child he found difficulty in sustained concentration on a printed text, although while still in the nursery he showed equal facility for speaking English, French and German, and he remained trilingual throughout his life. Yet Albert and Stockmar, analysing reports on the prince as though he were a scientific specimen, were convinced his slow progress sprang from natural laziness rather than from inappropriate teaching methods. Henry Birch, who was the prince's tutor from 1849 to 1852, handled him strictly but sympathetically and his cautious comments suggest he saw a need for elasticity in the prescribed teaching programme. His successor, Frederick Gibbs, a Fellow of Trinity College, Cambridge and a barrister, was a pedantically unimaginative as Stockmar himself. From shortly after the prince's tenth birthday until his seventeenth, Gibbs sought to impose his dry and humourless personality on his pupil. Yet Gibbs's published diary shows the difficulties of his task: the boy was bad-tempered and rebellious. Monday, March 8, was 'a very bad day': 'The P. of W. has been like a person half silly', Gibbs wrote, 'I could not gain his attention. He was very rude, particularly in the afternoon, throwing stones in my face. During his lesson in the morning, he was running first in one place, then in another. He made faces and spat.' Gibbs agreed wholeheartedly with Prince Albert that it would be best for the Prince of Wales and his brother, Alfred, to receive so much formal tuition, physical exercises and drill each day that they were left without the energy or spirit for mischief. As an experiment, Gibbs increased lesson time to forty-two hours a week. The queen was surprised to see her eldest son looking so weary and she was worried over his recurrent fits of incoherent rage. Fortunately the combined advice of the prince's other tutors and instructors induced Albert to cut lesson time back to thirty-six hours a week before Bertie succumbed completely to nervous exhaustion.[5]

Every essay and exercise written by the prince was submitted by his tutors to his father for inspection and comment. The queen believed the Prince of Wales suffered from unfavourable comparison with the Princess Royal, whose precocious academic gifts made her Albert's favourite child. If so, the prince showed no jealousy, for he treated his elder sister with warm affection throughout her life. His father's unwillingness to offer him any praise – a characteristic shared by Gibbs – seems to have demoralized him. Moreover, tuition was maintained for long hours outside the schoolroom. Walks in Scotland were educational and informative undertakings. There was little relaxation at any time. Bertie was expected to have some practical knowledge of horticulture, housekeeping, and even of housebuilding, at the miniature Swiss Cottage built in the grounds of Osborne House, on the Isle of Wight – his predecessor as Prince of Wales had similarly been encouraged to play at farming at Kew, also to please his father. On the eve of Bertie's confirmation, Prince Albert insisted that his son should submit to an hour-long oral examination of his religious beliefs which was conducted by the Dean of Windsor in the presence of the Archbishop of Canterbury as well as of his parents. 'Bertie acquitted himself extremely well', wrote Albert to Stockmar after that ordeal was over; but he was displeased by his son's inability to converse with eminent scientists brought as guests to raise the intellectual tone of the Prince of Wales's dinner table.[6] Albert continued to watch his academic progress like a masochistic hawk; the weaknesses on which he pounced seem to have caused him genuine suffering. It is hardly surprising if the chief emotion felt by Bertie towards so imperceptive a father was fear. Although by nature a straightforward young man, he was driven to dissimulate over petty matters largely through his father's inability to distinguish minor lapses in behaviour from offences which were morally reprehensible. Yet again a Prince of Wales was being asked by his parents to attain and maintain an impossible standard of conduct.

Gibbs, despite his limitations, saw the folly of allowing the Prince of Wales to grow up in isolation from his future subjects. He wished him to study and converse with boys of his own age. But the Queen and the Prince Consort (as Albert became in June 1857) reacted like the parents of the two previous Princes of Wales: they feared outside contact. Albert, after long thought and an exchange of views with Stockmar, began to encourage Bertie to find companionship in a group of selected schoolboys from Eton College at the age of twelve. The experiment was not a success: the Prince of Wales was rough and aggressive, probably from resentment at being an outsider pushed into a society whose members had long known the rules and conventions of agreeable behaviour. He had become a little more civilized by the summer of 1857 when four Etonians – all slightly older than himself and including the eldest son of the future prime minister, Gladstone – were chosen to accompany the prince to the Rhineland 'for the purposes of study'. Bertie was expected to keep a detailed diary and write letters to his parents full of his 'impressions of things'. But he was still not yet sixteen: much that he did, much that he saw, and much that was said to him remained as puzzling as the table-talk of the scientists. On 16 August he was entertained at Johannisberg by the 84-year-old Prince Metternich. Host and guest shared little in common. Metternich had first visited London in 1794 and remembered the then Prince of Wales as 'one of the handsomest men I ever saw'. He liked this new young prince, too, but found him sad and embarrassed. Bertie duly recorded in the diary which he knew his father would inspect that Metternich was 'a very nice old gentleman' who reminded him of 'the late Duke of Wellington'. Some of the prince's 'embarrassment' may well have sprung from sentimental Bonapartist sympathies. Two summers previously the Prince of Wales and the Princess Royal accompanied their parents on a state visit to Paris as guests of Napoleon III and the Empress Eugénie. These ten dazzling days at St Cloud, Versailles and St Germain made a vivid and lasting impression on the thirteen-year-old boy. Then he had stood respectfully beside his mother at the tomb of Napoleon I as veterans of the *Grande Armée* lit the side-chapels of the Invalides with their torches, and thunder rolled outside. Now, at Johannisberg, he was expected to admire the reminiscences of a retired Austrian diplomat whose name meant little to him but who seemed to preen himself on having outwitted the great Napoleon, inflicting the Waterloo of statecraft.[7] No doubt 'the late Duke of Wellington's' tales were more succinct and easier to follow.

Queen Victoria thought the few weeks spent by the Prince of Wales in Germany and Switzerland had 'done him good', helping him to grow 'so handsome'. His father, however, remained a grim task-master, for he was determined that his son should receive a university education. After three months intensive cramming at Edinburgh he went up to Christ Church, Oxford, in October 1859. There was no precedent for having a Prince of Wales in undergraduate society, and he was treated with great deference. His father decreed he should live outside college, in Frewen Hall off Cornmarket Street, a quarter of a mile north of Christ Church. 'The only use of Oxford', the Prince Consort insisted, 'is that it is a place for *study*'. Books were purchased to line the shelves of Frewen Hall, dons even crossed Cornmarket Street so as to impart wisdom to the heir of England in his own rooms; but it is hard to see that prince or university benefited from his four terms of almost residence. His greatest gain was self-confidence, and that sprang, not from his experiences at Oxford, but from his visit to Canada and the United States in the Long Vacation of 1860. It was in Ottawa that he fulfilled the first major public engagement of his life, laying the foundation stone of the Canadian parliament house. He then travelled by train to Washington, where he was guest of President Buchanan at the White House for a week. The Americans were pleased that a great-grandson of George III should have travelled down the Potomac to Mount Vernon and planted a chestnut sapling close to George Washington's grave, while the prince was most impressed by the size of the crowd which cheered him down Broadway during his few days in New York. His tact and amiability made him popular, for he showed dignity without being pompous. 'Come back in four years time and run for President', he heard a voice shout from the crowd in New York.[8] Those four years were to reveal the bitterest divisions in the Republic's history. Seventeen days after the prince left their shores, the Americans elected Lincoln president. Many of the West Point cadets who paraded for General Winfield Scott and the Prince of Wales on 15 October faced each other in opposing armies at Bull Run forty weeks later.

By then the prince himself was undergoing ten weeks intensive military training at the Curragh Camp, near Dublin, receiving promotion once a fortnight and passing out as a colonel attached to the Grenadier Guards. He was embarrassed by his father's insistence that he should not be 'detained longer at any one grade than would be necessary for his thoroughly mastering it'. The prince, who would have liked to make his career in the army, felt his father was showing a civilian's contempt for military affairs. The rift between father and son deepened after Bertie's return from America, partly because he was no longer a boy, but also because the Prince Consort knew well enough that he could never have fired the enthusiasm of a crowd as the prince did in New York. Albert, so conscientious that he was ruining his health with overwork, clamped down on his son's leisure activities as soon as he returned from America. After four terms at Oxford, he went up to Trinity College, Cambridge, for a year. He lived at Madingley Hall, a pleasant country house four miles out of town. The prince, though still under strict surveillance, gained more socially from Cambridge than from Oxford. But in his third term, a few days after his twentieth birthday, he received a letter from his father heavy with grief because of rumours that, during his weeks at the Curragh, he had spent an evening entertaining an actress in his rooms. The Prince of Wales admitted the substance of the report in a contrite letter; and on 25 November the Prince Consort came to Cambridge and appeared satisfied by assurances from his son. A week later Albert collapsed and late at night on 14

December he died, apparently from typhoid. The queen was almost mentally unhinged by this disaster. She blamed her eldest son for his father's illness: Bertie's escapade at the Curragh, she maintained, had cast Albert 'utterly down' because it confirmed the failure of the great experiment in moral education; and, not only had Bertie forced his exhausted father to come to Madingley, but he had even lost the way on a walk, and left Albert physically fatigued. Nothing could change what Lord Palmerston called 'the Queen's unconquerable aversion to the Prince of Wales'. Everything must now be determined by what Victoria imagined would have been Albert's wishes. There had been talk of sending Bertie on a four months' tour of archaeological and biblical sites in Egypt, Syria and the Holy Land; and the queen was relieved to see her son set out on this final educational venture seven weeks after his father's death. The Princess Royal — by now married to the Crown Prince of Prussia — urged her mother to recognize Bertie's good points, but without success.[9]

Even before the 'disgraceful affair' at the Curragh, Albert believed the time had come to find a bride for the Prince of Wales. The Almanach de Gotha could now be supplemented by photographs and there was little danger that Bertie would make so disastrous a mistake as had his great-uncle in agreeing to marry Princess Caroline. The Princess Royal liked all she heard of Prince Christian of Denmark's eldest daughter, Alexandra, and the Prince of Wales much admired her photograph. A 'chance meeting' was arranged when Bertie and Alexandra were sightseeing in Speyer Cathedral on 24 September 1861; and the Prince Consort was able to tell old King Leopold that 'the young people seem to have taken a liking to each other', before he learnt of the Curragh scandal. By the summer of 1862 Victoria regarded it as her duty to press forward arrangements for the 'Danish marriage'.[10] The engagement was announced on 16 September and 'the young people' were married at Windsor on 10 March 1863.

The new Princess of Wales, who was three years younger than her husband, was received in England with great enthusiasm. It was pleasant to cheer a fair skinned, auburn haired, gracefully thin eighteen-year-old through the streets, especially as the queen, at forty-three, insisted on retreating into a sombre and secluded widowhood. Tennyson caught the public mood when he welcomed the 'sea-king's daughter from over the sea', inviting 'all things youthful and sweet' to 'scatter the blossom under her feet'. But it was not only the Poet Laureate who was moved to verse by the royal wedding. As yet, the Welsh had seen little of their prince: a distant view of a five-year-old boy 'in glazed hat, blue jacket and white trousers' when the royal yacht moored off Caernarfon in 1847 as Victoria and Albert sailed up the west coast on their annual visit to Scotland. Despite the persistent royal neglect of Wales, the coming marriage of their titular prince aroused interest among a people accustomed to express their patriotism in poetry and music. At the Caernarfon Eisteddfod of August 1862 it was agreed that the poet Ceiriog Hughes and the musician Henry Brinley Richards should collaborate on a princely anthem. By Christmas Hughes had written two verses of *Ar Dywysog Gwlad y Bryniau* ('On the Prince of the Land of Hills'). Hughes's words were freely translated into English by George Linley and an additional verse added to the anthem, the title of which was changed to 'God Bless the Prince of Wales'. In this anglicized form Brinley Richards' composition was played and sung during the marriage celebrations. It remained popular as a loyal tribute to the heir to the throne throughout the empire until 1935, but the English words nowadays seem dated and the tune is a thin substitute for the traditional airs inspired over the centuries by a genuine Welsh patriotism. The bride and bridegroom of 1863 accepted the anthem as a graceful gesture from a musical nation; and five years later they received a rapturous welcome at Caernarfon Castle.[11]

By then the Princess was the mother of two sons and a daughter, and was expecting her fourth child. As in earlier reigns the Prince of Wales was recognized as the head of an alternative court. But whereas 'Leicester House' and 'Carlton House' had cocked an eighteenth-century snook at the sovereign's politics, the 'Marlborough House set' of the 1860s was politically neutral. The Prince reckoned MPs and peers from both the main parties among his friends, and he never considered organizing them into a pressure group. His companions were mostly rich, for his favourite pursuits were expensive, but they came from a more varied background than was customary in English court society. His close personal circle included industrialists and bankers as well as the landed nobility. Some of his friends were Jewish, some were Roman Catholic. They were cosmopolitan, too – Americans, French, Italians,

Hungarians, Portuguese. He liked them to be interested, as he was, in horses, yachts, hunting and the theatre. If they enjoyed food and good cigars, cards and a little gambling, so much the better. He would entertain them either at Marlborough House, his London home overlooking the Mall and St James's Park, or on his new estate at Sandringham in Norfolk, which was purchased for him with accumulated capital from the Duchy of Cornwall revenue in the last months of his father's life. In return he received hospitality in England and on the continent, visiting a circuit of great homes much as the Regent had done in the years after Waterloo, although railways enabled the prince to travel farther and faster. A whispering campaign of scandal linked his name with a 'troop of fine ladies' after only a few years of his married life. Alexandra treated his behaviour with tolerance, and it is possible that at times his 'affairs' were no more than heavy-handed flirtations with good-looking, quick-tongued women of wit and charm, many of whom were 'professional beauties'. The Prince of Wales was recognized as being gregarious, generous, and loyal, disliking uncharitable gossip and wrangling, whether public or private. He possessed an unquestioned flair for living, a quality that won for him – as for George IV – the double-edged distinction of being dubbed 'a prince of pleasure'.

Queen Victoria was puzzled and irritated by her son's success as arbiter of fashionable society. This was not what Albert and Stockmar had planned: she was saddened that he should show such a 'want of feeling'; and she thought that 'dear Alix' encouraged his giddy way of life, although she could also write of her daughter-in-law, 'I think her lot is no easy one'.[12] Most of all the queen blamed the vice and dissipation of London, much as had her grandfather eighty years before. Now and again the Prince of Wales's apparent extravagance provoked a blast from the radical press, a paragraph of reproach in one of the nonconformist dailies, or a headmasterly editorial in *The Times*. In the spring and summer of 1870 the prince received a bad reception in a London theatre and at Ascot races after he had been required to give court evidence in a divorce suit brought by his friend, Sir Charles Mordaunt, against his young wife. Although the prince was not cited as a co-respondent, the hearing encouraged a widespread belief that in his private life he remained an eternal playboy. But several journalists were righteously indignant at the high moral tone of their censorious colleagues and the prince was never unpopular with the public at large, as his great-uncle had been. In December 1871 the Prince of Wales almost died from typhoid fever, the disease which had cut short his father's life exactly ten years previously. Relief at his survival was widespread and genuine, and criticisms were swiftly forgotten in a wave of sentimental loyalty to the crown and its heir.[13]

Gladstone, the prime minister, thought the time right to seek for the prince a recognized post of responsibility which would ease the burden of business on the queen. It had been the Prince Consort's intention that his eldest son should 'early be initiated into the affairs of state'. But in this instance the queen ignored her dead husband's wishes. No use was made of those long, tedious years of preparation. It would, Victoria told the Home Secretary in 1864, be 'most undesirable . . . to place the Prince of Wales in a position of competing, as it were, for popularity with the Queen'. He was allowed to lay foundation stones, open public buildings, and serve as honorary colonel-in-chief of three regiments; but he was not consulted over the great problems of state, and active military service was denied him, as in the previous century to 'poor Fred' and 'Prinny'. Personally the prince looked upon himself as a soldier *manqué*, although he assured Gladstone that he was prepared to serve in a civilian administrative capacity if suitable employment could be found for him. Gladstone proposed he should take over the duties of a viceroy in Ireland, but the prince was far from enthusiastic over this suggestion, while the queen disliked the idea of her son representing the sovereign in any general sense, although she was glad for him to deputize for her on specific occasions. He himself suggested he might be attached successively to each of the great government departments in Whitehall so as to 'learn their habits of business'. No one liked this proposal, and the prince's further suggestion that he might serve as a member of the Indian Council to gain knowledge of the sub-continent was ignored. He kept up his round of foundation-stone laying but received no official post. Like his great-uncle, he enjoyed the few occasions when he took part in military parades. Indeed he showed a remarkable knowledge of uniforms and decorations. When in 1875 he became at thirty-three the first Prince of Wales to receive a field-marshal's baton (as opposed to helping himself to one, like the Prince Regent) veteran campaigners among Her Majesty's generals made some wry comments. But the prince was about to undertake a four-month tour of India which was intended to display the full majesty of the British Raj. As he disembarked at Calcutta no doubt the dress of a field marshal contributed to the aura of distant sovereignty, sustaining a rank worthy of the maharajahal magnificence awaiting him. A few weeks later, at Delhi, the field-marshal had the opportunity to lead the 10th Royal Hussars, 'Prince of Wales's Own', in a cavalry charge – on manoeuvres.[14]

The Prince Consort had encouraged his son to be interested in the affairs of Europe. It was therefore natural that, soon after his marriage, the prince should ask his mother for permission to see the most important Foreign Office despatches: this was the decade in which Italy and Germany completed their unification, changing the map of Europe and the fate of some of Bertie's closest relatives. But, although Albert had possessed his own key to the red boxes of Foreign Office papers, Victoria denied any such privilege to her son, fearing he would be 'unwise in his talk'. In 1870, when the ailing Napoleon III rashly allowed public opinion to force him into sending an ultimatum to Berlin, the Prince of Wales's sympathies were divided. He felt the French had provoked the war and he admired the professional skill of his brother-in-law, Fritz, the Prussian Crown Prince, during the early battles, but he was saddened to see the country he loved most on the continent ravaged by invading troops. That summer the prince was, as usual, in Scotland, staying at Abergeldie while the armies were locked in battle around Metz; he hated the inactivity. On 21 August he wrote to the queen, 'If only something could be done to stop this terrible war. I cannot bear sitting here and doing nothing, whilst all this bloodshed is going on. How I wish you could send me with letters to the Emperor [Napoleon III] and the King of Prussia with friendly advice.' But the Gladstone government could think of no way in which the Prince of Wales might mediate. Privately, like his mother, the ministers distrusted his would-be forays into diplomacy, thinking him indiscreet. Napoleon III was captured at Sedan, France became a republic, Paris was besieged, Fritz and Bismarck stage-managed the proclamation of a German Empire in occupied Versailles; and the Prince of Wales moved from Abergeldie to Marlborough House, and on to Sandringham and across to Windsor and back to London again, restless, frustrated, and easily bored. Yet despite his Francophile inclinations, by the summer of 1871 the prince was travelling in Germany, receiving a hostile press in London for gambling at Homburg but successfully concealing the fact that he had been shown round the battlefields of Sedan and Metz by the victors.

Sometimes he tired of being a privileged tourist. He was glad to be asked by the French to help organize the British section of the Paris Exhibition of 1878, a task he threw himself into with relief and enthusiasm. While in Paris that year he was able, by tactful conversations, to allay French suspicions over British policy in the eastern Mediterranean and in particular over the British occupation of the island of Cyprus. At home it was assumed that the Prince of Wales visited Paris for the delights of the theatre and the seductive charm of a gallery of pretty women: there was already talk in London of his infatuation for Mrs Lily Langtry, whom he first met in May 1877. But the prince did not spend all his time in Paris frivolously enjoying himself. He found it easier to exchange views with men and women of culture in France than in England and he was able to meet French politicians of the Right and the Left. Léon Gambetta, who in 1870 had proclaimed the Republic at the Hotel de Ville and who still remained the most influential political figure in Paris, regularly met the prince informally between 1879 and 1881: 'It is no waste of time to talk with him even over a merry supper at the Café Anglais', Gambetta told a friend, 'He loves France both in a gay and a serious sense, and his dream of the future is an *entente* with us'. This casual remark by Gambetta was prophetic, for in 1904 (twenty-two years after Gambetta's death) Edward VII's government concluded a convention with France which was accepted as the *Entente Cordiale* and which remained the cornerstone of British foreign policy for many years. But Gambetta was using the word '*entente*' in its true sense, as an 'understanding' rather than as a key agreement; and the Prince of Wales's views on diplomacy were based on the admirable and honest ideal of understandings between Great Britain and all the nations, not merely France. That had been his father's wish too.[15]

Thirteen years before the first of his suppers with Gambetta, the Prince had used the phrase '*entente cordiale*' in writing to the prime minister, Lord Palmerston, but he then applied it to his hopes for Anglo-Russian relations rather than to France. The British and Russian empires comprised between them a third of the land surface of the world, and successive British governments feared Russian ambitions in the Far East and in the Indian sub-continent. The Prince of Wales hoped to take advantage of family links with the Romanov dynasty so as to reduce Anglo-Russian tension: his wife's favourite sister was married to the Russian Grand-Duke who, in 1881, came to the throne as Tsar Alexander III and who was the father of the last Tsar, Nicholas II (reigned 1894–1917). This family connection encouraged the prince to make three visits to Russia before his accession as well as to hold numerous talks with his brother-in-law on private holidays in Denmark. Unfortunately the Russians, accustomed to autocratic government, thought little of the diplomatic overtures made by an heir to a constitutional monarchy; and his efforts in St Petersburg achieved far less than in Paris. He also paid six visits (as Prince of Wales) to Austria-Hungary, becoming a friend of the Emperor Francis Joseph, eleven years his senior. But in Vienna, as in St Petersburg, little store was set by the prince's conversations on world politics. In both capitals he sometimes found himself at a disadvantage because of his mother's continued refusal to allow him to see Foreign Office papers, a ban which Victoria only lifted under strong pressure from the government in 1892. Socially the Prince of Wales knew more about Europe's courts and capitals than any of his predecessors; he was a splendid emissary of friendship; but he continued to read little and only rarely did he penetrate beneath the surface of political life. He could size up individual statesmen and rulers – 'as weak as water' was his snap judgment on Tsar Nicholas II – but he assessed strength of arms by parade-ground appearances, an error that had led him to overrate Austrian prospects in the war of 1866 and French prospects in 1870. Popular legend attributed to him more influence and greater knowledge than he possessed.

The European capital with which the Prince of Wales had the closest family contact was Berlin. His eldest sister, 'Vicky' (officially styled the 'Empress Frederick' from 1888 until her death in 1901) served for more than forty years as the family go-between, easing the frequent tension which marred the relations of the English queen and her heir. The prince, for his part, tried to champion this liberal-minded sister in her struggles with 'Prussianism', as exemplified in Berlin by the policies of Chancellor Bismarck and later by the attitude of her eldest son, who was to reign as Kaiser William II from June 1888 until November 1918. The Prince of Wales never shared Victoria's indulgent affection for this first-born grandson. Bertie travelled to Berlin in 1874 and reported favourably on Willy's bearing during the ordeal of a Lutheran confirmation, but by 1880 he was criticizing his arrogance and brusque manners. It was, however, the tragic illness of 'Fritz', the Prince of Wales's brother-in-law, which first led to friction between Willy and his Uncle Bertie. Cancer of the throat cut Fritz's reign to a mere ninety-nine days (March-June 1888) ; his agony and early death saddened the Prince of Wales, who was intensely angered by his nephew's inconsiderate behaviour towards the widowed empress in the early months of his reign. The prince made no attempt to hide his contempt for the pretensions of 'William the Great', who duly declined to meet his uncle in October 1888 during a state visit to Vienna. His grandmother was exasperated by the young Kaiser's 'madness' in wishing to 'be treated in private as well as in public as "His Imperial Majesty"'.[16]

On this occasion the quarrel between uncle and nephew was soon patched up. The Kaiser visited England in the following summer : to his great delight he was made an Admiral of the Fleet, and was proposed as a member of the Royal Yacht Squadron by the Prince of Wales. For the next six years the Kaiser was a regular participant in the regatta at Cowes, frequently irritating his uncle by his obvious intention to steal the show. Both men enjoyed what Queen Victoria testily termed 'fishing for uniforms' : the Prince of Wales induced his mother to make the Kaiser honorary colonel-in-chief of the First Royal Dragoons ; and in return he was made an honorary colonel of the Prussian Hussars. But his German rank soon proved a source of embarrassment to the prince. In the summer of 1891 he had once more to appear in a court of law as witness in an action arising from allegations that a colonel of the Scots Guards had cheated while playing baccarat with the prince and some friends at Tranby Croft in Yorkshire the previous September. The British public, self-righteously nonconformist over such matters, momentarily turned against an heir to the throne whom the press revealed as a gambler ; and the Kaiser sent Queen Victoria a formal letter of protest, regretting that a Prussian honorary colonel should have become involved with a group of young men in a dispute over cards and gambling. It says much for the prince's desire not to aggravate Anglo-

German relations that he restrained a natural impulse to return his Prussian Hussar commission to Berlin.[17]

The Kaiser believed 'Uncle Bertie' was jealous of his status as an imperial autocrat and master of the most powerful army in the world: the Prince of Wales thought his nephew envied him social successes. Each man oversimplified the other's temperament and emotions; for the Kaiser, who suffered from an inner nervous uncertainty, needed praise and resented his uncle's occasionally malicious criticism, while the prince, a tolerant man at heart, had no desire to play the autocrat, although he was irritated by the importance attached to every word and gesture William made. At times the prince was much annoyed by his nephew's conversational asides. In 1884 and again in 1893 the prince had served on royal commissions which examined working-class housing conditions and the feasibility of introducing state pensions for the aged poor. He took these tasks extremely seriously, delivering a moving speech in the House of Lords on the poverty he observed in the slums of north London; but the Kaiser viewed his uncle's concern over such matters with lofty disdain. In Berlin he, too, had sought welfare legislation for the labourers: as he reminded his yachting friends at Cowes in 1893, it had been sufficient for the emperor to demand reform; not even Bismarck could thwart the imperial will. It is not surprising that uncle and nephew parted coolly after Cowes Week that August. The regatta always brought out the restless competitiveness in each of them. Two years later a series of ill-considered acts by the Kaiser deeply offended his hosts. On one occasion, while dining with the Prince of Wales, William remarked on the possibility that Anglo-French colonial rivalry in southern Asia might lead to war. Slapping his uncle heartily on the back, the Kaiser jokingly said, 'So you'll soon be off to India again, and we'll see at last what you're really good for as a soldier!' Over such matters 'fat old Wales', as he was called by the Kaiser's suite, remained acutely sensitive. It proved to be the last German imperial visit to Cowes Week.

The Prince of Wales invariably distinguished between essentially trivial family quarrels and the grave tension of two great competing empires, rivals in Africa and the Far East. Early in 1896 public feeling in London became furiously anti-German because of the Kaiser's telegram congratulating President Kruger of the Transvaal on the failure of a conspiracy by British colonialists to overthrow his government (the 'Jameson Raid'); but the prince, like his mother and the prime minister, behaved with masterly dignity, conscious that ill-considered words or deeds might prove as disastrous to the cause of peace as in Paris during the summer of 1870. The Prince of Wales helped entertain the Kaiser on a state visit to England in the autumn of 1899, soon after the start of the Boer War. Subsequently there were some sharp exchanges between uncle and nephew, when William tendered unsolicited advice on the best attitude to take towards the troubles in South Africa, but the prince was resolved to avoid provocative remarks. As he told a leading German diplomat, he would do all he could to improve the public appearance of relations between Britain and Germany 'whatever I may think of my nephew in private'. The Kaiser, for his part, remained deeply attached to his grandmother, and when the queen's health failed in January 1901 he cancelled his engagements in Germany and hurried to her deathbed at Osborne, supporting her with his one sound arm throughout the last hours of her life. This act of sentimental devotion deeply touched the hearts of many in England, including the new king, who hoped it presaged a fresh understanding between the two nations.[18]

The king chose to be known as Edward VII rather than as Albert I. It was a name which, as one of the parliamentary correspondents wrote, 'had a good Plantagenet ring about it'. But he had been Prince of Wales for fifty-nine years, longer even than Prinny, and it was difficult to think of him by any other title. The new heir to the throne was his second-born son, George Frederick Ernest Albert, who was thirty-five at his father's accession. Prince George and his elder brother were trained for the navy, serving 'before the mast' in sailing-vessels. Unlike his brother, who was created Duke of Clarence in 1890, George remained in the navy, serving in the Mediterranean for more than two years and taking command of a gunboat and a torpedo-boat, with the rank of Commander. The Duke of Clarence, a dissolute and witless young man much loved by both his parents, died from influenza and pneumonia in January 1892. Four months later Prince George was created Duke of York and in July 1893 he married his second cousin once-removed, the London-born Princess Mary ('May') of Teck, who had been engaged to the unfortunate Clarence at the time of his death. The Duke of York retired from the navy when he became second in line of succession to the throne but he retained a love of sailing and the sea, together with a naval officer's saltiness of language and keen sense of duty. At times he was overawed by his father's formidable presence but there were close bonds of affection and understanding between them, 'more like brothers than Father and son', as the new king had once written to him.[19] He lacked any confidence of style, and at first his world-vision was limited, but soon after Edward VII's accession the duke, with his duchess, set out on an eight-month trip to Australia, New Zealand, South Africa, Canada and Newfoundland, emphasizing the unity of empire and seeing for himself the impact of the British peoples in three distant continents. His journey forced him to become, with some reluctance, a public figure. On 5 December 1901, five weeks after his return to London, he delivered a long speech at the Guildhall in which he urged 'my fellow countrymen' to 'wake up' so as to safeguard the pre-eminence of the 'Old Country', which he saw threatened by what he described as 'foreign competition'. The vigour of his remarks surprised the Press. For the first time in many years a phrase of a British prince caught the world's headlines. Significantly, his diary recorded next day a personal visit by the German ambassador.[20]

He was already Prince of Wales when he sounded this reveille at the Guildhall. Edward VII chose his sixtieth birthday to honour his son. In authorizing the patent of creation, so the king told the prince, he was 'marking my appreciation of the admirable manner in which you carried out the arduous duties in the colonies which I entrusted you with'. There was no suggestion of any investiture, private or public. Although Welsh national feeling was more vociferous than for many centuries it was concerned with the politics of religion and education, rather than with narrowly dynastic matters. George agreed to become Chancellor of the University of Wales, a post his father had held for several years, but otherwise nobody thought he need interest himself in specifically Welsh topics. Nevertheless Edward VII authorized a gesture which he hoped would please Welsh patriots: in the second week of December 1901 the king commanded that the traditional badge of the red dragon should be added to the heraldic 'achievement' of a Prince of Wales.[21]

Having as he hoped woken up England, the prince was content to retire modestly into the background and allow his father to bask in the glitter of regal splendour. King and prince collaborated as amicably as

Edward III and his son had done. All important despatches from overseas found their way to the prince's desk as well as to the king's; he was consulted over naval and military affairs; and in the winter of 1905–6 he was encouraged to visit India and Burma, receiving homage there as son of the King-Emperor. In July 1908 he crossed the Atlantic, in one of the most modern and powerful cruisers, to open the Plains of Abraham in Quebec as a National Park, a voyage which emphasized the growing commitments of an heir to the throne towards the peoples of distant dominions. At home he paid visits to the House of Commons, taking his place in the peer's gallery for important debates so as to observe the political animal in its natural habitat. His persistence in going to the Commons pleased *Punch*: at the end of one parliamentary session an artist sketched him listening intently to a debate; 'A visitor as welcome as his appearance was frequent', ran the caption.

Cartoonists were occasionally tempted into malicious satire by earlier and later Princes of Wales; but never by the future George V. So free was his life from real scandal that, towards the end of his principate, a sensational tale was circulated by gossips in various levels of society. It was said he had contracted a secret marriage with an admiral's daughter while serving with the Mediterranean Fleet. This nonsense, which seems to have originated as a joke in the early 1890s and was then forgotten, finally appeared in print in a scurrilous periodical, the *Liberator*, published abroad but circulating through Britain. The *Liberator*'s editor, Edward Mylius, was eventually (in 1911) brought to trial; the story was exposed as a fabrication; and he went to jail for twelve months for criminal libel. It is curious so improbable a yarn should have gone the rounds at such a time: did it, perhaps, start as a muddled rumour in 1905, the year in which documentary proof was first given that an earlier Prince of Wales had made a secret marriage? But there was no Fitzherbert skeleton in this George's cupboard. His private life was blameless, although his tally of shot pheasants and stalked deer was later to offend the sensitivity of his official biographer ('For seventeen years he did nothing at all but kill animals and stick in stamps', wrote Sir Harold Nicolson with exasperated exaggeration to his wife). He was most at home amid the firs, bracken and heathland of Norfolk, for he was more naturally cast for the role of squire in Sandringham than ever his father had been.[22]

Edward VII continued as king his habit of travelling extensively on the continent. He believed, with some justification, that he was promoting international goodwill by his unruffled affability and tact. His state visit to Paris in May 1903 was a remarkable personal triumph: he was greeted with little enthusiasm and heard shouts, not merely of '*Vive les Boers*' but even of '*Vive Jeanne d'Arc*', for French patriots have a long sense of the past: he left, four days later, cheered by thousands of Parisians who were delighted by what they had seen, heard and read of his public activities and private gestures of appreciation; now it was '*Vive le Roi Édouard*'. In such a world the prince could not possibly compete with his father. George never liked 'abroad', nor did he understand foreign politics. In March 1890 father and son had been together in Berlin in the days immediately following the Kaiser's dismissal of Chancellor Bismarck and they duly paid a courtesy call on the fallen statesman: the future Edward VII noted Bismarck's prediction of disasters for a Europe deprived of his leadership; the future George V was only interested in the fluency of the great man's English. But, as Prince of Wales, George was prepared to assist the king in the external show of dynastic diplomacy. The Prince and Princess of Wales undertook a ceremonial visit to Vienna, where they were amazed by the stiff protocol of the Habsburg court; and in May 1906 they travelled to Madrid for the wedding of their cousin, Princess Ena of Battenberg, to King Alfonso XIII. On this occasion the bride and bridegroom's state coach – only three places ahead of that carrying George and Mary – was wrecked by an anarchist's bomb, and Alfonso and Ena were fortunate to escape death. A visit in that same summer to Trondhjem for the coronation of Norway's first king in modern times, the prince's brother-in-law, Haakon VIII, passed off more peacefully.[23]

It was, however, the Anglo-German dynastic bonds which continued to cause the greatest worry. Despite the sentimental pledges of family loyalty around Queen Victoria's deathbed, Kaiser and king quarrelled easily enough from the summer of 1901 onwards, although there were also frequent reconciliations. More serious was the deterioration in the relations between their two governments. The British were alarmed by the rapid growth of a German High Seas Fleet, while many leading figures in Berlin convinced themselves that Edward VII and his ministers were seeking to 'encircle' Germany, notably through the *ententes* with

France in 1904 and with Russia in 1907. The Prince of Wales undertook two visits to Germany, hoping to dispel the suspicions of the Kaiser and the more aggressive anglophobes of the younger generation. His three days in Berlin at the end of January 1902 were a marked success: the Kaiser treated 'Georgy' with irritating condescension, but was not provoked into any of those abrasive displays of arrogance which marred most encounters of nephew and uncle. In March 1908, with great reluctance, the Prince of Wales donned German uniform and travelled to Cologne to inspect the Cuirassier regiment of which he was honorary colonel-in-chief.[24] Once more the Kaiser was pleased by his cousin's apparent friendliness. He over-rated Georgy's influence on the shaping of foreign policy, both as Prince of Wales and as king, but he was right to assume that his cousin felt towards him none of that deep-rooted animosity which strained the customary kindliness of both Edward and Alexandra.

Sooner or later, as Edward realized, the King of England would have to satisfy the Kaiser's desire to receive him, and not merely the Prince of Wales, on a state visit to Berlin. At last he agreed to make the journey in February 1909. He found William on 'his best behaviour', an attentive and charming host. Yet the visit was hardly a success. The king was ageing rapidly: he coughed and wheezed his way down palace corridors; he fell asleep at the opera; he fainted and nearly choked after luncheon at the British Embassy. His physicians encouraged him to seek rest and sunshine at Biarritz, a resort which had long delighted him. He was glad to picnic or drive into the foothills of the Pyrenees, he liked to stroll along to the casino and watch the Atlantic rollers beating against the lighthouse or breaking over the brown rocks beyond the little harbour. At Biarritz his health rapidly improved. Unfortunately he returned to a protracted political crisis. The House of Lords threw out the 'People's Budget' proposed by the Liberal Chancellor of the Exchequer, David Lloyd George, and the king learnt that the prime minister, Asquith, wished to create sufficient Liberal peers to swamp the built-in Tory majority in the upper house. The king's conscience was uneasy over this tactic, he spent many hours discussing constitutional issues with his advisers and ministers, without resolving the problem. A general election in January 1910 confirmed the Liberals in office but left the king uncertain of his next move. Once more his health gave way, and in the second week of March he escaped again to Biarritz.

Spring seemed late that year on the Basque coast. The king developed bronchitis and could rarely leave his hotel. By the time he returned to London (29 April) he was seriously ill with asthma. Few people knew it, and he did not relax either his social activities or his public business. Shortly after noon on 5 May he collapsed, and his huge frame was shaken by a succession of heart attacks. The Prince of Wales hurried from Marlborough House to Buckingham Palace; and he was able to tell his father that one of the royal fillies had won the 3.30 race at Kempton Park. It was the last item of news which penetrated the king's consciousness. A quarter of an hour before midnight he died. 'I have lost my best friend and the best of fathers', his son wrote in his diary with all sincerity.[25] More formally, Europe mourned 'Edward the Peacemaker'; it was a title which would have pleased Albert and Stockmar.

Windsor

T HE body of Edward VII was taken from Westminster to Windsor for interment in St George's chapel on 20 May 1910. Nine reigning sovereigns and the heirs-apparent of five European monarchies followed on foot as the gun-carriage bearing the coffin was hauled up the hill from the railway station to the castle gate. At the head of the procession was King George V, with his uncle the Duke of Connaught to his left and his cousin the German Kaiser to his right. All three wore the full-dress uniform of a British field-marshal, the blue ribbon of the garter across their scarlet tunics, the feathers of their cocked hats caught by a light breeze. Immediately behind the Kaiser, watching him intently so as to remain in step at this slow and unfamiliar pace, came a slightly built naval cadet wearing the simple blue jacket with brass buttons and white collar-tabs of Dartmouth. For the past fortnight, the cadet – known to his family as 'David' – had been accustoming himself to the title 'Duke of Cornwall'. In four weeks' time he would become the twentieth of the English Princes of Wales.

Prince Edward Albert Christian George Andrew Patrick David was a month short of his sixteenth birthday at his grandfather's funeral, although he looked no more than twelve.[1] He was born during Ascot week at White Lodge, Richmond Park, which in 1894 was the home of his mother's parents, the Duke and Duchess of Teck, and which now houses the junior residential section of the Royal Ballet School. Most of the prince's childhood was spent at Sandringham, not in the 'Big House' but in its suburban annexe, York Cottage. At the age of eight his education was entrusted to a Norfolk-born schoolmaster, Henry Hansell, a history graduate from Magdalen College, Oxford, who once taught at Rossall. The masters' common rooms of English public schools were full of Hansells in the first years of the century, and for long after: muscular pipe-smoking Christians, strong on grammar and the fifteen decisive battles of the world but weak in imagination and needing outside help for mathematics, French and German. Hansell, who enjoyed golf and sailing and had gained school colours for football and cricket at Malvern more than twenty years before, was not so inhibiting as Frederick Gibbs in the 1850s, and Princes Edward and Albert (the future King George VI) liked him. He was honest enough to tell their father that he thought the princes would benefit from some terms at a preparatory school. But George V wanted his eldest sons educated as he had been himself: private tuition followed by a short, sharp spell in the navy. Hansell accommodated himself as best he could to the wishes of the family: he fitted up a schoolroom at Sandringham, and secured permission for the princes to play – or play at – cricket and football with children from the village school, ensuring that his charges were less socially isolated than their father or grandfather had been. But the task was too much for Hansell, a humourless man equally troubled by Prince Edward's mischievousness and by his father's gruff advice on what needed to be learnt and what did not. It was difficult in those days for a tutor to reconcile his responsibility for imparting a general, sound education with a parental ban on Latin and Greek as the Royal Navy had no use for either language. When the prince took the entrance examination for the naval college in February 1907, his educational attainments were praised in a report which surprised his father. The curriculum, however, soon revealed a weakness in mathematics, and from the prince's own later autobiographical writings it is clear he knew little about literature, drama, art or music. But the fault is not entirely Hansell's: neither of the prince's parents possessed intellectual interests or artistic tastes.

Edward was frightened of his father and ill-at-ease with his mother. King George was not a bully, nor did he ever neglect the welfare of his children: he had, however a brusque, hectoring manner and he hated innovation, whether in politics or fashion or convention. Moreover he was impatient, disinclined to listen to the explanations of any member of a younger generation. Queen Mary had greater mental flexibility and was more sympathetic than her husband to a widening of experience, but she deliberately restrained her interests and repressed her emotions as a duty within the family circle. Her official biographer quotes a revealing remark by Queen Mary to a friend about her sons, 'I have always to remember that their father is also their king'.[2] This parental stiffness checked the growth of any affectionate understanding between George V and his heir : they were never 'like brothers'.

Until George V's accession, the public as a whole took little notice of the 'young princes'. The sudden announcement that the king had created his eldest son Prince of Wales on his sixteenth birthday aroused widespread interest, especially within the principality. By the late autumn it was reported that the royal family intended to revive the long-lapsed ceremony of investiture. Traditionally the decision to associate the king's son once more with the Welsh people is attributed to David Lloyd George, the Liberal radical whose influence within the cabinet ensured that Welsh affairs received a better hearing at Westminster than at any time since the Tudors. Yet in 1910–11 Lloyd George, as Chancellor of the Exchequer, had other problems at the forefront of his mind. It is unlikely he would have thought of a public investiture for the young prince without the prompting of an old political enemy, a Welsh patriot Tory, the Right Reverend A. G. Edwards, Bishop of St Asaph for the past twenty-one years and an outspoken defender of an established 'Church' threatened by mass support for 'Chapel' interests. Dr Edwards (who was to become the first Archbishop of Wales in 1920) maintained in his memoirs that the Empress Frederick had broached with him the possibility of reviving investiture and presentation of the princes of Wales while she was staying at her mother's court as long ago as 1893. In the early autumn of 1910 the bishop wrote to Lloyd George emphasizing how much such a ceremony would heal divisions within Wales and remind the English of the separate identity of the principality. Lloyd George reviewed the merits of an investiture in talks at Balmoral at the end of September. King, queen and prince welcomed the idea. A committee on which both the Bishop of St Asaph and the Chancellor of the Exchequer served decided in favour of a public ceremony which was to include religious as well as secular symbolism. Although the possibility of investiture at Cardiff was duly considered by the committee, Caernarfon appeared the natural setting, even though the castle was in a poor state of preservation. The Marquess of Anglesey presented stone from the original quarries in order to renovate the nine towers and curtain walls. Remarkably this work, which necessitated the building of a special light railway to the Inner Ward, was completed within a few months. Seating was arranged for nearly 8,000 people inside the castle, with another 2,500 in the moats around the walls.[3]

The summer of 1911 – which was, fortunately, one of the finest on record – provided the young prince with a succession of ceremonial pageants. On 16 May he was, once again, beside the king, the Kaiser and the Duke of Connaught at the unveiling of the monument to Queen Victoria at the head of The Mall, outside Buckingham Palace. Three weeks later he was created a Knight of the Garter, walking in procession to the service in St George's Chapel, Windsor, a custom which had lapsed in the eighteenth century. His father's coronation on 22 June was followed by a naval review and other celebrations. Finally, on 13 July, the great ceremony of investiture was held at Caernarfon, a reigning sovereign coming to the castle for the first time since Henry IV marched his army there in October 1400. Considerable care was taken to satisfy English and Welsh sentiment during the investiture. The king, replying to a formal welcome by the mayor, told the corporation of the town that 'by his descent through the House of Tudor, my dear son derives a natural and intimate claim upon your allegiance'. The formal terms of the Letters Patent detailing the investiture were read, not by a Welshman, but by the Home Secretary, Winston Churchill; but in a short speech after the investiture the prince included some phrases in the Welsh language, an exercise for which he had been coached by Lloyd George at the chancellor's official residence, 11 Downing Street. Hymns were sung in both Welsh and English, and the closing benediction given by the Bishop of St Asaph in Welsh. The ceremony, which lasted for an hour and forty minutes, made a great impression on the participants, both because of its wealth of pageantry and its emphasis upon the principality as a live institution rather than an archaic relic.[4] After July 1911 the title 'Prince of Wales', long a remunerative courtesy bestowed by a sovereign on a male heir, recovered its territorial significance as a bond associating the royal house with a people who have nourished a monarchical loyalty through many centuries.

Queen Mary thought the investiture and presentation to the Welsh people 'a most picturesque and beautiful ceremony' in which despite 'awful' heat, 'David looked charming . . . and did his part very well'. The king, too, was pleased: 'The dear boy did it all remarkably well and looked so nice', he wrote in his diary. But the prince himself, who recalled later that he had been 'half fainting with heat and nervousness' resented having to wear what he called a 'fantastic costume'. White satin breeches, a purple velvet surcoat edged with ermine and golden embroidery, a purple silk sash around the waist also fringed with gold, white silk stockings, and black shoes with golden buckles did not suit an extremely youthful seventeen-year-old. Yet photographs of the Prince of Wales in 'this preposterous rig' (again his own phrase) sold well, in England as well as in Wales.[5] It was a summer of much industrial discontent, with more than eight hundred strikes or lockouts, and some newspapers encouraged their readers with harmless gossip about the royal family as a distraction from gloomier events. Inevitably there was speculation who would marry 'this young Prince Charming'. Even before the ceremony at Caernarfon there was talk of a 'romance' between the Prince of Wales and the Kaiser's daughter, Princess Victoria Louise, who accompanied her parents to London in the spring of 1911 and who was noticed beside the Prince of Wales at the unveiling of the memorial to their great-grandmother, Queen Victoria. Writing about these 'whispers' of romance more than half a century later, the princess recalled that her second cousin was 'very nice, but looked so terribly young, younger than he actually was'. She was, in fact, twenty-one months his senior in age and seemed far more mature and self-assured. 'The Kaiser would have some weighty words to say on the subject', the *Daily Express* assured its public while the 'whispers' were at their loudest. Perhaps fortunately, he was not required to deliver them. Princess Victoria Louise looked elsewhere, married the Duke of Brunswick in the spring of 1913, and did not meet her cousin again in England until 1934.[6]

The king had no wish to see his son turned into a London social idol so soon. Less than a month after the investiture at Caernarfon the Prince of Wales was posted as a midshipman to HMS *Hindustan*, a pre-dreadnought battleship attached to the Home Fleet. For twelve weeks he learnt watch-keeping duties and all the responsibilities of a junior naval officer at sea, trying to absorb these skills as rapidly as his grandfather had picked up parade-ground soldiering at the Curragh Camp fifty years previously. Then in early November the king summoned his son to Sandringham and told him he was to travel in France and Germany so as to widen his education, before going up to Oxford University for a few terms. This was an unexpected decision, and one that was unwelcome to Edward. Moreover, by a curious arrangement his tutor, Henry Hansell, was once again attached to the prince's suite, as also was Frederick Finch, who first looked after him in the nursery and remained as his personal servant until he became a naval cadet. A painfully immature young man, who had successfully sustained the buffeting of a naval gunroom and thereby acquired some self-confidence, was now thrust back into dependence upon the guidedogs of his boyhood. When, in April 1912, he made his first visit to Paris a wit at the embassy was heard to remark that the unfortunate prince was suffering from an excess of Hansell, and no Gretel.

Magdalen College, Oxford, welcomed Edward in October 1912. He enjoyed greater freedom than his grandfather had done at Christ Church, despite the presence of Hansell, Finch and a major from the Tenth Hussars sent by the king as an equerry who would improve his son's horsemanship. Sometimes his rooms in Magdalen were virtually besieged by sightseers, but he was able to join in the social and scholastic life of the university although he had the advantage of being excused all examinations. He drove a Daimler car, rode and hunted, played some football, cheered the college eight along the towpath, punted on the river Cherwell. His studies were general rather than specialized. He sat at the feet of Grant Robertson as he lectured on recent history (Bismarck), discussed problems of the constitution with Sir William Anson at All Souls, and listened to the idiosyncratic wisdom of the Reverend Lancelot Phelps, then Vice-Provost of Oriel, who as a former member of the Poor Law Commission was able to give him a donnish view of 'political economy', with special reference to problems of vagrancy. Each Thursday the prince, together with a half a dozen other Magdalen undergraduates, attended a tutorial seminar on the humanities in general given by Dr Warren, the President of the college. Soon after Edward left Oxford, Dr Warren wrote a report published in *The Times*, showing the advantages of providing the future king with six terms of residence at Oxford: 'Bookish he will never be', said the recently knighted Sir Herbert Warren with studied understatement, but he claimed that at Oxford the prince had been able to discover Englishmen 'both individually and still more in the mass', gauging character and seeing how it responded within a closed society. No one believed that he was, as yet, educated for the world and his diary entries for the summer of 1914 remain astonishingly naïve.[7] Yet he was, by now, at ease himself and able to make others at ease by his pleasantries of speech and manner.

This gift, enjoyed by Edward's grandfather, came to George V only in his later years.

The greatest formative influence on the Prince of Wales, as on so many of his generation, was what he called 'the grim school of war'. Sir Herbert's comments appeared in *The Times* on 18 November 1914: the remark that the prince had, in his leisure moments, 'shot at various country houses round Oxford' produced a wry smile on the charivaria page of *Punch*. For by now the world of weekly tutorials and drives out to Nuneham Courtenay and Blenheim was veiled in a distant past. Edward himself was with the British Expeditionary Force in France, hoping for service in the front line. He had entered the Grenadier Guards as soon as the Oxford term ended; when war came, suddenly in August, he asked for permission to go with his regiment across the Channel. At first he was faced with the veto which had kept at home many of his predecessors. At Whitehall he was told by the Secretary of State for War, Lord Kitchener, that while it might not matter if the heir to the throne were killed, 'I cannot take the chance of the enemy taking you prisoner'. The king could understand his son's attitude and, as the casualty list mounted, it was agreed that the prince had a duty to serve alongside his brother officers in France. He was attached to General Headquarters at St Omer, some twenty miles from the front line, and only permitted occasionally to enter the forward zone. But gradually this restriction was eased. By the autumn of 1915 he was serving on the staff of the Guards Division, under the command of the Earl of Cavan. He was present at the battles of Loos, the Somme and Passchendaele Ridge, although never allowed to participate in trench warfare. For two months in 1916 he was sent to the Mediterranean, arriving at headquarters in Ismailia on the Suez Canal at a time when the Turks still threatened to advance westwards into Egypt. During the winter of 1917–18 he observed the fighting in yet another theatre of war, following Lord Cavan to the Italian front after the disastrous battle of Caporetto. For the final months of the war he was back in northern France and Flanders, accompanying the Canadians as they advanced towards Brussels. Although trained as a naval officer, the Prince of Wales served in warships for only nine days of the four-year struggle. He thought of himself as a soldier, and it was as a soldier that his father's subjects remembered him in the twenties and thirties.

The prince had not been especially popular in Oxford; but the shared ordeal of war made this slightly built and diffident young man a familiar figure who was liked by thousands of men in the ranks. No one expected the heir to the throne to run the risks of a subaltern in the trenches, but it was heartening to see a future sovereign in the 'hot spots' on the Western Front, discovering the living hell of fighting in mud or marshland for king and country. On what Wellington would have called 'the other side of the hill', enemy troops were occasionally given a fleeting glimpse of Edward's second cousin, Crown Prince William ('little Willy'), as he was driven to headquarters in his official car as commanding general of the German Fifth Army. The Prince of Wales, by contrast, was a junior officer, who had won promotion to the rank of major by armistice day. His actions remained modest and he shunned formality. Although he had a Daimler car with him in France, he made frequent use of a bicycle. To see him cycling down the road to Poperinghe, or one of the other ruined villages along the Franco-Belgian border, left British troops with a memory which corresponded closely to their own experiences. They respected his courage and enterprise. So, too, did the forgotten army in Egypt, where British and Anzac veterans from Gallipoli were light-heartedly impressed by the spectacle of the prince, in shorts and sandals, on a training run before breakfast along the shore of the lake at Ismailia. It seemed fitting he should be deflating the pomp within the British monarchy at such a time, when more gilded dynasties were tottering to disaster.[8]

Technically in the eyes of the king, his son was still to make his 'entry into public life': he had not yet assumed the customary civic duties of an heir to the throne in a modern democracy. That entry came almost as soon as peace was signed in 1919, and it was on a grand scale. The prince sailed from Portsmouth in the first week of August aboard the battlecruiser *Renown* for Newfoundland, Canada and the United States. He was away for four months and then, after only fifteen weeks at home, he was off on a second voyage, again in *Renown*. This time he visited Barbados, Panama, Hawaii, Fiji, both islands of New Zealand, the great cities of Australia, Samoa, Trinidad, British Guiana and Bermuda, a seven month voyage. A year later the prince (and *Renown*) were off again, leaving Portsmouth on 26 October 1921 and not returning to Plymouth until 20 June 1922, having visited India, Burma, Ceylon,

Malaya, Hong Kong, Borneo, Japan and Egypt, a journey of over 40,000 miles. A fourth official overseas tour from March to October 1925 took him to the British colonies in west Africa, Rhodesia, the Union of South Africa and across to Argentina, Chile and Uruguay. These voyages enabled him to see – and be seen in – forty-five countries, whether dominions, colonies, dependencies or independent states. To the tours may be added semi-official visits to East Africa in 1928 and 1930 and a mission intended to boost British trade links in South America, a journey he undertook in the spring of 1931, after taking diligent lessons in spoken Spanish. These exhaustive tours, which were made almost entirely by sea or rail and never by air, served three main purposes: they perpetuated imperial bonds of wartime comradeship; they encouraged 'British Empire Trade' during years of bitter economic competition; and they identified the heir to the throne with his father's overseas territories at a time when 'dominion status' was conceding claims for freedom and nationhood. The prince showed himself to be a ready speaker, a sympathetic listener, a good salesman, and as fervent a believer in the moral trust of 'Empire' as any late-Victorian celebrating the Diamond Jubilee of his great-grandmother. Occasionally fatigue or irritation prompted a 'royal snub' and a sudden switch of temper from boyish spontaneity into the sullen peevishness of thwarted adolescence. No doubt there was justification for the worries of experienced observers in London who wondered if Prince Charming was now content to play Peter Pan. Old photographs and newsreels captured a gallery of hearty handshakes and genial smiles from a prince disinclined to grow up. Sometimes, in later tours, he was criticized for allowing private relaxations to cast aside the official programme of public events. But there is no doubt he worked hard to fulfill his duties of state.

Edward was at his best with ex-servicemen, principally with sailors, soldiers and airmen from the 'Great War' but also with veterans from South Africa, Boer and British alike; and while in Canada during his first overseas tour he was photographed asking a bearded survivor of Balaclava about the Crimean medals on his chest. In each of the dominions, and in the United States, he visited hospitals and convalescent homes for the war wounded, for he felt a deep compassion towards any who had suffered during 'the war to end war'. The *Prince of Wales' Book*, a 'pictorial record of the voyages of H.M.S. *Renown*' was published by the prince 'for the benefit of St Dunstan's, the home for blind sailors and soldiers'; and there were many similar fund-raising ventures which flourished under his patronage. He was an especially active supporter of the British Legion, the principal ex-servicemen's association in the United Kingdom, and was its official patron from its foundation in 1921 until his accession.[9]

The private life of the prince in the twenties and early thirties seemed frivolous to most of his father's generation. So, indeed did the activities of hundreds of other ex-officers, fortunate enough to enjoy wealth and social standing in the promised land fit for heroes. 'The public would be relieved to read a little less in the encomiums of the Press about the jazz drum and the banjo side of the Prince's life', wrote the sixty-year-old Liberal newspaper editor, A.G. Gardiner, in 1926.[10] But was Gardiner sure of the public mood? There were plenty who enjoyed speculating on whom the Prince of Wales would marry, others who wished their husbands or young men to follow his examples in casual dress, others still who were content to see him 'off-duty', at the races, on the golf-course, relaxed at a theatre, or at a night club. 'I've danced with a man who's danced with a girl who's danced with the Prince of Wales', ran the refrain of a popular song, reflecting the star adulation offered by younger and less censorious members of the public than Gardiner knew. By earlier and by later standards the British press was generously discreet in reporting the prince's social life. Nothing was said of the close friendship he enjoyed with Mrs Freda Dudley Ward from 1918 to 1934, nor of the presence with him on safari in 1928 of Thelma, Lady Furness ('Borne along on the mounting tide of his ardour, I felt myself being inexorably swept from the accustomed moorings of caution', she was to write with heart-throb imagery and deceptive candour some thirty years later).[11] This newspaper reticence may have come from the 'Press Barons'' resolve to keep journalists out of their own social set. It may, too, have sprung from a conviction that a staid, respectable monarchy was essential for stability in a world slipping too easily towards radical upheaval. There was sufficient novelty about the prince for editors to ignore stories which the public, still overwhelmingly conservative in moral outlook, would not wish to know. For most readers it was enough that he should be the first Prince of Wales to fly a plane, to be photographed smoking a cigarette, to ride winners in point-to-point steeplechases, to play polo, to ski, to popularize plus-fours and cairn terriers or to take a private holiday in Canada on his own ranch. His popularity ensured that he was always good for news provided it was good news: it needed to conform to the image in which the public saw their idol. He was the best known of all British princes; his voice, with its curiously flat Sandringham vowel sounds, was recognized by thousands of listeners to 'the wireless'. A people proud to possess the Prince of Wales, and conscious that other peoples envied them their possession, would not welcome columnists' gossip suggesting he was as much a playboy as any exiled princeling from the Balkans.

In the last weeks of the year 1928 the newspaper public identified itself with the prince in a shared emotion. While he was on safari in Tanganyika he learnt that the king was seriously ill with acute septicaemia and pneumonia. The British Press reported on 1 December that the cruiser *Enterprise* was on its way from Aden to bring the prince back to Europe. The 'eleven day dash from the wilds of Africa' excited readers who enjoyed their Jules Verne. Now they could follow *Enterprise* with 'her propellers thrusting her across the glazed, burning sea' from Dar-Es-Salaam to Suez in four and a half days; then a delay of twenty hours for passage of the Suez Canal; and on to Brindisi, completing a voyage of 4,700 miles in eight days. At Brindisi Mussolini placed his personal train at the prince's disposal and magisterially cleared the railway tracks of Italy for a rapid run to the Swiss frontier. Finally the evening papers of 11 December gave the worrying news that the prime minister had gone down to Folkestone to accompany the heir to the throne back to Victoria. The headlines next day said how 'silent crowds' gave him 'a quiet homecoming'; and a reporter at the station wrote, 'The anxious days through which H.R.H. had passed had left their mark on him, and there were many sympathetic references to the look of strain that overclouded his usually smiling face.' This was the respectful treatment which the public expected in their newspapers. Had they been told that the king, stirring from unconsciousness, opened half an eye and greeted his son with 'Damn you, what the devil are you doing here?', they would probably not have believed it. Regrettably the story may well be apocryphal.[12]

George V's will to live narrowly pulled him through his illness, but left him virtually an invalid throughout most of the following year. The prince accordingly spent more time in London, interesting himself in domestic political issues rather than in the Empire. In 1930 he asked his father for permission to turn Fort Belvedere, an eighteenth-century country house near Virginia Water, from a dilapidated 'grace-and-favour' mansion into his personal residence. 'What could you possibly want that queer old place for?' the king grumbled, 'Those damn weekends, I suppose';[13] but the Fort duly became the prince's retreat, where he was able to enjoy privacy and satisfy his enthusiasms for golf and gardening. Yet he did not scamp his duties. These years saw unemployment sharply rising as a result of the great economic Depression following the bursting of the American speculative bubble and the so-called 'Wall Street crash' of October 1929. Edward, visiting areas of mass unemployment in northern England, Scotland and the principality, developed a nagging social conscience over urban squalor. By temperament he was impatient for change: he thought little of Ramsay MacDonald's fumbling direction of affairs, and even less of the prime minister's specialist on unemployment problems, the Lord Privy Seal, J.H. Thomas, a Labour politician whom the king welcomed as a personal friend. In 1928 the Prince of Wales had become patron of the National Council of Social Service, and during the Depression he tried to ally the NCSS with the British Legion in a massive effort of voluntary service to relieve the social burden on the unemployed and, even more, to bolster morale in working-class families disillusioned with community life by the slump. He spoke out vigorously at a rally in the Albert Hall in January 1932, his speech broadcast throughout the kingdom; and in the spring he began a series of personal visits to clubs for the unemployed, encouraging men and women to find new occupations. A sustained personal drive of this character was new to the British concept of monarchy. Physically the prince's activity strained his nervous constitution and, in his precipitate desire for change, he was often intolerant of the politicians.

To some die-hards the prince seemed 'almost a socialist'. This he was not. But to several contemporaries it appeared as if Edward, like so many idealists who had found manhood under the discipline of war, was sympathetic to the romantic authoritarian creed of Mussolini's fascists. The prince had served on the Piave Front in the winter of 1917–18 when the allies were bolstering up the Italians after their rout at Caporetto.

The next time that he set foot in Italy was when he landed at Brindisi in December 1928 and was escorted to the Duce's private train : the contrast between the demoralized Italian soldiery in 1917 and the apparent orderliness and efficiency of the 'sixth year of the Fascist Era' was impressive. Not that the Prince of Wales was any more fascist than he was a socialist. He always scrupulously observed the neutral above-party role of the royal family, apart from allowing his car and chauffeur to carry copies of the government's official newspaper to Wales in the General Strike of 1926. Sir Oswald Mosley, organizing a 'New Party' with a radical right-wing solution for the Depression of 1931, claimed that the prince was 'sympathetic'. Some of the Fort Belvedere set were active supporters, although they broke with Mosley before the party became the British Union of Fascists. There is no indication that Edward was interested in the blackshirts of London. He made private visits to Italy twice before his accession, in August 1932 and September 1934, but never met Mussolini. Yet throughout the strained relations with Italy because of the war in Ethiopia (1935–6), the prince made it clear to British ministers that he was not a League of Nations supporter ; and, as king, he rejected Anthony Eden's proposal that he should receive the exiled Emperor Haile Selassie when he came to London.[14]

The advent of Hitler in January 1933 was greeted by many English people with satisfaction : here, they believed in their insular ignorance, was a strong man who would resist Bolshevism more effectively than any weak democracy. There is no evidence for supposing that the Prince of Wales viewed developments in Berlin quite so naïvely but he had long favoured Anglo-German friendship. He knew German, he remained in touch with several of his German relatives, and he had pleasant memories of a three-month visit to the Kaiser's Germany in 1913. Moreover in June 1932 Leopold von Hoesch was appointed German ambassador in London and in his four years at the embassy he became a trusted and valued friend of the prince, whom he had known in that last summer before the Great War. Hoesch had for many years worked for close collaboration between Germany, France and Russia. Over several points the Prince of Wales found his views coincided with those of Hoesch, for he had always believed that the Treaty of Versailles was unduly hard on Germany and stood in need of revision. More than once he had said as much to Hoesch's predecessor, Baron von Neurath, who became

German Foreign Minister in the summer of 1932, holding the post until February 1938. With Hoesch, Edward was even more at ease and relaxed, for he was so obviously a non-Nazi aristocrat popular with every society hostess in London. The prince had no idea that, from early 1934 onwards, his casual comments were treated with greater earnestness when reported to Berlin than such table-talk ever warranted.[15]

The king repeatedly warned his son against verbal indiscretions over foreign affairs: he had himself been misunderstood in pre-war times. By now old links were being cautiously restored with the fallen dynasties. In the summer of 1934 the king was pleased to entertain the Kaiser's daughter, the Duchess of Brunswick, and her husband (a first cousin of the king) at Buckingham Palace. The duchess found the Prince of Wales 'very forthright . . . extensively informed, particularly regarding Germany . . . unbiased'. On their return to Germany the Brunswicks received a visit from the Nazi party adviser on foreign affairs, Joachim von Ribbentrop, who told them that Hitler would favour a marriage between the Prince of Wales and their seventeen-year-old daughter, Frederica, who was then completing her education at a school in Kent. The duchess, recalling how in pre-war days 'it had been suggested that I should marry my cousin', refused to oblige the Führer, and Princess Frederica duly became the bride of the future King Paul of Greece in January 1938.[16] This proposed marriage intrigue of 1934 although attributed to Hitler himself bears all the marks of Ribbentrop's amateur diplomacy. He continued to show some interest in bride-hunting for the Prince of Wales during a special mission to London in 1935.

While in Britain Ribbentrop, like any other well-champagned celebrity, was entertained by Lady Cunard at Grosvenor Square. Twice in the same week Mrs Wallis Simpson was a fellow-guest with Ribbentrop (and so, on one occasion, was Churchill). Soon afterwards, on 10 July 1935, Mrs Simpson and her husband, a former Coldstream Guards officer working for a London shipping firm, were invited to a dinner at the German Embassy where the guest of honour was the Prince of Wales. There was nothing sinister in this: London hostesses had accepted for the past eighteen months that Mrs Simpson was the favourite companion of the prince, who barely concealed from his circle of friends the deep love he felt towards her. The embassy invitation merely confirmed the political significance now being attached to his infatuation with an American-born divorcee, living with her second husband in a first-floor flat in Bryanston Square, near Marble Arch. No mention was made of Mrs Simpson in the English newspapers or magazines.

The prince and Wallis Warfield Simpson first met in November 1930 as weekend guests of Lady Furness in Leicestershire.[17] They did not, however, begin to see each other regularly until the summer of 1933, when Edward frequently entertained Mrs Simpson and her husband at 'the Fort', as he called his Virginia Water home. In August 1934 Mrs Simpson, chaperoned by an aunt, spent a month with the prince at Biarritz, later sailing with him in a chartered yacht from Corunna to Genoa and extending the holiday for a week on Lake Como. She joined him again for winter sports at Kitzbühl in February 1935. Unexpectedly he decided to go on to Vienna and Budapest at a traditional carnival time, the last week before Lent. They visited both cities again seven months later. Throughout the spring and summer of 1935 the king and queen (who celebrated their Silver Jubilee on 4 May) were aware of their son's infatuation, but it is not clear if they also appreciated that he had ended all past romantic associations. The king, often 'feeling rotten' with bronchitis, had long been made anxious by the prince's preference for friends socially unacceptable at court, but he was reluctant to provoke a family crisis by criticizing his son's private affairs. If, as appears probable, the Prince of Wales was already considering renouncing his rights to the throne in order to marry the woman he loved, nothing was said between father and son of so dramatic a break in the stately rhythm of succession.

Tension did, however, arise between the king and the prince in the summer of 1935 over foreign affairs. In a speech at the Albert Hall on 11 June the prince urged that British ex-service men should 'stretch forth the hand of friendship to the Germans'; and his words were given exaggerated significance by the Nazi Press. The king sharply reprimanded his son for expressing views which conflicted with official government policy but Edward was unrepentant. He resented curbs on his self-expression. 'How would you like to make a thousand speeches and never once to be allowed to say what you think yourself?' he remarked to Winston Churchill.[18] A few days after the Albert Hall meeting the prince was at Berkhamsted School where, as he later wrote,

'I spoke not from notes but from the heart', conscious that his father would be displeased 'because I had embroiled myself again – and so soon – in politics'. For at Berkhamsted, an independent public school in Hertfordshire, the prince praised the virtues of martial patriotism, roundly condemning 'misguided cranks' on the London County Council who banned the use of imitation guns by boy cadets drilling at their schools. The speech aroused interest in the newspapers at home and abroad: it was thought of sufficient importance to merit a separate file of comments among the archives of the Foreign Office. Yet no one seems to have noticed that the Prince of Wales was, at the time, angry with the leader of the Labour-controlled LCC, Herbert Morrison, for rejecting a housing experiment he had proposed to set up on Duchy of Cornwall land in south London. The Berkhamsted School speech well illustrates the prince's immaturity of mind and judgment. Like a spoilt child he was defying his father and ridiculing someone who had given him an authoritative 'No'.[19]

George v was worried by his son's behaviour. He confided some of his fears to his close personal friend, the Archbishop of Canterbury, Dr Lang; and he remarked to Stanley Baldwin, the prime minister, 'After I am dead the boy will ruin himself in twelve months' – a shrewd prophecy, though it is significant that the king should still have thought of his heir, at forty-one, as 'the boy'. The king seems, however, to have shown some interest in the prince's desire for reconciliation with Germany for in November 1935 he took the unusual step of asking Sir Robert Vansittart, the Permanent Under-Secretary at the Foreign Office, for an assessment of the possibilities of reaching an understanding with Germany. Vansittart, an early believer in the Nazi menace, was convinced that an attempt 'to do a deal' would end 'in ignominy'. Soon after this enquiry from the king Sir Robert and Lady Vansittart invited Mrs Simpson to spend a night at their home in Buckinghamshire. Courtesy – coupled, perhaps, with knowledge of Vansittart's considerable influence – prompted Mrs Simpson to accept the invitation, even though she had no more than a slight acquaintance with her host and hostess. In her memoirs she recalls how uneasy she felt throughout the visit, as if Sir Robert were 'dissecting' her.[20] No doubt he was asking himself, as others did in the foreign service, whether it was mere chance that the social ascendancy of this attractive and amusing conversationalist coincided with the Prince of Wales's mounting sympathies for Europe's right-wing regimes. There is not the slightest evidence that Mrs Simpson was being 'used' by any foreign government. The British, however, had remained on guard against female interlopers in diplomacy ever since the Congress of Vienna, and the popularity of biographical studies of this period in the early 1930s may have tempted Whitehall into seeing Mrs Simpson as a latter-day Princess Lieven, or a Duchess of Sagan with a Maryland accent. Such roles were not for her.

At five minutes before midnight on 20 January 1936 King George died at Sandringham, the Prince of Wales and other members of his family at his bedside. The new sovereign flew to London next morning, where he was proclaimed King Edward VIII. It was an innovation for a king to be airborne, and it was a further innovation for him to broadcast an accession message to his empire : 'I am better known to most of you as the Prince of Wales – as a man who, during the war and since, has had the opportunity of getting to know the people of nearly every country in the world under all conditions and circumstances. And, although I speak to you as the King, I am still the same man who has had that experience and whose constant effort it will be to continue to promote the well-being of his fellow men'. Soon the new king's desire to modernize the traditions of court life was to arouse resentment and uneasiness, but he ensured that the funeral of his father was conducted with dignity and all the appropriate ceremonial. There was some consternation in the Foreign Office when he proposed, in a letter written in his own hand, that the German Crown Prince should be invited to represent the House of Hohenzollern at the funeral, but when it was pointed out to the king that, rightly or wrongly, the Crown Prince had been arraigned for alleged 'war crimes' under Article 228 of the Treaty of Versailles, he accepted instead that the fallen dynasty of Prussia should be represented by one of the Kaiser's grandsons.[21] Even so the list of official mourners includes some unexpected names: Baron von Neurath and General von Rundstedt from Germany; Marshal Mannerheim, the strong man of Finland; Prince Starhemberg, leader of the Austrian *Heimwehr*, a non-Nazi fascist movement; Marshal Pétain, representing the French army; and General Francisco Franco from Spain, where he was to plunge the country into civil war six months later. Only Pétain and Neurath had ever been presented to George V. Among the family mourners was George V's first cousin, the Duke of Saxe-Coburg-Gotha, a *Gruppenführer* among the Nazi stormtroopers. The duke sent to Berlin an extraordinary report on his talks with the new king who is alleged to have expressed a wish to meet Hitler, either in Britain or in Germany, and to have indicated he had every intention of concentrating government in his own hands.[22] If Edward VIII really spoke in these terms, then he was talking greater constitutional nonsense than any monarch on his accession since George III. Probably the Duke of Coburg was exaggerating, but it is a pity the German government should at such a time have been told that British policy would be shaped by a strong ruler who wanted an Anglo-German alliance. Within six weeks of George V's funeral Hitler's troops had entered the demilitarized Rhineland and torn up the treaties of Versailles and Locarno.

Edward VIII reigned for a mere 326 days. Thirty-three of them were spent with Mrs Simpson on a cruise in the Adriatic and Aegean, followed by yet another visit to Vienna and Budapest. Soon after his return he held a house party at Balmoral, attended by many members of the royal family, several of whom were disagreeably surprised to find Mrs Simpson behaving more as a hostess than a guest. American and continental newspapers and magazines were by now printing sensational stories concerning the king's private life, but the British press remained silent. Pictures of the king and Mrs Simpson on their holiday cruise aboard the yacht *Nahlin* appeared abroad: in England the photographs were edited so as to exclude His Majesty's companion. Under pressure from Lord Beaverbrook and the Rothermere family, the newspapers gave no publicity to the divorce proceedings at Ipswich Assizes where, on 27 October, Mrs Simpson was granted a decree nisi against her husband. But many public figures, from the Archbishop of Canterbury down to backbench MPs, were by then receiving anxious letters from members of the public who had seen American, Canadian and European press reports of an impending marriage between the king and his close companion. On Monday, 16 November, Edward let his prime minister, Baldwin, know that he intended to marry Mrs Simpson when her divorce became absolute and that if the government regarded such a marriage as out of the question, he was prepared to abdicate.

There followed three and a half weeks of crisis, most of it concealed from the public until the last days. On Wednesday and Thursday, 18–19

November, the king visited the distressed areas of South Wales, talking to the unemployed, listening to their problems, showing the sympathy he had displayed during the war years and in his dominion tours: 'Something must be done to find them work', he was heard to say to one of his official escorts as he listened, deeply moved, to hundreds of unemployed singing one of the Welsh hymns in a derelict area near Merthyr Tydfil. His concern raised hopes, and his evident determination to lift the blight from the principality won praise in the press. Subsequently it was alleged by some opponents of Baldwin that Edward was hustled into abdication because of his outspoken championship of the poor. There is no evidence that in the cabinet meetings of November and December anyone discussed the king's political initiatives in home or in foreign affairs: the sole problem was whether the British and Dominion governments believed their peoples would accept union between the sovereign and a woman who had divorced her two previous husbands. In Britain it was thought difficult to reconcile such a union with the king's status as 'Supreme Governor' of the Church of England; nor was there support for a morganatic marriage, which would have denied the king's wife the rank of queen. The Australian prime minister, Joseph Aloysius Lyons (a Roman Catholic), was strongly opposed to the marriage, morganatic or not; and so, less vehemently, were the premiers of South Africa, Canada and New Zealand. After the British press broke silence (on 2 December) a 'Stand By the King' campaign united Churchill, Beaverbrook, a few Liberal intellectuals and the British Union of Fascists in a short-lived Front. There was no show of support for the king: the working class was largely indifferent, apart from a vague feeling that 'they' were getting at 'him'; the lower middle class disliked the proposed marriage, not least because past speculation had conjured up for the Prince of Wales the image of a far more interesting bride, somebody with the glamour of Princess Marina, who had married the Duke of Kent in 1934, or with the natural charm of the Duchess of York and the Duchess of Gloucester. Among the remainder of the people there were many who, while prepared to tolerate divorce and remarriage in their own circle of acquaintances, deplored any lowering of standards in the monarchy. The king had not expected such hostility, which may well have been intensified by shock at the sudden revelation of a romance about which millions of his subjects had remained ignorant until the beginning of December. By Saturday, 5 December, the king had accepted the need to abdicate, if he wished to marry Wallis Simpson.[23]

An instrument of abdication was prepared on 9 December, signed next day at the Fort, and became effective at 1.52 pm on Friday, 11 December 1936. That evening 'Prince Edward' broadcast to the Empire from Windsor Castle, explaining that he found it impossible 'to discharge my duties as King as I would wish to do without the help and support of the woman I love'. He left for France a few hours later. His brother, King George VI immediately created him Duke of Windsor, a title intended to emphasize his membership of the royal dynasty, which had assumed the name 'Windsor' in place of 'Saxe-Coburg-Gotha' in 1917. The duke spent most of the remaining months of the winter at Enzesfeld, near Vienna. He married Mrs Simpson at the Château de Candé, near Tours, on 3 June 1937. A protracted honeymoon was spent at Wasserleonburg, near the Wörther See in Carinthia. Four months later the duke and duchess were Hitler's guests in Germany, Edward spending an hour alone with the Führer and his interpreter at the Obersalzberg above Berchtesgaden. They discussed the progress apparently made in social welfare under the Third Reich. After the duke and duchess left, Hitler remarked to his interpreter, 'She would have made a good Queen'.[24]

The duke's thirty-five years of happy married life as an exile, mostly spent in France, were in many ways a tragic waste of talent. He had possessed as a young man such a gift for identifying himself with the crowds who flocked to see and hear him that Lloyd George called him 'our greatest ambassador'. Some of these qualities were revealed once more during the four and a half years in which he served as Governor of the Bahamas (curiously enough, one of the few outposts never visited by him as Prince of Wales). Yet unfortunately he remained a poor judge of politics, politicians and the public mood. His behaviour in the summer of 1940 was extraordinarily inept, comparing unfavourably with the dignity and sense of proportion shown by the future George IV when England was threatened with an earlier invasion. For in July 1940 the Duke of Windsor sought to bargain with Churchill, attaching conditions to his return to England which included trivial matters concerned with the social status of the duchess. This long-distance wrangle, conducted from Madrid and Lisbon, became known to the

Germans, and Ribbentrop as Foreign Minister authorized his agents in Spain and Portugal to show willingness to meet 'any desire expressed by the Duke, especially with a view to the assumption of the English throne by the Duke and Duchess'.[25] Such heavy-handed intrigue never made the duke's loyalty waver. In 1957, however, it caused him some embarrassment when selections from the German foreign-office archives were made available in the original German and in English translation.

The duke continued to command affection among some of his former subjects throughout the fifties and sixties, and he was well received on his occasional visits to Britain. A public opinion poll conducted twenty-eight years after the abdication and twelve years after his niece's accession showed he was the 'favourite member of the royal family' to three per cent of those asked. On his death in Paris on 28 May 1972 his coffin was flown to England and lay in state for two days in St George's Chapel, Windsor; 57,000 people filed past the catafalque. He was buried at Frogmore, in Windsor Great Park, as Duke of Windsor and an inscription on his coffin recalled that he had reigned as King Edward VIII from 20 January to 11 December 1936. But to many he remained, as he had been for a quarter of a century, 'the Prince of Wales'. In her memoirs, *The Heart has its Reasons*, the Duchess of Windsor describes the difficulties she and her husband experienced in June 1940 when the French gendarmerie threw barricades across the roads along which they were seeking to escape to neutral Spain and Portugal. Credentials were inspected, progress slowed down in town after town until the duke remembered his open-sesame: '*Je suis le Prince de Galles. Laissez-moi passer, s'il vous plaît*'.[26] Even in the dying days of the Third Republic every barrier was lifted to please a Prince of Wales.

CHAPTER ELEVEN

The Twenty-First Prince

THROUGHOUT the reign of King George VI the heir-presumptive was his daughter, Princess Elizabeth, who had reached
her eleventh year at the time of her uncle's abdication. The prospect of female succession created an unusual situation. Apart from twelve
months in 1840–41 there had been no occasion when the heir was the
young daughter of a reigning sovereign since the days of Henry VIII.
From time to time during the war articles in newspapers and periodicals
speculated on a possible title for the future queen. As she approached her
eighteenth birthday, which fell in April 1944, it was thought likely that a
group of Members of Parliament would organize a Commons petition to
the king asking him to create his elder daughter 'Princess of Wales'. Such
a change of style would have been welcomed, especially in Wales, as a
reaffirmation of the traditional links between the community and the
dynasty, a sentiment emphasized by the shared experiences of wartime
bombing and suffering. The king, however, disliked the idea: he was a
practical man, tidy-minded and correct over such matters. 'Princess of
Wales', he argued, was a social rank borne by the wife of a Prince of
Wales. He did not see how he could give the title to his daughter, for he
was puzzled over the style she should then carry if she were married and,
indeed, over the position of her husband: it did not seem right that the
consort of a 'Princess of Wales' should be a 'Prince of Wales'. The king
accordingly issued a press statement before any Commons petition could
be prepared. On 12 February 1944 he officially denied that 'any change
in the style and title of the Princess Elizabeth' was contemplated 'on the
occasion of her approaching eighteenth birthday'.[1] Nothing more was
heard of the suggestion. When his elder daughter was married, on 20
November 1947, she became 'H.R.H. the Princess Elizabeth, Duchess of
Edinburgh'. The principality had to wait for several more years before
being given once again a titular head.

This discussion of the official title of the king's elder daughter was an early example of the wide interest being taken in the royal family by newspapers and by their public. The cinema and radio made kings and queens better known; and so, too, did the motor-car. By the end of the Second World War the monarch was a living person, not just a profile on a coin or postage-stamp. Gradually protocol and ceremonial were ceasing to be formidable barriers separating crown from people. As the monarchy became less aloof, so it could count more and more on the affection of ordinary men and women. They came to identify themselves with their sovereign's family fortune, bringing 'down the pride of sovereignty to the level of petty life', as Walter Bagehot wrote in the 1860s or 'wallowing in the royal soap-opera' as a less elegant critic said a century later. This humanizing of institutional monarchy implied an increasing loss of privacy. An enterprising journalist, seeing the Tsar of Russia return to his London hotel in 1814, thought it sufficient to write, 'His Imperial Majesty turned round to the people and most condescendingly took off his hat.' A hundred and forty years later newspaper readers were demanding something more than they could see projected on a screen. Uninhibited probing by reporters, many of them from foreign newspapers or agencies, began with the royal honeymoon of 1947 but was to become more intensive and obtrusive after the birth of Princess Elizabeth's first child, on 14 November 1948 at Buckingham Palace. Soon columnists and editors began to offer to the royal parents all the unsolicited advice which it was believed a paper's readers wished to see being given to 'England's No. 1 family'. Prince Charles Philip Arthur George, it was said, should be educated free from the fustiness of a palace, alongside his future subjects at their desks in the schools of the country. Well-intentioned letters, full of advice on rearing young children, began to arrive at Clarence House, Princess Elizabeth's London residence.[2] After her accession in February 1952 the flow of letters followed her, as queen, across the Mall to Buckingham Palace. For many of Her Majesty's subjects the new heir to the throne was 'our prince', with strongly possessive emphasis on the pronoun.

The queen recognized the truth in some of the press comments. Long ago it was accepted, even by Prince Albert, that it was foolish to isolate the royal children completely and successive tutors had stressed the stimulus of mental competition. But at what age and to what extent could princes and commoners mingle? At first Prince Charles received lessons from a Scottish governess, Miss Catherine Peebles, who taught him in an improvised schoolroom fitted out on the third floor of Buckingham Palace as soon as the prince reached his fifth birthday. Three years later he became a pupil at Hill House, a pre-preparatory school off Knightsbridge. There, for the first time in British history an heir-apparent was taught his lessons alongside other eight-year-old dayboys from families who were prepared to pay fees for their sons' education. Left-wing critics maintained that the prince should have been sent to the local state primary school: security considerations made nonsense of this emotive argument, such as it was.[3] From Hill House the prince moved on in September 1957 to his father's old preparatory school, Cheam, on the Berkshire Downs between Newbury and Basingstoke. Once again this was an innovation. Although the last three kings of England had been sent away from home for training as naval cadets at the age of twelve, none received an education which conformed to the usual pattern of mental training and character building for the British upper classes – boarding at a preparatory school until thirteen or fourteen, followed by four or five years at an independent public school and probably by three years at Oxford or Cambridge. In sending Prince Charles to Cheam School the queen and the Duke of Edinburgh showed that they had no intention of permitting a future king to be educated in segregated isolation. Press comment – and the newspapers found something to say about the prince or the school on sixty-eight of the eighty-eight days of his first term there – suggested that Prince Charles's name had been entered at birth for Eton. Several members of the royal family were Etonians, for the college had been closely linked with Windsor Castle since the reign of George III. But Cheam also prepared its pupils for Harrow, Winchester, Stowe, Charterhouse and many other ancient or distinguished foundations, while the best-known of Cheam's old boys, the Duke of Edinburgh, had gone on from the legendary, character-building Schloss Salem to Kurt Hahn's new school at Gordonstoun in the mid-1930s. There was, however, no need to map out Prince Charles's scholastic course in detail before competition with other boys afforded some clues to his character and aptitude.

Prince Charles had automatically become Duke of Cornwall at his mother's accession, although the title was rarely used, apart from its inclusion in the Mattins and Evensong prayers for the royal family of the Church of England. The queen had no wish to see any of her children involved in the pomp of public life until they were old enough to understand the significance of ceremonial. When Prince Charles accompanied his parents on a visit to Brecon, Tenby and Haverfordwest in August 1955 there was speculation that his mother might use the occasion to order the passing of Letters Patent to create him Prince of Wales, but the queen particularly wished to associate this act of great personal significance with an event of importance to all her subjects. It was therefore decided that the queen would announce the creation of her son as Prince of Wales during the closing ceremonies of the Commonwealth Games at Cardiff Arms Park in the summer of 1958. This decision was kept secret from the newspapers and the general public although Prince Charles himself was told, and so was his headmaster at Cheam. Early in July the queen was unwell with sinus trouble and had to have an immediate minor operation, which prevented her going to Cardiff. The Duke of Edinburgh therefore went to the Arms Park alone, on 26 July 1958, and the queen sent a recorded message which was broadcast through loudspeakers to competitors and spectators alike during the end of the competitive events. 'The British Empire and Commonwealth Games in the capital, together with all the activities of the Festival of Wales, have made this a memorable year for the Principality', the queen declared, 'I have therefore decided to mark it further by an act which will, I hope, give as much pleasure to all Welshmen as it does to me. I intend to create my son, Charles, Prince of Wales today. When he is grown up I will present him to you at Caernarfon.' The new prince, looking at a television screen in Berkshire ninety miles away, then saw and heard thousands of Welsh voices in the stadium burst spontaneously into Brinley Richards' anthem 'God Bless the Prince of Wales' which had not been sung for twenty-three years.[4] Never before had the creation of an English Prince of Wales been first announced at a ceremony within the principality.

A few weeks later the young prince accompanied his parents when they landed from the royal yacht in Anglesey, but he continued to be kept free from official engagements of his own until after his sixteenth birthday. At Cheam his work showed intelligence and he enjoyed playing cricket and both codes of football, singing in the choir, acting and taking part in all the out-of-classroom activities offered by a preparatory school with ninety pupils in a pleasant part of the English countryside. Occasionally there were security alerts and tiresome problems raised by intrusive reporters. This difficulty counted against Eton when the time came to consider the prince's further education. By contrast, Gordonstoun had the advantage of being over 170 miles north of Edinburgh and nearly six hundred miles away from Fleet Street. Prince Charles seems to have been slightly deterred by rumours of Gordonstoun's toughness and by the natural instinct in a son against wishing to appear as a carbon-copy of his father. An informal visit from Balmoral in the autumn of 1961 convinced the prince that Gordonstoun was not as 'gruesome' as it sounded; and he joined the school in the following summer term.

In 1920 Prince Max of Baden, who two years previously had been the last Chancellor of the Kaiser's Germany, founded a school in his castle at Salem on Lake Constance in order to encourage imaginative leadership and enterprise as well as academic attainments in the young. Prince Max had close links with Britain: he had married a niece of Queen Alexandra; and, after his death, his son was to marry the Duke of Edinburgh's second sister, Princess Theodora. But he did not wish Salem to become a modernized English public school with a foreign accent. It looked back to traditions of the German Enlightenment and, further still, to the educational theories of Plato. As headmaster Prince Max appointed his former political adviser, Dr Kurt Hahn, who like so many German liberal educationists, was a good classicist (and had, indeed, completed his university education at Christ Church, Oxford). Dr Hahn was a Jew; in 1933 he was arrested by the Nazis, while his school was closed for being a 'corrupting influence'. Under British pressure, the Nazis released Kurt Hahn and he was allowed to settle in Scotland, where he re-kindled Prince Max's ideal at Gordonstoun in the summer of 1934. By 1962 the school's curriculum was necessarily corresponding more closely to the general pattern of the British examination system, but the spirit of adventure, physical fitness and self-reliance marked Gordonstoun off from all other independent schools.[5] Dr Hahn retired in 1953 but his successor as headmaster, Mr F.R.G.Chew, had first taught at Salem when Prince Max was still alive and could therefore maintain at Gordonstoun the traditions of experiment which first surprised the educationists of Europe during the hopeful twenties. Prince Albert, one feels, would have approved of Gordonstoun and have recognized what it was seeking to achieve.

His great-great-great-grandson studied the normal subjects taught in the British public schools of the 1960s: mathematics, English, Latin, French, history, some geography and a certain amount of non-specialist science (mainly physics and chemistry). This was a wider syllabus than anything imposed on his recent predecessors as Princes of Wales although narrow by the standards of most other lands. Outside the classroom he had the opportunity to act, enjoy music, and play rugby or cricket. Active training with mountain-rescue teams, coast-guard watchers and surf life-savers was of greater value than any mere formal tuition; and the prince learnt endurance in long expeditions by canoe or by sailing ketch, going as far as the Outer Hebrides. Along with more than a quarter of a million other young people, the prince sat for his General Certificate of Education at Ordinary Level in the summer of 1964. He passed in five subjects but failed in two, including mathematics, which he gained at a later attempt. Normally the Advanced Level course takes two years, but the prince seems to have found the pace of life at Gordonstoun over-exacting and, like many sixteen-year-olds, was eager to break the monotony of term following upon term. As Dermot Morrah was to write, in the 'privileged account' of the prince's life, he had 'spent three years trying with his innate conscientiousness . . . to follow in his father's footsteps in all school activities, and in most of them with a creditable measure of success; but he was doing it against the grain'.[6] The prince therefore welcomed the opportunity to spend six months in Australia. At the suggestion of Australia's elder statesman, Sir Robert Menzies, the prince became a pupil at Geelong Grammar School, in Victoria, spending most of his time not at the main part of the school near Melbourne but at Timbertop, some two hundred miles to the north-east, an outpost on the foothills of the Great Dividing Range with gum-trees emerging from thick undergrowth. His experience of six months in the bush seems to have helped the prince overcome a certain introspective diffidence; and a trip to Papua-New Guinea gave him a new interest, anthropology.[7] He returned to Gordonstoun for his final year of schooling in September 1966.

While he was at Timbertop considerable thought was given, in

England, to his further education. On the Tuesday before Christmas in 1965 the queen invited to dinner at Buckingham Palace the Archbishop of Canterbury, the prime minister, the Chief of the Defence Staff (Earl Mountbatten, Prince Charles's great-uncle), the Dean of Windsor (Dr Robin Woods, who had prepared the prince for confirmation), and the chairman of the university vice-chancellors (Sir Charles Wilson).[8] These five guests were then asked to form an impromptu committee which that same evening would advise the Duke of Edinburgh on details of a general plan, agreed by the prince and his parents in private exchanges. This must have been a formidable task, even for such eminent men, and much was left open. It was, however, decided that the prince should go to at least one university and then enter the armed services without any long spell of training at the specifically service colleges of Dartmouth, Sandhurst or Cranwell. The prince himself chose Cambridge and, on the recommendation of Dr Woods, selected Trinity College, where his grandfather had spent a couple of terms in 1919–1920. But the Prince of Wales was determined to enter Cambridge on his own merits; and in July 1967 he therefore sat the Advanced Level of the Oxford and Cambridge Schools Examination Board, passing in History and French. The history papers included an optional 'S-Level' General Paper, on which Prince Charles gained a distinction. This was a good academic achievement, for the S-Level paper has always emphasized mature ability of judgment rather than any sheer accumulation of facts. To gain his distinction the prince will, for example, have needed to understand the role of successive historians in interpreting the past by the standards of their own age, and it will have helped him if he possessed ideas about the influence of geography on different civilizations or about the historical impact of the authorized version of the bible.[9] These matters require a skill in generalizing from a wide range of knowledge. No more appropriate examination paper could be devised for assessing the educational attainments of a modern prince, unless of course it is assumed he should speak a dozen languages and be capable of knocking together a nuclear reactor in the palace grounds.

At Trinity, Cambridge, the prince at first specialized in anthropology and archaeology.[10] He joined university societies and lived a more normal undergraduate life than had his great-uncle at Magdalen, Oxford, fifty-five years before. In 1969 he was awarded a half-blue for polo, his favourite sport. It was reported that his closest acquaintances came from the older public schools, such as Eton and Winchester, but he met many other types of student, particularly in college theatricals. He appeared in the Trinity revue *Revulution*, mocking an old cliché of his critics by standing solemnly beneath an umbrella and lugubriously intoning 'I lead a sheltered life'. To several columnists – and possibly to Prince Charles himself – it seemed improbable that he would buckle down to three years of academic work, reading for the Tripos like any other undergraduate. He sat for the first part of the Archaeology and Anthropology Tripos in the summer of 1968, passing with good Second Class Honours. He then transferred to the faculty of history, but took his sixth term at Cambridge off, so as to spend April to June in 1969 at the University College of Wales at Aberystwyth where he studied Welsh history, language and culture. So far as possible with this interruption to the Cambridge course, he continued to read for the History Tripos, taking his finals in May 1970. His name duly appeared under the 'Class 2 (ii)' heading of the Modern History Tripos list, and he proceeded to take his Bachelor of Arts degree. 'He would have made a very good schoolmaster', one of his tutors is reported to have remarked wistfully. It is a comment applicable to none of his predecessors.

Inevitably, by the age of twenty, royal functions were beginning to intrude on his academic pursuits and his moments of leisure. The most important of these events was his investiture at Caernarfon Castle on 1 July 1969, when the responsible department of state, the Welsh Office, encouraged a mood of patriotic exuberance, greater even than the celebrations of 1911. Extremist members of the Welsh national party, *Plaid Cymru*, deplored the continuance of 'Anglo-Norman' supremacy in their homeland, the so-called Free Wales Army rudely dubbing Prince Charles 'this German oaf'. Thirteen small bombs were exploded by nationalist fanatics in the twenty-one months preceding the investiture but without causing death or serious injury except to two bombmakers themselves. Even on the day of the investiture the royal train was delayed for an hour at Crewe while the police removed a hoax bomb, consisting of plasticine and a discarded alarm clock, from a bridge near Chester Station, and a young man threw a banana skin under the hooves of the Windsor Greys drawing the royal coach to the castle. Yet. despite these protests, most of Wales welcomed the investiture. Many had been pleased by a speech in Welsh given a few weeks earlier by the prince at Aberystwyth. During the investiture ceremony itself he replied to the loyal address in both languages. 'It is my firm intention to associate myself in word and deed with as much of the life of the Principality as possible', he declared; and on the day after the ceremony he began a four-day progress through the principality, travelling by road, by helicopter and by the royal yacht *Britannia*. More attention was given to Welsh patriotic sensitivities than ever before, but television enabled millions to share the delights of all this rich pageantry with the Welsh people in the royal borough itself. Much of the colourful ceremonial followed a ritual prescribed in 1911: the Earl of Snowdon now held Lloyd George's post as Constable of the Castle while the responsibilities of the Home Secretary, once fulfilled by Winston Churchill, were carried out in 1969 by James Callaghan. Fortunately for Prince Charles's dignity, the style of both coronet and robes had been modernized, thus shaking off the Fauntleroy image which had so distressed his predecessor.[11]

The prince, as Earl of Chester, took his seat in the House of Lords in February 1970, during his penultimate term at Cambridge, but he did not make his maiden speech until 25 June 1975, when he contributed to a debate on the value of voluntary service within the community. During most of the five years which followed the prince's graduation from Cambridge, he tried to divide his time between fulfilling public engagements, honouring his pledge to the Welsh, and gaining experience of life in the Royal Air Force and the Royal Navy. His first training flight took place at Tangmere during the Long Vacation of 1968 and he had flown solo before he left the university. To qualify for his 'wings' as an air force pilot at Cranwell he had to learn to fly jets, as well as co-piloting a supersonic Phantom and voluntarily making a parachute drop into the Channel. He passed out from Cranwell, after completing the advanced flying course, in August 1971. Two months later he was at Dartmouth as a Sub-Lieutenant, Royal Navy. He was posted to several vessels, including the Leander class frigate, HMS *Jupiter*, in which he served as communications officer as she sailed across the Atlantic and the Pacific in 1974. After qualifying as a helicopter pilot aboard the commando-carrier *Hermes*, he was given command of the minehunter HMS *Bronington* at Rosyth in January 1976, serving mainly in the North Sea. At the end of

August 1976 he took *Bronington* into the Baltic to the German port of Lubeck, thus renewing a family acquaintance with the waters around Kiel which went back nearly ninety years but had not always been so amicable.

The Prince of Wales retired from active service in the Royal Navy in December 1976 because of the pressure of official duties. Conscience impelled him, however, to take on yet another gruelling course of training in 1978. As colonel-in-chief of the Parachute Regiment he believed it wrong for him to contemplate wearing their uniform without being trained himself as a paratrooper. He therefore undertook the full paratroop-officer's course so that he might proudly add a parachutist's wings to his military insignia. Yet for most of the period after his retirement from the navy the prince concentrated on his official duties. There were, for example, a reservoir to be opened at Mold in Clwyd and a new steelworks in which he was interested at Cardiff; and he undertook in March 1977 a twenty-five-day visit to Ghana and the Ivory Coast. For a year, from April 24 1977 until May 4 1978, the prince was primarily concerned with furthering the Queen's Silver Jubilee Appeal, a campaign of which he was president 'to help young people help themselves'. Already he had chaired many meetings to plan the campaign and he is reported to have shown himself a good public relations man, raising sixteen million pounds for causes which matter for him. 'I cannot help feeling that there is a great deal of untapped enthusiasm amongst young people in this country who want to involve themselves in the more challenging and adventurous aspects of community services but who find it difficult to know where to begin', he said.[12] These were sentiments Dr Hahn would readily have understood.

Like his immediate predecessors, the Prince of Wales has kept in close personal touch with the old dominions and former colonies. He has also made several visits to the United States, and he scored considerable personal success in communist Yugoslavia. Air travel has eased the burdens of long journeys, but he has been left with one far greater problem than his predecessors. Photographers and journalists shadow him relentlessly, eager for an off-the-cuff comment or a snap of him in the company of an attractive girl. It must seem sometimes to him that 'next-queen-spotting' is the most popular speculative recreation of three continents. He has had to accustom himself to projecting a personality on to the tiny screens of people's sitting rooms throughout vastly different communities in the English-speaking world. This difficult and accident-prone task – something far harder than the radio broadcasts of his great-uncle – he has accomplished with all the confidence of someone who enjoyed making an ass of himself in a college revue. His television appearances have been marked by good humour and a revelation to viewers of his unusually wide range of interests and sympathies. In November 1975 a documentary programme struck a fine balance between his duties as a serving naval officer, his ceremonial obligations as Great Master of the Most Honourable Order of the Bath, and his leisure activities, including his love of music and delight in Goon Show comedy: 'I would have been committed to an institution long ago were it not for my ability to see the funny side of life', he declared. Occasionally light-hearted throw-away lines recoil and almost trip him up. It was, for example, safe for him to say in November 1975 that he thought thirty was about the right age to marry: by November 1978 he may well have wished he had followed Aristotle and kept the reporters at bay for another seven years by opting for thirty-seven.[13]

'All the world and all the glory in it, whatever is most attractive, whatever is most seductive, has always been offered to the Prince of Wales of the day, and always will be', wrote Walter Bagehot in 1867: 'It is not rational to expect the best virtue where temptation is applied in the most trying form at the frailest time of human life', he added, casting a critical eye at a monarchy which he saw as represented by 'a retired widow and an unemployed youth.'[14] If Bagehot's scathing words seem no longer applicable, it is because a conscious effort has been made to give the concept of Prince of Wales both status and mission, as in the days of the Black Prince. Common sense now once again associates the prince with the principality whose name he bears. The training of a Prince of Wales is recognized as a step towards kingship, something marked by collaboration between sovereign and heir rather than a senseless and suspicious conflict of generations. Outwardly there seems little resemblance between earlier Princes of Wales and this present jet-flier, naval commander, helicopter pilot, parachutist, polo half-blue, tank-driver, 'cellist, comedy-actor, BA(Cantab) who is also a keen anthropologist, Welsh linguist and active patron of 170 institutions. Yet there is both continuity and familiarity, a sense of the past brought into the later twentieth century. For the wide interests, skills and enthusiasms of Prince Charles reflect the varied needs of a modern society: he can do much more than his predecessors, just as Henry Stuart or Henry Tudor could achieve far more than the recognizably medieval figures of the earliest English princes. There is little doubt that, through seven centuries, every generation has had the Prince of Wales it deserves.

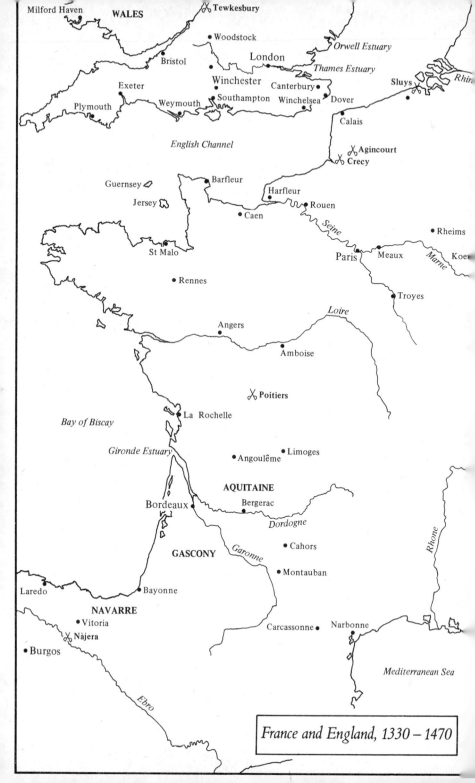

Milford Haven
WALES
⚔ **Tewkesbury**
● Woodstock
Orwell Estuary
● Bristol
London
Thames Estuary
Winchester
Canterbury
Sluys ⚔
Rhin
Exeter
Southampton
Winchelsea
Dover
Plymouth
Weymouth
● Dover
Calais ●
English Channel
⚔ **Agincourt**
⚔ **Crecy**
Guernsey ⬦
● Barfleur
Harfleur ●
● Rouen
Jersey ⬦
● Caen
Seine
● Rheims
Koe
St Malo
Paris ●
● Meaux
Marne
● Rennes
● Troyes
Loire
● Angers
● Amboise
⚔ **Poitiers**
Bay of Biscay
● La Rochelle
Gironde Estuary
● Limoges
● Angoulême
AQUITAINE
● Bergerac
Bordeaux ●
Dordogne
● Cahors
GASCONY
Garonne
● Montauban
Laredo ●
● Bayonne
Rhone
NAVARRE
● Vitoria
Carcassonne ●
Narbonne ●
⚔ **Nàjera**
● Burgos
Mediterranean Sea
Ebro

France and England, 1330 – 1470

England and Wales in the
fourteenth and fifteenth centuries

///// Principality of Wales

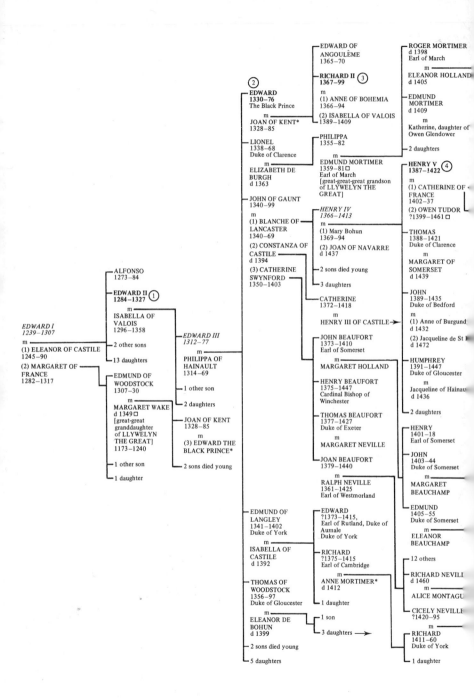

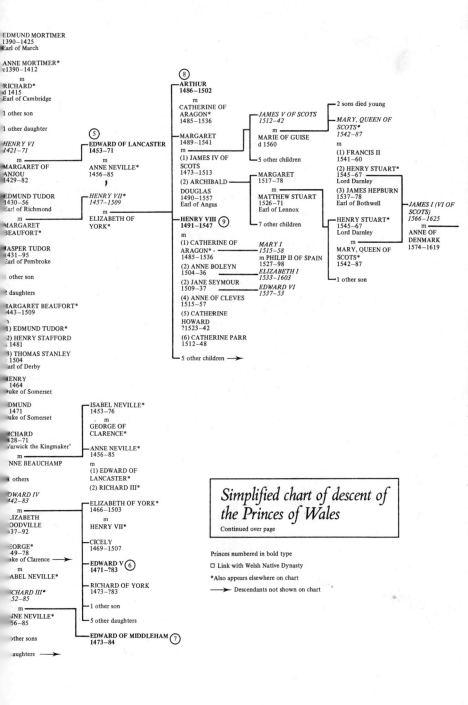

EDMUND MORTIMER
1390–1425
Earl of March

ANNE MORTIMER*
c1390–1412
m
RICHARD*
d 1415
Earl of Cambridge

1 other son

1 other daughter

HENRY VI
1421–71
m
MARGARET OF ANJOU
1429–82

EDMUND TUDOR
1430–56
Earl of Richmond
m
MARGARET BEAUFORT*

JASPER TUDOR
1431–95
Earl of Pembroke

1 other son

2 daughters

MARGARET BEAUFORT*
1443–1509
m
(1) EDMUND TUDOR*
(2) HENRY STAFFORD d 1481
(3) THOMAS STANLEY d 1504 Earl of Derby

HENRY
1464
Duke of Somerset

EDMUND
1471
Duke of Somerset

RICHARD
1428–71
'Warwick the Kingmaker'
m
ANNE BEAUCHAMP

4 others

EDWARD IV
1442–83
m
ELIZABETH WOODVILLE
1437–92

GEORGE*
1449–78
Duke of Clarence
m
ISABEL NEVILLE*

RICHARD III*
1452–85
m
ANNE NEVILLE*
1456–85

other sons

daughters →

EDWARD OF LANCASTER (5)
1453–71
m
ANNE NEVILLE*
1456–85

HENRY VII*
1457–1509
m
ELIZABETH OF YORK*

ISABEL NEVILLE*
1453–76
m
GEORGE OF CLARENCE*

ANNE NEVILLE*
1456–85
m
(1) EDWARD OF LANCASTER*
(2) RICHARD III*

ELIZABETH OF YORK*
1466–1503
m
HENRY VII*

CICELY
1469–1507

EDWARD V (6)
1471–?83

RICHARD OF YORK
1473–?83

1 other son

5 other daughters

EDWARD OF MIDDLEHAM (7)
1473–84

ARTHUR (8)
1486–1502
m
CATHERINE OF ARAGON*
1485–1536

MARGARET
1489–1541
m
(1) JAMES IV OF SCOTS 1473–1513
(2) ARCHIBALD DOUGLAS 1490–1557 Earl of Angus

HENRY VIII (9)
1491–1547
m
(1) CATHERINE OF ARAGON* 1485–1536
(2) ANNE BOLEYN 1504–36
(2) JANE SEYMOUR 1509–37
(4) ANNE OF CLEVES 1515–57
(5) CATHERINE HOWARD ?1523–42
(6) CATHERINE PARR 1512–48

5 other children →

JAMES V OF SCOTS
1512–42
m
MARIE OF GUISE
d 1560

5 other children

MARGARET
1517–78
m
MATTHEW STUART
1526–71
Earl of Lennox

7 other children

MARY I
1515–58
m PHILIP II OF SPAIN
1527–98

ELIZABETH I
1533–1603

EDWARD VI
1537–53

---

2 sons died young

MARY, QUEEN OF SCOTS*
1542–87
m
(1) FRANCIS II 1541–60
(2) HENRY STUART* 1545–67 Lord Darnley
(3) JAMES HEPBURN 1537–78 Earl of Bothwell

HENRY STUART*
1545–67
Lord Darnley
m
MARY, QUEEN OF SCOTS*
1542–87

1 other son

JAMES I (VI OF SCOTS)
1566–1625
m
ANNE OF DENMARK
1574–1619

Simplified chart of descent of the Princes of Wales

Continued over page

Princes numbered in bold type

□ Link with Welsh Native Dynasty

*Also appears elsewhere on chart

→ Descendants not shown on chart

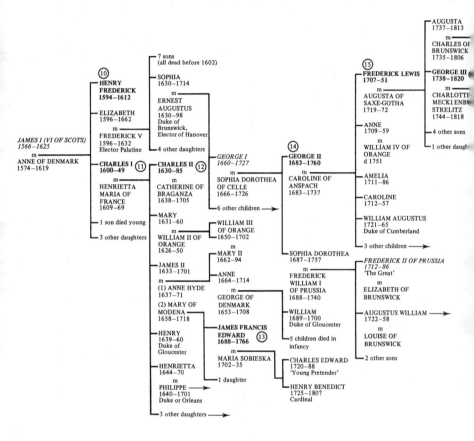

JAMES I (VI OF SCOTS) 1566–1625
m
ANNE OF DENMARK 1574–1619

⑩ **HENRY FREDERICK** 1594–1612

ELIZABETH 1596–1662
m
FREDERICK V 1596–1632 Elector Palatine

7 sons (all dead before 1602)

SOPHIA 1630–1714
m
ERNEST AUGUSTUS 1630–98 Duke of Brunswick, Elector of Hanover

4 other daughters

⑪ **CHARLES I** 1600–49
m
HENRIETTA MARIA OF FRANCE 1609–69

1 son died young

3 other daughters

⑫ **CHARLES II** 1630–85
m
CATHERINE OF BRAGANZA 1638–1705

GEORGE I 1660–1727
m
SOPHIA DOROTHEA OF CELLE 1666–1726

6 other children ⟶

MARY 1631–60
m
WILLIAM II OF ORANGE 1626–50

WILLIAM III OF ORANGE 1650–1702
m
MARY II 1662–94

JAMES II 1633–1701
m
(1) **ANNE HYDE** 1637–71
(2) **MARY OF MODENA** 1658–1718

ANNE 1664–1714
m
GEORGE OF DENMARK 1653–1708

HENRY 1639–60 Duke of Gloucester

JAMES FRANCIS EDWARD 1688–1766 ⑬
m
MARIA SOBIESKA 1702–35

1 daughter

HENRIETTA 1644–70
m
PHILIPPE ⟶ 1640–1701 Duke or Orleans

3 other daughters ⟶

⑭ **GEORGE II** 1683–1760
m
CAROLINE OF ANSPACH 1683–1737

SOPHIA DOROTHEA 1687–1757
m
FREDERICK WILLIAM I OF PRUSSIA 1688–1740

WILLIAM 1689–1700 Duke of Gloucester

5 children died in infancy

CHARLES EDWARD 1720–88 'Young Pretender'

HENRY BENEDICT 1725–1807 Cardinal

⑮ **FREDERICK LEWIS** 1707–51
m
AUGUSTA OF SAXE-GOTHA 1719–72

ANNE 1709–59
m
WILLIAM IV OF ORANGE d 1751

AMELIA 1711–86

CAROLINE 1712–57

WILLIAM AUGUSTUS 1721–65 Duke of Cumberland

3 other children ⟶

FREDERICK II OF PRUSSIA 1712–86 'The Great'
m
ELIZABETH OF BRUNSWICK

AUGUSTUS WILLIAM ⟶ 1722–58
m
LOUISE OF BRUNSWICK

2 other sons

AUGUSTA 1737–1813
m
CHARLES OF BRUNSWICK 1735–1806

GEORGE III 1738–1820
m
CHARLOTTE MECKLENBURG STRELITZ 1744–1818

4 other sons

1 other daughter

CAROLINE OF
BRUNSWICK
1768–1821

m
GEORGE IV (17)
1762–1830

m (not legally)

MARIA
FITZHERBERT
1756–1837

FREDERICK
1763–1827
Duke of York

m

FREDERICA OF
PRUSSIA
1767–1820

WILLIAM IV
1765–1837

m
ADELAIDE OF
SAXE-MEININGEN
1792–1849

EDWARD
1767–1820

m
VICTORIA OF
SAXE-COBURG
1786–1861

5 other sons

6 daughters

CHARLOTTE
1796–1817

m
LEOPOLD OF
SAXE-COBURG
1790–1865

2 daughters died
in infancy

VICTORIA
1819–1901

m

ALBERT OF
SAXE-COBURG
1819–61

VICTORIA ADELAIDE
1840–1901

m
FREDERICK III
1831–88
German Emperor

EDWARD VII (18)
1841–1910

m
ALEXANDRA OF
DENMARK
1844–1925

ARTHUR
1850–1942
Duke of Connaught →

m
LOUISE OF PRUSSIA
1860–1917

2 other sons →

3 daughters →

WILLIAM II
1859–1941
German Emperor

m
AUGUSTA OF
SCHLESWIG-
HOLSTEIN
1858–1921

7 other children →

ALBERT VICTOR
1864–92
Duke of Clarence

GEORGE V (19)
1865–1936

m
MARY OF TECK
1867–1953

2 daughters

(20)
EDWARD VIII
1894–1972

m
WALLIS WARFIELD
SIMPSON
b 1896

GEORGE VI
1895–1952

m
ELIZABETH
BOWES-LYON
b 1900

3 other sons →

1 daughter →

ELIZABETH II
b 1926

m
PHILIP
MOUNTBATTEN
b 1921
Duke of Edinburgh

MARGARET ROSE
b 1930

m
Antony
Armstrong-Jones
b 1930

(21)
CHARLES
b 1948

ANNE
b 1950

m →
MARK PHILIPS
b 1950

ANDREW
b 1960

EDWARD
b 1964

Dates of the Princes of Wales

PRINCE	BIRTH		IDENTIFICATION	CREATED PRINCE		
	DATE	PLACE		ON	AGE	AT
1 Edward	25 April 1284	Caernarfon	Edward II	7 Feb. 1301	16.9	Lincoln
2 Edward	15 June 1330	Woodstock	'Black Prince'	12 May 1343	12.11	Wesminste
3 Richard	16 Jan. 1367	Bordeaux	Richard II	20 Nov. 1376	9.10	Havering-Atte-Bow
4 Henry	16 Sept. 1387	Monmouth	Henry V	15 Oct. 1399	12.1	Westminst
5 Edward	13 Oct. 1453	Westminster	'Edward of Lancaster' Son of Henry VI	14 March 1454	.5	Westminst
6 Edward	2 Nov. 1470	Westminster Abbey	Edward V	26 June 1471	.7	Westmins
7 Edward	1473(?)	Middleham	'Edward of Middleham' Son of Richard III	24 Aug. 1483	9.0(?)	Pontefrac
8 Arthur	20 Sept. 1486	Winchester	Elder son of Henry VII	29 Nov. 1489	3.2	Westmins
9 Henry	28 June 1491	Greenwich	Henry VIII	18 Feb. 1504	11.2	Westmin
10 Henry Frederick	19 Feb. 1594	Stirling	Elder son of James I	4 June 1610	16.3	Westmin
11 Charles	19 Nov. 1600	Dunfermline	Charles I	4 Nov. 1616	15.11	Westmin
12 Charles	29 May 1630	St James's Palace	Charles II	Circa 1640	10.0	London(
13 James Francis Edward	10 June 1688	St James's Palace	'The Old Pretender'	4 July 1688(?)	.1	St James's Palace
14 George Augustus	30 Oct. 1683	Hanover	George II	27 Sept. 1714	30.11	Westmin
15 Frederick Lewis	20 Jan. 1707	Hanover	'Poor Fred'	8 Jan. 1729	22.0	St James' Palace
16 George William Frederick	4 June 1738	Norfolk House, St James's Sq.	George III	20 April 1751	12.11	St James Palace
17 George Augustus Frederick	12 Aug. 1762	St James's Palace	George IV	17 Aug. 1762	5 days	St James Palace
18 Albert Edward	9 Nov. 1841	Buckingham Palace	Edward VII	7 Dec. 1841	28 days	Windso
19 George Frederick Ernest Albert	3 June 1865	Marlborough House	George V	9 Nov. 1901	36.5	Bucking Palace
20 Albert Edward Christian George Andrew Patrick David	23 June 1894	White Lodge, Richmond	Edward VIII	23 June 1910	16.0	Windsc
21 Charles Philip Arthur George	14 Nov. 1948	Buckingham Palace	Eldest son of Elizabeth II	26 July 1958	9.8	Cardiff

INVESTITURE HELD		LENGTH OF PRINCIPATE		PRINCESSES OF WALES
ON	AT	TIME	UNTIL	
:b. 1301(?)	Lincoln(?)	6 yrs 5 mths	July 1307, acceded	
May 1343	Westminster	33 yrs 1 mth	8 June 1376, died	Joan of Kent, married at Windsor, 10 Oct. 1361
t invested		7 mths	21 June 1377, acceded	
)ct. 1399	Westminster	13 yrs 4 mths	21 March 1413, acceded	
ne 1454	Windsor	(1) 6 yrs 6 mths	25 Oct. 1460, father deposed	
		(2) 15 days	Feb.–March 1461, reinstated father deposed	
		(3) 23 days	11 April–4 May 1471, killed at Tewkesbury	
invested		11 yrs 9 mths	9 April 1483, acceded	
pt. 1483	York	8 mths	9 April 1484, died	
eb. 1490	Westminster	12 yrs 4 mths	2 April 1502, died	Catherine of Aragon, married at St Paul's Cathedral, 14 Nov. 1501
eb. 1504	Westminster	5 yrs 2 mths	21 April 1509, acceded	
ne 1610	Westminster	2 yrs 5 mths	5 Nov. 1612, died	
)v. 1616	Westminster	8 yrs 5 mths	27 March 1625, acceded	
invested		*Circa* 9 yrs	30 Jan. 1649, acceded in exile	
invested		5 mths	11 Dec. 1688, father deposed	
invested		12 yrs 8 mths	10 June 1727, acceded	Caroline of Anspach, married at Hanover, 1706
invested		22 yrs 2 mths	20 March 1751, died	Augusta of Saxe-Gotha, married at St James's Palace, 27 April 1736
invested		9 yrs 6 mths	24 Oct. 1760, acceded	
invested		57 yrs 5 mths	29 Jan. 1820, acceded	Caroline of Brunswick, married at St James's Palace, 8 April 1795
invested		59 yrs 1 mth	22 Jan. 1901, acceded	Alexandra of Denmark, married at Windsor, 10 March 1863
invested		8 yrs 6 mths	6 May 1910, acceded	Mary of Teck, married at St James's Palace, 6 July 1893
y 1911	Caernarfon	25 yrs 7 mths	20 Jan. 1936, acceded	
1969	Caernarfon			

Reference Notes

Since I have used books and articles covering so many different periods of history it seems to me of more value to the reader if I relate details of the sources to the appropriate chapter rather than give the customary alphabetical bibliography. Full titles and place of origin for books and articles are given on first citing in the notes. 'L.' indicates publication in London. Other abbreviations:

CSP   Calendar of State Papers
EHR   English Historical Review (L.)
HJ   Historical Journal (Cambridge)
L & P   Letters and Papers
TSC   Transactions of the Honourable Society of Cymmrodorion (L.)
WHR   Welsh History Review (Cardiff)

CHAPTER ONE: EDWARD OF CAERNARFON

1 The king's movements may be traced in H. Gough, *Itinerary of Edward I* (Paisley 1900), I, pp. 150–62. For the general background of events in Wales see: J.E. Lloyd, *History of Wales from the earliest times to the Edwardian Conquest* (L. 1911), II, pp. 767–854; J.E. Morris, *Welsh Wars of Edward I* (Oxford 1901), especially Chapter 4; F.M. Powicke, *The Thirteenth Century* (Oxford 1953), pp. 381–444; A.H. Dodd, *Short History of Wales* (L. 1977), pp. 1–55.

2 A.J. Taylor in H.M. Colvin (ed.), *History of the King's Works* (L. 1963), I, pp. 371–4, also printed separately with same pagination as *History of the King's Works in Wales* (L. 1974).

3 Gough, op. cit., I, p. 154.

4 Contrasting views on the imperial significance of Caernarfon are given in Taylor, loc. cit., pp. 369–72 and in Hilda Johnstone, *Edward of Caernarvon* (Manchester 1946), pp. 6–9. See also Taylor's article on the birth of Edward in *History* (L. 1950), XXXV, pp. 256–61.

5 Johnstone, op. cit., p. 10.

6 Ibid., p. 9.

7 Harold F. Hutchinson, *Edward II, the Pliant King* (L. 1971), pp. 8–11; N. Denholm-Young (ed.), *Vita Edwardi Secundi* (L. 1957), f. 192, p. 40.

8 Johnstone, op. cit., pp. 27–30.

9 G.L. Haskins, 'A Chronicle of the Civil War of Edward II', *Speculum* (Cambridge, Mass. 1939), XIV, pp. 73–81; Johnstone, op. cit., p. 42.

10 H.S. Altham, *History of Cricket* (L. 1962), I, pp. 20–1.

11 Antonia Gransden (ed.), *Chronicle of Bury St Edmunds* (L. 1964), f. 201, p. 157; Johnstone, op. cit., p. 46.

12 Ibid., pp. 54–62; Hutchinson, op. cit., pp. 33–4; Francis Jones, *Princes and Principality of Wales* (Cardiff 1969), pp. 61–4.

13 H.T. Riley (ed.), *Willelmi Rishanger, Chronica et Annales* (L. 1865, Rolls Series), p. 464.

14 Johnstone, op. cit., pp. 62–3.

15 Edward to Louis of Evreux, 26 May 1305, H. Johnstone, *Letters of Edward, Prince of Wales* (Cambridge 1931), p. 11.

16 Edward to Earl of Lincoln, 14 June 1305, ibid., p. 30; Johnstone, *Edward of Caernarvon*, pp. 97–8.

17 Edward to Queen Margaret, August 1305, Johnstone, *Letters . . .* , p. 73. For the reconciliation, see Johnstone, *Edward of Caernarvon*, p. 101.

18 Ibid., pp. 107–8, 117.

19 Hutchinson, op. cit., p. 49; J. Stevenson (ed.), *Chronicon de Lanercost* (Edinburgh 1839), I, p. 210.

20 Robert of Reading, a monk at Westminster, cited by May McKisack, *The Fourteenth Century* (Oxford 1959), p. 1. For contemporary comments on Gaveston, see Denholm-Young, op. cit., ff. 168–81, pp. 14–28. See also T.F. Tout, *Place of Edward II in English History* (rev. edn, Manchester 1936), pp. 83–170.

21 Hutchinson, op. cit., pp. 77–85; McKisack, op. cit., pp. 35–9, 70.

22 Ibid., pp. 71–91; Hutchinson, op. cit., pp. 116–35.

23 J. Beverley Smith, 'Edward II and the Allegiance of Wales', *WHR*, December 1976, VIII, no. 2, pp. 139–71.

24 See 'Death and Captivity of Edward II' in Tout, *Collected Papers* (Manchester 1920), III, pp. 167–89; Hutchinson, op. cit., pp. 141–2.

25 G.P. Guttimo and Thomas W. Lyman, 'Where is Edward II?', *Speculum* (Cambridge, Mass. July 1978), LIII, no. 3, pp. 522–44, with the inscription in the abbey of San Alberto di Burtio reproduced on p. 531. See also Tout, *Collected Papers*, III, pp. 178–9.

26 H.T. Riley (ed.), *Historia Anglicana Thomas Walsingham* (L. 1863, Rolls Series), p. 83. On the activities of Hywel and Rhys ap Gruffydd, see Beverley Smith, loc. cit., pp. 167–9.

CHAPTER TWO: WOODSTOCK AND BORDEAUX

1 The fullest recent biography of the Black Prince is Richard Barber, *Edward, Prince of Wales and Aquitaine* (L. 1976), pp. 12–46 for his early life. Barbara Emerson, *The Black Prince* (L. 1976) is very readable. Much detail on his personal life is in the *Register of Edward the Black Prince* (L. 1930–33), four volumes: see, for example, IV, pp. 74, 75, 76 for entries on gambling habits. For Woodstock manor, see H.M. Colvin (ed.), *History of the King's Works* (L. 1963), II, pp. 1009–17.

2 J. Viard and E. Deprez (eds), *Chronique de Jehan le Bel* (Paris 1904–5), II, p. 72; cf. Geoffrey Brereton (ed.) *Froissart Chronicles* (L. 1968, Penguin), p. 71.

3 Barber, op. cit., pp. 49–79; McKisack, *Fourteenth Century*, pp. 134–6; Perroy, *Hundred Years War* (L. 1951), pp. 119–21.

4 Barber, op. cit., pp. 99–101; Brereton, op. cit., pp. 113–19.

5 McKisack, op. cit., pp. 250–2; Barber, op. cit., pp. 83–93; C. Hibbert, *The Court at Windsor* (L. 1964), pp. 10–21; A.R. Myers (ed.), *English Historical Documents*, IV, pp. 91–2.

6 H.J. Hewitt, *The Black Prince's Expedition, 1355–57* (Manchester 1958), pp. 100–39, superbly reconstructed mediaeval military history. Contemporary material on Poitiers campaign, Myers, op. cit., pp. 92–9. See also K.B. McFarlane, *Nobility of Later Mediaeval England* (Oxford 1973), pp. 22, 30, 195.

7 Black Prince and Chester: P.H.W. Booth, 'Taxation and Public Order in Cheshire', *Northern History* (Leeds 1976), XII, pp. 16–31, a valuable corrective. Black Prince and Wales: D.L. Evans, 'Some Notes on the Principality in the time of the Black Prince', TSC for 1925–6, pp. 25–107; H.J. Hewitt, op. cit., pp. 15, 16, 20, 21, 49, 68 and Appendix C; H.J. Hewitt, *Organization of War under Edward III* (Manchester 1966), p. 48; A.D. Carr, 'Welshmen and the Hundred Years War', *WHR* (June 1968), IV, no. 1, pp. 1–46.

8 Barber, op. cit., pp. 172–4; M. Galway, 'Joan of Kent and the Order of the Garter', *Univ. of Birmingham Historical Journal* (1959), VIII, pp. 18–35; A. Gransden, 'The alleged rape by Edward III of the Countess of Salisbury', *EHR* (1972), LXXXVII, pp. 333–44.

9 Mildred K. Pope and Eleanor C. Lodge (eds), *Life of the Black Prince by the Herald of Sir John Chandos* (L. 1910), p. 148.

10 P.E. Russell, *The English Intervention in Spain and Portugal in the Times of Edward III and Richard II* (Oxford 1955), pp. 84–107; Perroy, op. cit., pp. 156–9; Barber, op. cit., pp. 192–206.

11 Ibid., pp. 207–27; Richard Barber effectively refutes earlier sensational

judgments on the sack of Limoges, ibid., pp. 224–6, but Froissart's account of the suffering remains impressive (Brereton, op. cit., p. 178). For Chandos Herald's comment on the 'mischances', see Pope and Lodge, p. 123.

12 On Owen Lawgoch see Edward Owen in TSC for 1899–1900, pp. 1–45, and the article by A.D. Carr, loc. cit., pp. 31 ff.

13 English grievances: George Holmes, *The Good Parliament* (Oxford 1975), pp. 21–62; M.A. Devlin (ed.), *The Sermons of Thomas Brinton, Bishop of Rochester* (L. 1954), Camden Society, Series 3, LXXXVI, (introduction) p. xxv, (sermon 12) pp. 43–8 and (sermon 69) pp. 315–21.

14 Death of Black Prince: Barber, op. cit., pp. 233–7; Holmes, op. cit., p. 106. Creation of Richard as Prince of Wales: ibid., p. 107; V.H. Galbraith (ed.), *Anonimalle Chronicle* (Manchester 1927), pp. 92, 94–5; Francis Jones, *Princes and Principality of Wales*, pp. 121–2.

15 Holmes, op. cit., pp. 185 and 190; Galbraith, op. cit., p. 104; E.M. Thompson (ed.), *Chronicon Angliae 1328–88* (L. 1874, Rolls Series), pp. 121–6.

16 K.B. McFarlane, *Lancastrian Kings and Lollard Knights* (Oxford 1972), pp. 14–19.

17 For the final section of this chapter I used the works already cited by McKisack and McFarlane together with: M.V. Clarke, *Fourteenth Century Studies* (Oxford 1937), pp. 66–77; Glyn Roberts, 'Wales and England', *WHR* (1963), I, no. 4, pp. 392–3; James Sherborne, 'Richard II's return to Wales', *WHR* (1975), VII, No. 4, pp. 389–402.

CHAPTER THREE: HARRY OF MONMOUTH

1 Francis Jones, *Princes and Principality of Wales*, p. 123: E.M. Thompson (ed.), *Chronicon Adae de Usk* (L. 1876), pp. 30–7; E.F. Jacob, *Fifteenth Century* (Oxford 1961), pp. 18–19.

2 K.B. McFarlane, *Lancastrian Kings and Lollard Knights*, pp. 28–9, 114–15; McFarlane, *Nobility of Later Mediaeval England*, pp. 152, 177.

3 M.W. Labarge, *Henry V* (L. 1975), pp. 9–11; McFarlane, *Lancastrian Kings* . . . , pp. 120–1.

4 J.E. Lloyd, *Owen Glendower* (Oxford 1931), pp. 28–52; Jacob, op. cit., pp. 37–40; Thompson, op. cit., p. 237.

5 Ibid., p. 85; McFarlane, *Lancastrian Kings* . . . , pp. 70–4, 122; Peter Earle, *Life and Times of Henry V* (L. 1972), pp. 50, 56–7; J.M.W. Bean, 'Henry IV and the Percies', *History* (L. 1959), XLIV, pp. 212–27.

6 Labarge, op. cit., pp. 20–1; J.A. Wylie, *Henry the Fourth* (L. 1884), I, pp. 354–65.

7 McFarlane, *Lancastrian Kings* . . . , p. 103; Wylie, op. cit., II, p. 249; III, p. 110.

8 The chronicle of Monstrelet, cited by McFarlane, *Lancastrian Kings* . . . , p. 106.

9 Ibid., pp. 107–8; Jacob, op. cit., pp. 101–6; Labarge, op. cit., pp. 34–6.

10 Jacob, op. cit., p. 112; Earle, op. cit., pp. 86–7.

11 McFarlane, *Lancastrian Kings* . . . , pp. 110–11; E. Tyrell and N.H. Nicols (eds), *Chronicle of London* (L. 1827), pp. 94–5; V.H. Galbraith (ed.), *St Albans Chronicle* (Oxford 1937), pp. 65–7.

12 Jacob, op. cit., pp. 116–17, 121–7; Labarge, op. cit., p. 39.

13 E.F. Jacob, *Henry V and the Invasion of France* (L. 1947) lays special emphasis on the elements of truth and propaganda in the Harry of Monmouth legends: Chapter Three considers the Oldcastle and Southampton conspiracies. See, also, Frank Taylor and John S. Roskell (eds), *Gesta Henrici Quinti* (Oxford 1975), pp. 3–5, 11, 188–90, and V.H. Galbraith, op. cit., pp. 69–79.

14 The outstanding contemporary source for the Agincourt campaign is the *Gesta* cited above, pp. 81–99. Sir N. Harris Nichols, *The Battle of Agincourt* (L. 1827 and reprinted 1970) is a collection of contemporary documents. A.H. Burne, *The Agincourt War* (L. 1956) and C. Hibbert, *Agincourt* (L. 1964) are modern military assessments.

15 Jacob, *Fifteenth Century*, pp. 200–2; McFarlane, *Lancastrian Kings* . . . , pp. 127–33.

CHAPTER FOUR: THREE PRINCE EDWARDS

1 Myers, *English Historical Documents*, IV, pp. 259–60; J. Haswell, *The Ardent Queen* (L. 1976), pp. 79–80; Jacob, *Fifteenth Century*, pp. 491–6.

2 McFarlane, *Nobility of Later Mediaeval England*, pp. 185–6.

3 Haswell, op. cit., pp. 79–80; Jacob, op. cit., pp. 476–7.

4 Myers, op. cit., pp. 259–60; Haswell, op. cit., pp. 97–107; Jacob, op. cit., p. 508; Philippe Erlanger, *Margaret of Anjou* (L. 1970), pp. 145–50.

5 The contemporary sources used by J.R. Lander, *Wars of the Roses* (L. 1965) are extremely useful: for this quotation from the Paston Letters see p. 70. See also Myers, op. cit., pp. 272–3, Haswell, op. cit., p. 100.

6 See, in general, K.B. McFarlane, 'Wars of the Roses', *Proceedings of the British Academy* (L. 1964), Vol. 50, pp. 87–119 and chapter 3 of his *Nobility of Later Mediaeval England*, as well as the introduction to Professor Lander's book, cited above. See also the stimulating contribution by Margaret Aston, 'Richard II and the Wars of the Roses' in F.R.H. du Boulay and Caroline

Barron, *The Reign of Richard II* (L. 1971), pp. 280–317. J.R. Lander, *Crown and Nobility, 1450–1509* (L. 1976) is a convenient compilation of articles which originally appeared elsewhere.

7 Lander, *Wars of the Roses*, pp. 111–22; Jacob, op. cit., p. 525; Haswell, op. cit., p. 147.

8 Myers, op. cit., p. 288.

9 Haswell, op. cit., pp. 169–71; Jacob, op. cit., pp. 309–16 and 530; C. Plummer (ed.), *Fortescue's Governance of England* (L. 1885).

10 Myers, op. cit., pp. 303–5; Haswell, op. cit., p. 191; Erlanger, op. cit., p. 221. For Edward's marriage to Anne, see P.W. Hammond, *Edward of Middleham* (Cliftonville 1973), pp. 9, 27–8.

11 Lander, *Wars of the Roses*, pp. 187–95; Myers, op. cit., pp. 310–15; Haswell, op. cit., pp. 197–205.

12 Elizabeth Jenkins, *Princes in the Tower* (L. 1978), pp. 95–8, 131–2.

13 Ibid., pp. 142–57; P.M. Kendall, *Richard III* (L. 1956), pp. 213–29; Jacob, op. cit., pp. 623–5.

14 Ibid., pp. 178–81.

15 Francis Jones, *Princes and Principality of Wales*, p. 126; Hammond, op. cit., pp. 29–30.

16 Ibid., p. 18; Jenkins, op. cit., p. 187; Jones, op. cit., pp. 127–8; H.T. Riley (ed.), *Ingulphus Chronicle of Croyland* (L. 1854), p. 490.

17 Ibid., pp. 496–7.

18 A.F. Pollard, *The Reign of Henry VII from Contemporary Sources* (L. 1913), I, p. 17.

CHAPTER FIVE: SONS OF PROPHECY

1 On Owen Tudor, see: H.T. Evans, *Wales and the Wars of the Roses* (Cambridge 1915); S.B. Chrimes, *Henry VII* (L. 1977), pp. 5–7; Glyn Roberts, 'Wyrion Eden' in his *Aspects of Welsh History* (Cardiff 1969), pp. 179–214; D. Williams, 'The Family of Henry VII', *History Today* (L. February 1954), IV, pp. 77–84.

2 Chrimes, op. cit., pp. 15–17.

3 W. Garmon Jones, 'Welsh Nationalism and Henry Tudor', TSC 1917–18, pp. 1–59; S. Anglo, 'The *British History* in Early Tudor Propaganda', *Bulletin of John Rylands Library* (Manchester 1961), XLIV, pp. 17–40; Francis Jones, *Princes and Principality of Wales*, p. 45. For the establishment of the dynasty, see Chrimes, op. cit., pp. 21–60.

4 Ibid., pp. 245–57; Christopher Morris, *The Tudors* (paperback edition, L.

1966), pp. 57–8; David Williams, *A History of Modern Wales* (second edition, L. 1970), pp. 21–4.

5 Leland, *De Rebus Britannicus, Collectanea* (L. 1774), IV, pp. 250–1; Francis Jones, op. cit., pp. 128–9; S. Anglo, *Spectacle, Pageantry and Early Tudor Policy* (Oxford 1969), pp. 52–3.

6 Arthur, Prince of Wales, to Princess Catherine, 4 October 1499, *CSP Spanish*, I, p. 253; G. Mattingly, *Catherine of Aragon* (L. 1942), p. 25.

7 Leland, *Collectanea*, V, pp. 352–4; *L & P, Henry VII*, I, pp. 404–5, II, pp. 103–4; Mattingly, op. cit., pp. 35–7.

8 Ibid., pp. 38–40; Leland, *Collectanea*, V, pp. 356–73; F. Grose and T. Astle, *Antiquarian Repertory* (L. 1807–9), II, pp. 249–302; Anglo, op. cit., pp. 56–94, 99–103.

9 Alleged remark to Maurice St John: *L & P, Henry VIII*, IV (iii), no. 2580. Prince Arthur to Ferdinand and Isabella, 30 November 1501, *CSP Spanish*, I, p. 265.

10 Quotation from Leland, *Collectanea*, V, p. 377. Leland has a considerable section on Arthur at Ludlow, ibid., pp. 373–81. For modern treatment, see Mattingly, op. cit., pp. 42–5. See also Grose and Astle, op. cit., pp. 322–3.

11 Ferdinand and Isabella to Puebla, 14 June 1502, *CSP Spanish*, I, p. 270. For Campeggio's conduct in 1528 see Mattingly, op. cit., p. 197.

12 Francis Jones, op. cit., pp. 130–1.

13 F. Morgan Nichols (ed.), *The Epistles of Desiderius Erasmus* (L. 1901), pp. 201–2; Marie Louise Bruce, *The Making of Henry VIII* (L. 1977), pp. 83–96.

14 Duke de Estrada to Queen Isabella, 10 August 1504, *CSP Spanish*, I, pp. 328–9.

15 *CSP Spanish*, I, pp. 379–86, contains a narrative of events, draft treaties and correspondence relative to the visit. Mattingly, op. cit., pp. 65–72; Bruce, op. cit., pp. 179–93.

16 Duke of Berwick and Alba (ed.), *Correspondencia . . . de Fuensalida* (Madrid 1907), p. 484: Ferdinand to Fuensalida, July 1508, *CSP Spanish*, I, pp. 457–8.

17 For Mary Tudor at Ludlow see H.F.M. Prescott, *Spanish Tudor* (L. 1940), p. 28. On the Dunstable decree see Chapuys to Emperor Charles V, 27 April 1533, *CSP Spanish*, IV(II), p. 647, and *L & P, Henry VIII*, VI, pp. 219, 230–1. For Catherine's last years at Kimbolton, Mattingly, op. cit., pp. 305–8.

18 Morris, op. cit., pp. 97–9.

19 William Rees, 'The Union of England and Wales', TSC, 1937, pp. 27–100; David Williams, op. cit., pp. 28–45.

20 J.J. Scarisbrick, *Henry VIII* (L. 1968), pp. 496–7; *L & P, Henry VIII*, XXI (ii), p. 389.

CHAPTER SIX: FOUR STUART PRINCES

1 D.H. Willson, *King James VI & I* (L. 1956), p. 161; on *Basilikon Doron*, pp. 132–6. The *Basilikon Doron* is printed in C.H. McIlwain, *Political Works of James I* (Cambridge, Mass. 1918), pp. 3–52.

2 E.K. Chambers, *The Elizabethan Stage* (Oxford 1923), III, pp. 250, 382–6, 391, 393.

3 For Connack, see Francis Jones, *Princes and Principality of Wales*, pp. 131–2.

4 Ibid., pp. 132–7.

5 H.M. Colvin (ed.), *History of the King's Works*, III, part 1, pp. 121–6.

6 C. Cornwallis, *Discourse on the Most Illustrious Prince, Henry, late Prince of Wales* (L. 1641), printed in *Harleian Miscellany*, IV, pp. 333–40: Willson, op. cit., pp. 280–2.

7 G. Goodman, *The Court of King James I* (L. 1839), I, pp. 250–1.

8 On Prince Henry and Ralegh, see A.L. Rowse, *Ralegh and the Throckmortons* (L. 1962), pp. 258–60 and J.H. Adamson and H.F. Folland, *The Shepherd of the Ocean* (L. 1969), pp. 375–6. Quotation from Ralegh about Spain cited by Eric Ecclestone, *Sir Walter Ralegh* (L. 1941), p. 86.

9 Goodman, op. cit., I, p. 168.

10 Cornwallis (*Harleian Misc.*), IV, p. 340; Willson, op. cit., p. 340; David Mathew, *The Jacobean Age* (rev. edition, L. 1971), pp. 79–83; Elizabeth Thomson (ed.), *The Chamberlain Letters* (L. 1966), pp. 68–71.

11 J.O. Halliwell, *Autobiography and Correspondence of Sir Simonds D'Ewes* (L. 1845), I, pp. 91–2; Edmund Howes, *The Annales or General Chronicle of England begun by John Stowe* (L. 1631), p. 1026; Francis Jones, op. cit., pp. 137–40.

12 Horatio Busino to Doge and Senate of Venice, 22 December 1617, *CSP Venice for 1617*, p. 80.

13 Willson, op. cit., pp. 407–8; Girolamo Lando to Doge and Senate of Venice, 30 January 1620, *CSP Venice for 1619–21*, p. 151.

14 J.R. Tanner, *English Constitutional Conflicts of the Seventeenth Century* (Students' Edition, Cambridge 1966), p. 48.

15 Prince of Wales to James I, 22 February 1623 from Paris, 10 March from Madrid, Sir Charles Petrie (ed.), *Letters of King Charles I* (L. 1935), pp. 7–11: Willson, op. cit., pp. 431–3; Carola Oman, *Henrietta Maria* (L. 1941), pp. 16–17.

16 Petrie, op. cit., pp. 25–31.

17 Oman, op. cit., pp. 31–62.

18 Francis Jones, op. cit., p. 141.

19 J.E.B. Mayor, *Two Lives* (Cambridge 1855), p. 136; M. Ashley, *Charles II, the Man and the Statesman* (L. 1971), pp. 2–3.

20 Giovanni Giustinian to Doge and Senate of Venice, 24 May 1641, *CSP Venetian*, XXV, p. 151.

21 C.V. Wedgwood, *The King's War, 1641–47* (L. 1958), p. 127: D. Williams, *Short History of Modern Wales*, p. 99.

22 For the prince's movements from Falmouth to Jersey, see G.E. Manwaring (ed.), *Life and Works of Sir Henry Mainwaring* (L. 1920, Navy Records Society), I, pp. 306–14; S. Elliott Hoskins, *Charles II in the Channel Islands* (L. 1854), I, pp. 413–14.

23 Pierre Adolphe Chervel (ed.), *Mémoires de Mlle. de Montpensier* (Paris, 1889), I, pp. 137 and 142–4.

24 M. Ashley, op. cit., pp. 29–30.

25 Sophia, Electress of Hanover, *Memoirs* (L. 1888), p. 24.

26 Carola Oman, *Mary of Modena* (L. 1962), p. 55.

27 Ibid., p. 110.

28 Henri and Barbara van der Zee, *William and Mary* (L. 1973), pp. 230–42 and 252–60; Lord (Michael Morris) Killanin, *Sir Godfrey Kneller and his Times* (L. 1948), p. 18; Oman, op. cit., pp. 113–14.

29 Ibid., pp. 123–32.

30 Letter written by Charles Lesley after a visit to the former Prince of Wales, A. Browning, *English Historical Documents, 1660–1714*, pp. 910–11.

31 Bill of Rights, ibid., pp. 122–8 and Act of Settlement, pp. 129–34.

CHAPTER SEVEN: HANOVER

1 Henri and Barbara van der Zee, *William and Mary*, pp. 400–1; Francis Jones, *The Princes and Principality of Wales*, pp. 93–7.

2 This comment by Thackeray appears in a satirical contribution to *Punch*, 11 October 1845, and anticipates by ten years his famous lectures on *The Four Georges* (published in book form, L. 1861). For a sympathetic modern biography of George I, see Ragnhild Hatton, *George I: Elector and King* (L. 1979). On revenues from the principality, see Jones, op. cit., pp. 86–7.

3 J.H. Plumb, *The First Four Georges* (L. 1956), pp. 38–51.

4 Romney Sedgwick (ed.), *Some Materials towards Memoirs of the Reign of King George II by John, Lord Hervey* (L. 1931), I, p. 29 and III, pp. 846–8.

5 Plumb, op. cit., p. 59; but, for a recent assessment, cf. Hatton, op. cit., pp. 201–9.

6 Sedgwick, *Hervey Memoirs*, I, p. 29.

7 Ibid., I, p. 95; A. Edwards, *Frederick Louis, Prince of Wales* (L. 1947), pp. 15–16; John Walters, *The Royal Griffin* (L. 1971), pp. 47–8.

8 Edwards, op. cit., p. 17.

9 J. Carswell and L.A. Dralle, *The Political Journal of George Bubb Dodington* (Oxford 1965), pp. xvii–xxii; A.N. Newman, 'The Political Patronage of Frederick Louis, Prince of Wales', *HJ* (1959), I, pp. 68–75.

10 Sedgwick, *Hervey Memoirs*, III, p. 681.

11 Ibid., III, pp. 759–93 (birth of Augusta), pp. 808–12 (expulsion from St James), pp. 877–917 (death of Queen Caroline), pp. 943–5 (king on his son); John Brooke, *King George III* (L. 1972), pp. 17–18.

12 A.N. Newman, 'Leicester House Politics', *Camden Miscellany*, XXIII (L. 1969), pp. 85–228, based on the Egmont papers, with the Duke of Virginia proposal on pp. 192–3. See, also, Dr Newman's earlier article, 'Leicester House Politics, 1748–51', *EHR* (1961), LXXVI, pp. 577–89.

13 Edwards, op. cit., pp. 181–8; Walters, op. cit., pp. 214–16; Brooke, op. cit., pp. 23–5; Dodington's journal for 6–21 March 1751, Carswell and Dralle, op. cit., pp. 104–5.

14 Dodington's journal, 25 January 1753, ibid., p. 199.

15 Quoted from a memoir of Lady Louisa Stuart by John Brooke, op. cit., p. 41: Dodington journal, 18 December 1753, Carswell and Dralle, op. cit., p. 244.

16 Horace Walpole, *Memoirs of the Reign of King George III* (L. 1845)?, I, pp. 297–300. There is an excellent brief study of Bute by John Brewer in H. van Thal (ed.), *The Prime Ministers* (L. 1974), I, pp. 105–13.

17 Waldegrave's report was included by Sir Lewis Namier in his perceptive 'study of the personality' of George III, *Personalities and Powers* (L. 1955), quotation from pp. 46–7. This study appeared originally in *History Today* (L. September 1953), III, pp. 610–21.

18 Romney Sedgwick (ed.), *Letters from George III to Lord Bute*: 'parcel of children' letter, 8 December 1758, p. 18; 'old king' letter, 28 July 1759, pp. 26–7.

19 Letter of 23 April 1760, ibid., p. 43.

CHAPTER EIGHT: FARMER GEORGE AND PRINNY

1 The fullest study of the Bute experiment will be found in L.B. Namier, *England in the Age of the American Revolution* (revised edition, L. 1961), pp. 120–70 and pp. 283–326, supplemented by R. Pares, *King George III and the Politicians* (paperback edition, Oxford 1957), pp. 99–109, 113–15. See also John Brooke, *King George III*, pp. 93–102. For the king's comment on Bute

as Newcastle's friend and for public hostility to Bute, see John Brewer's contribution to H. van Thal, *The Prime Ministers*, I, pp. 108–9, and his article, 'The Misfortunes of Lord Bute', *HJ* (1973), XVI, no. 1, pp. 3–44. The king's letter of April 1763 is in Sedgwick, *Letters of George III to Lord Bute*, p. 208.

2 'New Berlin Almanack' letter, winter 1758–9, ibid., p. 40. The care with which George sought a bride is emphasized in Romney Sedgwick's article 'The Marriage of George III', *History Today* (L. June 1960), X, pp. 371–7.

3 Francis Jones, *Princes and Principality of Wales*, p. 53 ; C. Hibbert, *George IV, Prince of Wales* (L. 1972), pp. 2–3.

4 Ibid., pp. 6–25.

5 For the rules of conduct see the king's letter to the prince of 22 December 1780, A. Aspinall (ed.), *The Correspondence of George, Prince of Wales* (L. 1963–71), I, pp. 36–8 ; and complaint about newspapers, 6 May 1781, p. 60.

6 A. Francis Steuart (ed.), *Last Journals of Horace Walpole* (L. 1910), II, p. 496.

7 Bonamy Dobrée, *Letters of George III* (revised edition, L. 1968), March 1782, pp. 154–5 ; March 1783, pp. 169–71 ; 'lustre of empire', King to Lord North, 7 September 1783, Fortescue, *Correspondence of King George III* (L. 1927), VI, pp. 443–4 ; Brooke, op. cit., pp. 221 and 261.

8 Hibbert, op. cit., pp. 40–1.

9 Ibid., pp. 44–59 ; Aspinall, op. cit., pp. 155–250 *passim*.

10 A. Palmer, *Life and Times of George IV* (L. 1972), pp. 39–40 ; Aspinall, op. cit., p. 313 ; Hibbert, op. cit., pp. 60–70 ; W.H. Wilkins, *Mrs Fitzherbert and George IV* (L. 1905), I, pp. 90–1.

11 For George III's illness and the prince's reaction see the account in Brooke, op. cit., pp. 328–36 based on J. Macalpine and R. Hunter, *George III and the Mad Business* (L. 1969). See also C. Chenevix-Trench, *The Royal Malady* (L. 1964). For newspapers see Aspinall, op. cit., II, pp. 3–4 and *The Times*, 13 August 1791.

12 Hibbert, op. cit., pp. 120–22 ; Palmer, op. cit., pp. 52–3 ; *The Times*, 5 August 1793 ; M. Brander, *The 10th Royal Hussars* (L. 1969), pp. 9–13 ; Clifford Musgrave, *Life in Brighton* (L. 1970), p. 108.

13 Earl of Malmesbury, *Diaries and Correspondence of James Harris, first Earl of Malmesbury* (L. 1844) Volume III, is the principal source for all information about the marriage arrangements: 'Harris, I am not well', ibid., III, pp. 217–18. For the wedding, Hibbert, op. cit., pp. 146–7.

14 The prince's last will and testament, Aspinall, op. cit., III, p. 132.

15 Brooke, op. cit., p. 351, paraphrasing Aspinall, *Later Correspondence of George III* (Cambridge 1963), II, pp. 481–2.

16 Mrs Fitzherbert at Brighton: Musgrave, op. cit., pp. 124–48 ; Willkins, op. cit., II, pp. 20–23 ; Shane Leslie, *Mrs Fitzherbert* (L. 1940), II, pp. 128–35 ;

John Gore (ed.), *Creevey, Selections* (L. 1948), pp. 30–1 and Mrs Creevey's comments, pp. 41–5.

17 Hibbert, op. cit., pp. 237–42. The 'naughty person' letter, 3 January 1811, Aspinall, *Correspondence . . . Wales*, VII, p. 138: cf. the delightful letter from Minny Seymour on the following St Valentine's Day, ibid., p. 234.

18 Lady Puleston's account, Edward Parry, *Royal Visits and Progresses to Wales* (L. 1851), pp. 414–15.

19 Prince of Wales to Lord Holland, 14 September 1806, Aspinall, *Correspondence . . . Wales*, V, pp. 428–9; the same to Lord Grenville, 8 October 1806, ibid., pp. 468–9; see ibid., p. 283 for Nelson reference.

20 Hibbert, op. cit., pp. 208–14.

21 Break with Mrs Fitzherbert, Shane Leslie, op. cit., II, pp. 133–5. Coming of the Regency, Brook, op. cit., pp. 382–4; Aspinall, *Letters . . . Wales*, VII, pp. 200–8; Hibbert, op. cit., pp. 280–1; *The Times*, 8 February 1811.

22 Regent and the Tsar, Alan Palmer, *Alexander I* (L. 1974), pp. 294–8, 300; Regent and the Austrians, Palmer, *Metternich* (L. 1972), pp. 125–9. Contemporary comment, H. W. V. Temperley, *Unpublished Diary of Princess Lieven* (L. 1925). Regent's letters to his mother 1812–14, Sir Charles Webster, *Foreign Policy of Castlereagh* (L. 1931), I, p. 28.

23 Queen Charlotte to the Prince Regent, 7 November 1817, Aspinall, *Letters of King George IV* (Cambridge, 1938), II, p. 212.

24 For the so-called Queen's Trial, see C. Hibbert, *George IV, Regent and King* (L. 1975), pp. 132–88 and Roger Fulford, *The Trial of Queen Charlotte* (L. 1968).

25 For the proposed 'Order of St David', see E. Parry, op. cit., p. 464.

26 Wilkins, op. cit., II, pp. 221–2.

CHAPTER NINE: ALBERT EDWARD AND SON

1 Philip Magnus, *King Edward VII* (L. 1964), pp. 3–4; *The Times*, 26 January 1842.

2 Reminiscences of Queen Victoria, written by her in 1872, A.C. Benson and Viscount Esher, *Letters of Queen Victoria* (L. 1908), I, p. 12.

3 Melbourne to Queen Victoria, 1 December 1841, ibid., I, p. 365; Queen to King Leopold, 29 November 1841, ibid., I, p. 364.

4 C. Woodham-Smith, *Queen Victoria, Her Life and Times, 1819–61* (L. 1972), p. 268; Magnus, op. cit., pp. 6–9.

5 Ibid., pp. 9–16; C. Hibbert, *Edward VII* (L. 1976), pp. 7, 12, 13: extracts from Gibbs's diary, *Cornhill Magazine* (L. spring 1951), p. 986.

6 Prince Consort to Baron Stockmar, 2 April 1858, Theodore Martin, *Life of the Prince Consort* (L. 1876–80), IV, p. 205.

7 Magnus, op. cit., pp. 20–22; A. Palmer, *Metternich*, pp. 336–7; Queen Victoria, *Leaves from a Journal, 1855* (L. 1961), pp. 115–17.

8 Magnus, op. cit., pp. 30–41.

9 Ibid., pp. 50–6; Woodham-Smith, op. cit., pp. 385–401; Elizabeth Longford, *Victoria R.I.* (L. 1964), pp. 295–304; E.C. Corti, *The English Empress* (L. 1957), p. 81.

10 Ibid., pp. 67, 72; Magnus, op. cit., pp. 56–68.

11 Francis Jones, *Princes and Principality of Wales*, pp. 55–6, and the same author's *God Bless the Prince of Wales* (Carmarthen 1969), pp. 11–31. For the boy prince's visit to the Menai Straits, 1847, E. Parry, *Royal Visits and Progresses to Wales* (L. 1851), p. 467.

12 E. Longford, op. cit., p. 364.

13 Ibid., pp. 385–90; Hibbert, op. cit., pp. 157–60; Magnus, op. cit., pp. 113–15.

14 Ibid., pp. 116–42.

15 Gordon Brooke-Shepherd, *Uncle of Europe* (L. 1975), pp. 66–71; A. Ramm (ed.), *Political Correspondence of Mr Gladstone and Lord Granville* (L. 1952), I, p. 131.

16 Alan Palmer, *The Kaiser* (L. 1978), pp. 23, 38–9; Lady Gwendolen Cecil, *Robert, Marquis of Salisbury* (L. 1932), IV, pp. 366–7; Magnus, op. cit., p. 211.

17 Ibid., pp. 222–9; Hibbert, op. cit., pp. 157–60.

18 Palmer, op. cit., pp. 58–61, 62, 71, 97–8.

19 Prince of Wales to Duke of York, 25 August 1894, Magnus, op. cit., p. 242. For Prince George see John Gore, *King George V, A Personal Memoir* (L. 1941), pp. 30–129 and Harold Nicolson, *King George V* (L. 1952), pp. 3–60.

20 Ibid., p. 73; *The Times*, 6, 7 and 9 December 1901.

21 Nicolson, op. cit., p. 75; *Punch*, 18 December 1901.

22 On the Mylius Case see Nicolson, op. cit., pp. 143–4 and Randolph S. Churchill, *Winston S. Churchill* (L. 1967), II, pp. 419–23. Killing animals and sticking in stamps, Nigel Nicolson (ed.), *Harold Nicolson, Diaries and Letters 1945–62* (L. 1968), p. 174.

23 Brook-Shepherd, op. cit., pp. 187–210; Alan Palmer, *Bismarck* (L. 1976), p. 257; Nicolson, op. cit., pp. 43, 94–5.

24 Ibid., pp. 97–9.

25 Ibid., p. 105; Magnus, op. cit., pp. 449–56.

CHAPTER TEN: WINDSOR

1 Frances Donaldson's *Edward VIII* (L. 1974) is a superb biography. *The Times* obituary of the Duke of Windsor, 29 May 1972, is judiciously phrased and shows a fine tact of omission. Frank Verney, *HRH* (L. 1926) and Evelyn Graham, *Edward P* (L. 1929) are entertaining mid-course laudations, while A.G. Gardiner, *Certain People of Importance* (L. 1926), chapter 8, is perceptive and politely critical, pp. 73–9.

2 James Pope-Hennessy, *Queen Mary* (L. 1959), p. 391. For the Duke of Windsor's views on his parents see his *A King's Story* (L. 1951), pp. 6, 7, 24–5, 27–8 and his *A Family Album* (L. 1960), pp. 54–5.

3 A.G. Edwards, Archbishop of Wales, *Memories* (L. 1927), pp. 242–53; Francis Jones, *God Bless the Prince of Wales*, pp. 82–3; *The Times*, 8 February, 22 March, 9 May 1911.

4 Edwards, op. cit., pp. 253–4; Jones, *Princes and Principality of Wales*, pp. 147–55; *The Times*, 14 July 1911.

5 Windsor, *A King's Story*, p. 79; Pope-Hennessy, op. cit., p. 444; Nicolson, *King George V*, p. 148.

6 Viktoria Luise, *Ein Leben als Tochter des Kaisers* (Hanover 1965), p. 69, slightly modified in the English version, *The Kaiser's Daughter* (L. 1977), p. 148.

7 For criticism of the decision to send the prince to Oxford, see Pope-Hennessy, op. cit., p. 445. The Duke of Windsor has written of his days at Oxford in *A King's Story*, pp. 93–6 and *A Family Album*, pp. 44–52 and 63. See also Donaldson, op. cit., pp. 38–48. For an entertaining character-sketch of Lancelot Phelps by J.I.M. Stewart, see Ann Thwaite (ed.), *My Oxford* (L. 1977), pp. 76–9. Sir Herbert Warren, *The Times*, 18 November 1914; *Punch*, 25 November 1914.

8 Donaldson, op. cit., pp. 49–55; Duke of Windsor, *A King's Story*, pp. 108–25.

9 The account of the prince's travels in Lady Donaldson's biography and in his memoirs may be supplemented by the 'pictorial record of the voyages of *HMS Renown* 1919–20', published as *The Prince of Wales' Book* (L. 1921).

10 Gardiner, op. cit., pp. 78–9.

11 G. Vanderbilt and T. Furness, *Double Exposure* (revised edition, L. 1961), p. 219.

12 Windsor, *A King's Story*, p. 222; Donaldson, op. cit., pp. 137–8; *The Times*, 4, 12, 13 December 1928; arrival at Victoria reported in *Oxford Mail*, 12 December 1928; Nicolson, op. cit., p. 430.

13 Windsor, op. cit., p. 235.

14 Ibid., p. 296 (Haile Selassie); Prince of Wales and Mosley's 'New Party', R. Skidelsky, *Oswald Mosley* (L. 1975), p. 255.

15 See *Documents on German Foreign Policy*, Series C, Volumes IV (L. and Washington 1962), pp. 48–50, 330–1 and V (L. and Washington 1966), pp. 106 and 193.

16 Viktoria Luise, *Kaiser's Daughter*, pp. 180 and 188.

17 Duchess of Windsor, *The Heart has its Reasons* (L. 1956), pp. 164–76. The duke's version of their meeting, *A King's Story*, p. 254.

18 For the Albert Hall speech, ibid., pp. 251–2: remark to Churchill, Martin Gilbert, *Winston S. Churchill* (L. 1976), V, p. 810.

19 Duke of Windsor, op. cit., p. 251 for dispute with Herbert Morrison, pp. 252–3 for Berkhamsted School speech. The file on the speech in the Foreign Office archives is indexed as C 4759/55/18. On the attitude of the LCC to military cadets at this time see B. Donoughue and G.W. Jones, *Herbert Morrison* (L. 1973), p. 202. Morrison's *Autobiography* (L. 1960) does not mention the Duke of Windsor as prince, king or exile.

20 On Vansittart and the king, Nicolson, op. cit., p. 529; on Vansittart's hospitality, Duchess of Windsor, op. cit., p. 218.

21 Edward VIII's letter is in the Foreign Office papers in the Public Record Office, F.O. 372/3186. See Alan Palmer, *The Kaiser,* pp. 222–3 for the background to this suggestion.

22 The report is printed in *Documents on German Foreign Policy*, Series C, IV, (L. and Washington 1962), pp. 1062–4. Extensive extracts are in Donaldson, op. cit., pp. 199–200.

23 Ibid., pp. 233–96. Duke of Windsor, op. cit., pp. 280–397; Duchess of Windsor, op. cit., pp. 220–84. Brian Inglis, *Abdication* (L. 1966) *passim*. Lord Beaverbrook, *The Abdication of King Edward VIII* (L. 1966), pp. 34–80. Philip Ziegler, *Crown and People* (L. 1978), pp. 34–9 and 60.

24 Paul Schmidt, *Hitler's Interpreter* (L. 1951), pp. 94–5; Duchess of Windsor, op. cit., pp. 307–8. The visit to Hitler is not mentioned in either of the duke's volumes of memoirs, nor is it in his obituary in *The Times*.

25 Donaldson, op. cit., pp. 358–77. For the Berlin–Lisbon–Madrid correspondence about the duke and duchess see *Documents on German Foreign Policy*, Series D, Volume X (L. and Washington 1957).

26 Duchess of Windsor, op. cit., p. 335.

CHAPTER ELEVEN: THE TWENTY-FIRST PRINCE

1 *The Times*, 12 February 1944: J.W. Wheeler-Bennett, *King George VI* (L. 1958), pp. 590–2.

2 Dermot Morrah, *To Be a King* (L. 1968). The Arundel Herald Extraordinary's account of the first nineteen years of the prince's life is 'privileged . . . written with the approval of H.M. the Queen'.

3 Ibid., pp. 45–65.

4 Francis Jones, *Princes and Principality of Wales*, p. 156: *The Times*, 28 July 1958.

5 H. Röhrs and H. Tunstall-Behrens, *Kurt Hahn* (L. 1970), pp. 1–21 on Hahn personally, pp. 22–38 on Salem, pp. 39–59 on Gordonstoun.

6 Morrah, op. cit., pp. 115–16.

7 Prince Charles's own account of life at Timbertop, originally printed in the *Gordonstoun Record*, forms an appendix to Geoffrey Wakeford, *The Heir Apparent* (L. 1967), pp. 225–7.

8 Morrah, op. cit., pp. 138–40; *The Times*, 23 December 1965; conversation with Harold Wilson reported in R.H.S. Crossman, *Diaries of a Cabinet Minister* (L. 1975), I, p. 420. See also the 'off-the-record interview' account in Robert Lacey, *Majesty* (paperback, L. 1977), pp. 406–7.

9 Morrah, op. cit., p. 147; *The Times*, 5 October 1967. The question papers set for History A-Levels, 1966–70, were published by the Oxford and Cambridge Schools Examination Board in 1971.

10 Academic aspects of the prince's Cambridge days are listed in the *Cambridge University Calendar*. For a lighter side, see the article by Ann Leslie in William Davis (ed.), *Punch and the Monarchy* (L. 1977), pp. 110–12.

11 Douglas Liversidge, *Prince Charles, Monarch in the Making* (L. 1975), pp. 76–8; *The Times*, 1, 2, 8 July 1969; Philip Ziegler, *Crown and People*, pp. 111, 116–17 and 132.

12 *The Times*, 25 April 1977. There is a succinct survey of the prince's service career in Ronald Allison, *Charles, Prince of Our Time* (L. 1978), pp. 8–9, 24.

13 *The Times*, 11 and 14 November 1978: *The Observer*, 12 and 19 November 1978. E. Barker (ed.), *The Politics of Aristotle* (Oxford 1947), Book VII, c. XVI, p. 383.

14 W. Bagehot, *The English Constitution* (Fontana edition, L. 1963), pp. 82, 96.

Index

Abbreviation used: P of W for Prince of Wales. The Princes of Wales who succeeded to the throne appear under their reigning titles. All kings and queens are of England or Great Britain unless otherwise identified.

Thomas of Walsingham, chronicler: (quoted) 19–20
Tower of London: 55, 70, 71, 73, 76
Townshend, Charles, Viscount: 126–7, 128
Towton, Battle of (*1461*): 69
Tudor, Edmund, Earl of Richmond: 81
Tudor, Jasper, Earl of Pembroke: 81–5, 92
Tudor, Owen: 80–2
Tudor family: 39, 45, 46, 80, 83–4, 92
Tudor historians on: first P of W, 4; Garter, 25; Henry V, 57; Wars of the Roses, 66

Union of England and Wales (*1536–43*), 98
USA: Edward VII visits, 171–2

Vansittart, Sir Robert: and Mrs Simpson, 203–4
Victoria, Queen: views on George IV, 166–7; and P of W, 166–8, 169, 171, 173, 175–7, 179; and Albert's death, 172–3; and Kaiser, 180, 182; dies, 182
Victoria, Princess Royal: 169, 173, 179–80, 190
Victoria Louise, Princess, Kaiser's daughter: 192, 201
Vincennes: Henry V dies at, 59–60

Wakefield, Battle of (*1460*): 68
Waldegrave, James, Earl, George III's governor: 139–40
Wales (and Welsh): Edward I in, 1–5; Edward II in, 5, 10, 17–18; soldiers in English service, 10, 29–30, 38–9, 85, 113; Lawgoch and, 34–5; Richard II in, 38–9; Glendower's rebellion, 45–50; Lancastrians in, 68,

81; Tudors and, 80–2, 84–5, 92; dragon of, 84–5, 183; union with England, 98; Charles II in, 113, 116; William III and, 123–4; Hanoverians and, 124; George IV visits, 157–8, 164; Edward VII and, 174, 183; University of, 183, 216; Edward VIII and (investiture), 190–2, 206; Prince Charles in, 212, 216–17, 218
Wales, Principality of: administration, 10–11, 16, 28–9, 96, 98; revenues, 29, 67, 92, 123–4, 132–3; *see also* Wales and Welsh
Wallace, William, Scots patriot: 8, 12
Walpole, Horace: 131, 143, 147–8
Walpole, Sir Robert: 126–9, 131, 135–6
Walter, Lucy, Charles II and: 116
Warren, Sir Herbert, President of Magdalen College, Oxford: on Edward VIII, 193–4
'Wars of the Roses': 66–73
Warwick, Richard Neville, Earl of ('Kingmaker'): Yorkist, 63, 64, 67–9; Lancastrian, 70–1
Washington, DC: Edward VII in, 171–2
Waterloo, Battle of (*1815*): 164, 165
Waterloo Bridge: George IV and opening of, 161
Wellington, Arthur Wellesley, Duke of: 160, 161–2, 164, 165, 166, 167, 171
West Indies: 135, 137
Westminster, royal residence: 55, 93, 94
Westminster Abbey: Edward II knighted, 12–13;

coronations: Henry IV, 41, Richard III, 76, George II, 129, George IV, 164; Henry IV dies in, 56; tombs: Richard II, 57, Henry V, 60; right of sanctuary, 73, 75–6; Edward V born in, 73
Westminster Hall: 7, 36, 41; investitures and, 86, 102–3
Whigs: 147–9, 152, 158, 159–60
William II, German Emperor (Kaiser): and Edward VII, 179–82, 185–6; and George V, 186, 188, 191, 192
William III: 118; accession, 120–1; and Wales, 123–4
William IV: 153–4, 157, 164
William, German Crown Prince: 195, 204
Windsor, Duke of: as title, 207; *see* Edward VIII
Windsor Castle: 8, 12, 15, 166, 173; Garter ceremonies at, 26, 34, 191; George III at, 152, 159, 162; George IV and, 161, 165; Edward VIII and, 207, 208
Woodstock, royal manor of: 21–2, 31, 86, 103, 105, 110
Woodville, Elizabeth, Edward IV's wife: 70, 73–4, 75–6
Worcester, Thomas Percy, Earl of, 47–9
World War I: 194–5
World War II: 207–8

York, Edmund Langley, Duke of: 42
York, Edward, Duke of: 54, 58, 62
York, Frederick, Duke of: 145, 152
York, Richard, Duke of: claimant to throne, 62–8
York, Richard, Duke of, Edward IV's son: 76
York: Parliament at (*1322*), 16–17; Richard III and, 75, 78, 79; investiture at, 78

18 05